SHOOT
THE MESSENGER?

Spanish Democracy and the Crimes of Francoism

The Cañada Blanch / Sussex Academic Studies on Contemporary Spain

Cristina Palomares, *The Quest for Survival after Franco: Moderate Francoism and the Slow Journey to the Polls, 1964–1977.*

David Wingeate Pike, *France Divided: The French and the Civil War in Spain.*

Hugh Purcell with Phyll Smith, *The Last English Revolutionary: Tom Wintringham, 1898–1949.*

Isabelle Rohr, *The Spanish Right and the Jews, 1898–1945: Antisemitism and Opportunism.*

Gareth Stockey, *Gibraltar: "A Dagger in the Spine of Spain?"*

Ramon Tremosa-i-Balcells, *Catalonia – An Emerging Economy: The Most Cost-Effective Ports in the Mediterranean Sea.*

Maria Thomas, *The Faith and the Fury: Popular Anticlerical Violence and Iconoclasm in Spain, 1931–1936.*

Dacia Viejo-Rose, *Reconstructing Spain: Cultural Heritage and Memory after Civil War.*

Richard Wigg, *Churchill and Spain: The Survival of the Franco Regime, 1940–1945.*

IN MEMORIAM
Amparo Barayón, assassinated on October 11, 1936,
and Violeta Friedman, Antonio Martínez Borrego,
José Casado Montado and Fernando Ruiz Vergara, all deceased.

DEDICATED TO
Isidoro Sánchez Baena, Dolors Genovés,
Marta Capín, Santiago Macías, Emilio Silva,
Dionisio Pereira and Alfredo Grimaldos.

ALSO TO
Ramón and Andrea Sender Barayón,
Magdalena Maes Barayón, Mercedes Esteban Maes,
Helen Graham and Paul Preston.

AND TO
The democratic jurists who understood and rigorously applied the
prevalence of the right to information over the right to honor.

SHOOT
THE MESSENGER?

Spanish Democracy and the Crimes of Francoism

From the Pact of Silence to the Trial of Baltasar Garzón

Francisco Espinosa-Maestre

Translation by Richard Barker

ACADEMIC
PRESS

Brighton • Portland • Toronto

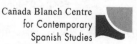

Cañada Blanch Centre
for Contemporary
Spanish Studies

2 4 6 8 10 9 7 5 3 1

First published in Spanish, titled *Callar al mensajero: La represión franquista, entre la libertad de información y el derecho al honor* (Barcelona: Ediciones Península, 2009). Published in English, 2013, in Great Britain, with additional chapter, "The Spanish Justice System, Baltasar Garzón and the Crimes of Francoism", by
SUSSEX ACADEMIC PRESS
PO Box 139, Eastbourne BN24 9BP

and in the United States of America by
SUSSEX ACADEMIC PRESS
920 NE 58th Ave   Suite 300
Portland, Oregon 97213-3786

and in Canada by
SUSSEX ACADEMIC PRESS (CANADA)
8000 Bathurst Street, Unit 1, PO Box 30010, Vaughan, Ontario L4J 0C6

Published in collaboration with the
Cañada Blanch Centre for Contemporary Spanish Studies.

British Library Cataloguing in Publication Data
A CIP catalogue record for this book is available from the British Library.
Library of Congress Cataloging-in-Publication Data
Espinosa Maestre, Francisco.
[Callar al mensajero. English] Shoot the messenger? : Spanish democracy and the crimes of Francoism : from the pact of silence to the trial of Baltasar Garzón / Francisco Espinosa Maestre ; translated from the Spanish by Richard Barker.
pages   cm
First published in Spanish, titled Callar al mensajero: La represión franquista, entre la libertad de información y el derecho al honor (Barcelona: Ediciones Península, 2009); first published in English, 2013, with one additional chapter, "The Spanish justice system, Baltasar Garzón and the crimes of Francoism" — Title page verso.
ISBN 978-1-84519-542-7 (paperback : alk. paper)   1. Political crimes and offenses—Spain—History—20th century. 2. Francoism. 3. Seditious libel—Spain. 4. Censorship—Spain. 5. Reparations for historical injustices—Spain. I. Title.
KKT4415.E87 2013
364.1'310946—dc23

2012047404

Typeset & designed by Sussex Academic Press, Brighton & Eastbourne.
Printed by TJ International, Padstow, Cornwall.

Contents

The Cañada Blanch Centre for Contemporary Spanish Studies

In the 1960s, the most important initiative in the cultural and academic relations between Spain and the United Kingdom was launched by a Valencian fruit importer in London. The creation by Vicente Cañada Blanch of the Anglo-Spanish Cultural Foundation has subsequently benefited large numbers of Spanish and British scholars at various levels. Thanks to the generosity of Vicente Cañada Blanch, thousands of Spanish schoolchildren have been educated at the secondary school in West London that bears his name. At the same time, many British and Spanish university students have benefited from the exchange scholarships which fostered cultural and scientific exchanges between the two countries. Some of the most important historical, artistic and literary work on Spanish topics to be produced in Great Britain was initially made possible by Cañada Blanch scholarships.

Vicente Cañada Blanch was, by inclination, a conservative. When his Foundation was created, the Franco regime was still in the plenitude of its power. Nevertheless, the keynote of the Foundation's activities was always a complete open-mindedness on political issues. This was reflected in the diversity of research projects supported by the Foundation, many of which, in Francoist Spain, would have been regarded as subversive. When the Dictator died, Don Vicente was in his seventy-fifth year. In the two decades following the death of the Dictator, although apparently indestructible, Don Vicente was obliged to husband his energies. Increasingly, the work of the Foundation was carried forward by Miguel Dols whose tireless and imaginative work in London was matched in Spain by that of José María Coll Comín. They were united in the Foundation's spirit of open-minded commitment to fostering research of high quality in pursuit of better Anglo-Spanish cultural relations. Throughout the 1990s, thanks to them, the role of the Foundation grew considerably.

In 1994, in collaboration with the London School of Economics, the Foundation established the Príncipe de Asturias Chair of Contemporary Spanish History and the Cañada Blanch Centre for Contemporary Spanish Studies. It is the particular task of the Cañada Blanch Centre for Contemporary Spanish Studies to promote the understanding of twentieth-century Spain through research and teaching of contemporary Spanish history, politics, economy, sociology and culture. The Centre possesses a valuable library and archival centre for specialists in contemporary Spain. This work is carried on through the publications of the doctoral and post-doctoral researchers at the Centre itself and through the many seminars and lectures held at the London School of Economics. While the seminars are the province of the researchers, the lecture cycles have been the forum in which Spanish politicians have been able to address audiences in the United Kingdom.

Since 1998, the Cañada Blanch Centre has published a substantial number of books in collaboration with several different publishers on the subject of contemporary Spanish history and politics. A fruitful partnership with Sussex Academic Press began in 2004 with the publication of Christina Palomares's fascinating work on the origins of the Partido Popular in Spain, *The Quest for Survival after Franco: Moderate Francoism and the Slow Journey to the Polls, 1964–1977*. This was followed in 2007 by Soledad Fox's deeply moving biography of one of the most intriguing women of 1930s Spain, *Constancia de la Mora in War and Exile: International Voice for the Spanish Republic* and Isabel Rohr's path-breaking study of antisemitism in Spain, *The Spanish Right and the Jews, 1898–1945: Antisemitism and Opportunism*. 2008 saw the publication of a revised edition of Richard Wigg's penetrating study of Anglo-Spanish relations during the Second World War, *Churchill and Spain: The Survival of the Franco Regime, 1940–1945* together with *Triumph at Midnight of the Century: A Critical Biography of Arturo Barea*, Michael Eaude's fascinating revaluation of the great Spanish author of *The Forging of a Rebel*.

Our collaboration in 2009 was inaugurated by Gareth Stockey's incisive account of another crucial element in Anglo-Spanish relations, *Gibraltar. A Dagger in the Spine of Spain*. We were especially proud that it was continued by the most distinguished American historian of the Spanish Civil War, Gabriel Jackson. His pioneering work *The Spanish Republic and the Civil War*, first published 1965 and still in print, quickly became a classic. The Sussex Academic Press/Cañada Blanch series was greatly privileged to be associated with Professor Jackson's biography of the great Republican war leader, Juan Negrín.

2011 took the series to new heights. Two remarkable and complementary works, Olivia Muñoz Rojas, *Ashes and Granite: Destruction and Reconstruction in the Spanish Civil War and its Aftermath* and Dacia Viejo-Rose, *Reconstructing Spain: Cultural Heritage and Memory after Civil War*, opened up an entirely new dimension of the study of the early Franco regime and its internal conflicts. They were followed by Richard Purkiss's analysis of the Valencian anarchist movement during the revolutionary period from 1918 to 1923, the military dictatorship of General Primo de Rivera and the Second Republic. It is a fascinating work which sheds entirely new light both on the breakdown of political coexistence during the Republic and on the origins of the violence that was to explode after the military coup of July 1936. The year ended with the publication of *France Divided: The French and the Civil War in Spain* by David Wingeate Pike. It made available in a thoroughly updated edition, and in English for the first time, one of the classics of the historiography of the Spanish Civil War.

An extremely rich programme for 2012 opened with Germà Bel's remarkable *Infrastructure and the Political Economy of Nation Building in Spain*. This startlingly original work exposed the damage done to the Spanish economy by the country's asymmetrical and dysfunctional transport and communications model. It was followed by a trio of books concerned with the International Brigades and the Republican medical services in the Spanish Civil War: Angela Jackson's rich and moving account of an extraordinary life – that of the left-wing nurse Patience Darton; the comprehensive account of the Republican medical services by Linda Palfreeman and the fascinating life of Tom Wintringham by Hugh Purcell and Phyl Smith.

They were followed by Helen Graham's *The War and its Shadow*, an extraordinarily original analysis of the afterlife of the Spanish Civil War, not just during the long dictatorship which was the institutionalization of Franco's victory but in Spain's present-day democracy. Especially striking is the way in which she relates the horrors of the Spanish Civil War to the mass violence taking place across Europe in the inter-war period. That work was matched in importance by Maria Thomas's ground-breaking work on the anti-clericalism that remains at the heart of many of the bitter on-going polemics about the Spanish war. *The Faith and the Fury: Popular Anticlerical Violence and Iconoclasm in Spain, 1931–1936* is an illuminating and even-handed account which fills a major gap in the literature.

An equally nutritious programme is envisaged for the series in 2013. It opens with two important works. David Lethbridge's perceptive study of the time spent in Spain by the remarkable Canadian surgeon Norman Bethune is a crucial addition to the literature on the Republican medical services during the Spanish Civil War. Alongside previous volumes in the series by Angela Jackson and Linda Palfreeman, David Lethbridge has made an outstanding biographical contribution. The series also welcomes Francisco Espinosa-Maestre, one of the most important historians of the Francoist repression during the Spanish conflict and its aftermath. He is best known for his many books on the terror in southern Spain but his contribution to the series is a unique addition to the literature. *Shoot the Messenger* lays out twelve cases in which investigation into atrocities committed in Spain has been blocked by various legal subterfuges and threats. It goes a very long way to explaining the maintenance of silence about the crimes of Franco.

PAUL PRESTON
Series Editor
London School of Economics

The Right to Know: A Foreword by Rafael Escudero Alday

The book you hold in your hands is another step forward in the research being carried out by some Spanish historians to reconstruct the Francoist repression. In this case, it is a work by Francisco Espinosa, renowned specialist in matters related to the so-called movement for "historical memory." The novelty of this work with respect to previous publications – in which he dealt with episodes such as "the death column" or "General Queipo de Llano's justice," among other topics – is that here the author takes up the question of the relationship between Law and Historical Memory. And he does so, it should be noted from the outset, with a facility for handling legal practices and terminology that many of the judges and magistrates that appear in these pages would do well to emulate.

In the last few years, and in the shadow of the development of the movement for the recuperation of historical memory, we have seen and heard all types of arguments against this process. Arguments that range from a stubborn resistance on the part of right-wing politicians and journalists to "reopening the wounds of the past" and breaking "the accord among Spaniards embodied in the transition to democracy,"[1] to the refusal by more than a few historians to accepting the very existence of something called "historical memory." With respect to the former, there is little I can add here to what has already been said by more authoritative voices.[2] Others have collected living testimonies – some of these researchers are portrayed in this book – from those abandoned by that "spirit of the Transition," which prescribed amnesia for the nascent Spanish democracy regarding what had happened, "fairness and balance" in the evaluation of the Republic and the Francoist military dictatorship, and ignominious indifference towards and disdain for the victims of the latter. Besides the seriousness of this silence when considered by itself, it has also had repercussions on the subsequent evolution of the Spanish democracy. As evidence, it is enough to quote Vicenç Navarro:

> one of the causes of the enormous deficiencies of the welfare state in Spain
> is the ignorance of what the Spanish Republic, the Civil War and the long

dictatorship that came in its wake represented. [Spanish youth] are unaware that these enormous deficiencies are derived precisely from the vast power exercised by conservative forces during the dictatorship and the democracy. It is difficult to build a future when we are so ignorant of our past.[3]

The Interrelatedness of History, Politics and Law: Democratic Memory

Some authors in the field of historiography launch attacks against "historical memory." Their arguments are born during conceptual discussions but, without a doubt, have repercussions in political and judicial spheres. They begin by denying the concept of a historical memory, go on to criticize the intrusion of Law in this debate and end by rejecting the existence of a people's right to historical memory.[4] But let us take it step by step in order to make a clear distinction between the different elements and levels of the debate.

As with so many other topics, conceptual clarity should prevail when dealing with matters related to historical memory. To that end, the concepts of memory and history must be defined with rigor and precision. But this should not lead us into a sort of "conceptual essentialism" that prevents us from recognizing the existence of certain realities that ought to be grouped by specific categories that may be useful when identifying the object of analysis and examination. One of these is historical memory, a concept that includes those dimensions that not only have to do with efforts to know the past, but also with those activities that tend to evaluate it and rescue it from indifference.[5]

Therefore, we had better be aware that the concept of "historical memory" refers to the understanding and evaluation of a specific reality. It is born with ties to concrete purposes and objectives. It does not claim to explain the beginning of time or to study history in the broader sense of the word, but rather to rehabilitate the memories of those who were, first, massacred for their personal, syndical or political convictions; and, second, were forgotten during the entire time of the military dictatorship that devastated the country for forty years. It responds, therefore, to a specific and concrete demand: to recuperate the memory of those who fought for democracy and the legality of the Republic or were massacred for opposing the *coup d'état* and the Franco dictatorship.

Consequently, the movement for the recuperation of historical memory is a partisan movement. Through scientific rigor and social action, it hopes to rescue from oblivion those persons who were victims of the dictatorship because of their convictions, activities and attitudes in defense of democratic values, respect for human rights, and the legal system in effect at the moment the *coup d'état* took place; indeed, the legal system in place at the time was one of the most advanced in matters such as freedom and political pluralism, gender equality, social politics and respect for international law as a way to resolve conflicts, among other things.

And, as it turns out, equally partisan was the law by which the Spanish Parliament attempted to address – with more shortcomings than successes, it must be said – the demands of this movement initiated by civil society. From its own Declaration of Purposes, Law 52/2007, of December 26 – popularly known as the Law of Historical Memory – which recognized and broadened rights and established measures favoring those who suffered persecution or violence during the Civil War or the dictatorship, delimits its measures "to all those who suffered injustices or affronts brought about by one or another ideological or political motive or by religious beliefs," as well as "to those who on different occasions fought in defense of democratic values."

Democratic memory: this is the concept that delimits the philosophy and content of the Law. And the memory that deserves reconstruction in a democratic regime such as the present one is that of those who suffered this specific form of violence, paying with their lives or their well-being for their personal and political struggle against dictatorship and fascism, which is to say, the memory of democracy, liberty and anti-fascism. The Law deliberately and consciously breaks with the principle of balance between dictatorship and democracy, fascism and anti-fascism.[6] For a democratic legislator, who attempts to lay the foundations for constructing an ever stronger democratic memory committed to human rights, the violence to be condemned is the violence of those who made up the dictatorship's side, because it was they who broke with the democratic Republican regime and whose work within the government was characterized by a continual violation of the most elemental and fundamental rights. The violence, in the words of the Law, that was utilized to "impose political convictions and establish totalitarian regimes contrary to the liberty and dignity of all its citizens."

In this sense, the memory to be rehabilitated is that of those who fought on the side of democracy, which was the side of Republican legality. A democratic regime is not obliged to rehabilitate the collective memory of persons or groups who fought against it. It is only obliged to do so in the case of those who fought on the side of democracy and liberty, which was the side of the pre-established legality.[7] Inherent to democracy is its radical opposition to all forms of autocracy, totalitarianism or fascism. This is the memory that fits in with the process of the recuperation of historical memory that has evolved in Spain. And it fits because its political objective is the same: to rehabilitate our democratic memory, our memory of the struggle for democracy and freedom.

The Right to Know as Part of the People's Right to Remember

What has just been set forth is the sense in which the concept of "historical memory" is used in its present context. This context goes beyond the field of historiography – as much as that might trouble some of its practitioners – to include the fields of law and politics. In fact, satisfying the demand – born in the social sphere and later transferred to the realm of politics – for a recuperation of historical memory requires the elaboration of juridical norms that would institutionalize the instruments necessary to achieve its objectives of rehabilitating and evaluating our democratic memory, all with the aim of creating more democracy for the future, a future with neither amnesty nor amnesia, but with justice and public policies that promote memory.[8]

It seems beyond doubt that the judicial system has a critically important role to play in the area of historical memory. The Law of Historical Memory is itself a good example of that. Its virtues and defects, its shortcomings and contributions, are open to debate, but what cannot be disputed is that it is a legal recognition of historical memory as understood in the terms we have set forth above. And it does so to the extent of defining a people's right to the recuperation of personal and family memory. This novel right – legally created and with legal status – encompasses a range of judicial intentions and activities that fall under the protection of the law's contents.[9] This right includes dimensions related to moral reparations to the victims and their families, the recuperation of personal and family memory, the general declaration of the illegitimacy of the repression, the right to indemnification and patrimonial rights, as well as the right to know, including the right to access information as well as the right to find out the location of disappeared persons.[10]

Consequently, whoever denies the existence of a citizen's right to memory, defined and configured by law, is confusing their wish that such a law not exist with judicial reality. It is as if someone who is opposed to private ownership of assets and the means of production denied the existence of the right to private property in Spanish law. What we would like there to be or not be is one thing, and what the judicial system institutes and protects is quite another. To confuse the two is a mistake – whether out of self-interest or not – that one is not allowed to make.

It is precisely one of these dimensions of this right to memory that takes on relevance in Francisco Espinosa's book. It deals with the right to know in relationship to the work of historians who attempt – with clearly partisan intentions – to lift the veil of darkness and silence that has protected those persons who actively participated in the Francoist repression. The book analyzes some cases in which the right to know is at stake, cases that reveal how the investigation of certain aspects of the Francoist repression pits the historian against the typical conflict between freedom of information and the "right to honor."[11]

Before analyzing this matter, it is fitting to consider another aspect of the right to know that is not dealt with directly in this book, although it is certainly related to what is discussed there. We are talking about the right to know the location of disappeared persons. On this point, the Law of Historical Memory delegates the responsibility for locating and disinterring victims to the private sphere. These tasks are left to the families and associations through the provision of subventions that barely cover the expense of their voluntary work in the identification and recovery of the victims' remains. In December 2008 the government announced the creation of an Office for the Victims of the Civil War and the Dictatorship which, supposedly, will elaborate protocols for conducting exhumations. Together with this vague announcement (in March 2009 the Office had still not begun to function) the government also let it be known that it intended to leave the final decisions regarding the opening of mass graves to town halls and to the regional governments. Once again, the government fails to fulfill its responsibilities: it is astonishing that these matters be left to the jurisdiction of local and regional entities when it is a question of the exhumation of cadavers. It is easy to foresee that some entities will refuse to act and that this will affect the principle of equality: some mass graves will be opened and others will be relegated to oblivion.

This panorama becomes even darker with the two following additions. On the one hand, during a plenary session on March 11, 2009, the Senate, with votes from both the Socialists and the Popular Party, rejected a proposal to reform the Law of Historical Memory that would have required the government to cover the expenses of identifying and exhuming the remains of persons who even today are still among the disappeared. On the other hand, there is the total lack of judicial activity with respect to this entire process. This inactivity has two dimensions. One is related to the investigation by the National Tribunal of crimes against humanity committed during the *coup d'état* and the Franco dictatorship. Let it be remembered that the decision by the head of the Fifth Central Chamber of National Tribunal to initiate criminal proceedings to clarify those crimes was followed by an appeal by the public prosecutor's office against it and a decision on December 2, 2008, during a Plenary of the Criminal Chamber of the National Tribunal, to declare it to be outside its jurisdiction to try such crimes.[12] As José Antonio Martín Pallín points out:

> If the National Tribunal tries crimes under international law committed outside Spanish territory, it seems absurd that its jurisdiction is diminished among the Spanish courts of first instance when crimes of this nature are committed in Spain. It has always been said that law is terrified by a vacuum but even more so by irrationality. If jurisdiction is universal, Spanish territory cannot be outside the universe. It is an absurd and insurmountable contradiction of terms.[13]

Besides, the courts of first instance have not intervened either. This is the second dimension of the previously mentioned lack of judicial action. Confronted by the appearance of human remains in mass graves, there are many judges who refuse to go to the scene of the crime, identify the cadavers or even take statements from witnesses or persons who could shed light on what happened. In short, these judges are not doing their duty, such as initiating criminal proceedings when confronted by the appearance of human remains, in many cases with hands bound and bullet holes. To allege that the 1977 Law of Amnesty – a law that violates the International Covenant on Civil and Political Rights, ratified by Spain in 1976 – prevents the investigation of these persons' assassinations reveals total ignorance of the laws applicable to crimes against humanity and violations of human rights.[14]

The Freedom to Engage in Research and the Formation of a Collective Historical Consciousness

In this book, Francisco Espinosa presents us with a series of cases in which the right to know has been questioned by those who claimed – and still claim – that the honor of the perpetrators should by safeguarded, and who point to the "right to honor" to prevent historians from disseminating the results of their research if it reveals the participation of specific persons in different aspects or at different moments of the Francoist repression. It is indeed grotesque that people who represent and vindicate the honor of those who actively participated in the repression of a democratic regime like the Spanish Republic are now the first to turn to the Constitution and its fundamental rights – which were ignored during the Franco dictatorship – for their defense.

But if the claim to a "right to honor" is grotesque, equally grotesque is the reception it has had in some of the media and certain institutions, including some judges who have not hesitated to interpret this supposed "right to honor" in a nearly categorical fashion, placing it above other fundamental rights such as freedom of expression and freedom of information. Throughout the pages of this book, Francisco Espinosa not only analyzes, with rigor and precision, the claims of both sides in each of the cases presented, he also dissects the motives for this new attempt to silence the past and emphatically lays out the consequences that would derive from accepting such theses.

The supposed conflict between the "right to honor," on the one hand, and the freedoms of information and scientific creation and production, on the other, is the thread that runs through the cases presented in these pages. It is a conflict which, in relation to the field of historiography, has been resolved from the constitutional point of view by the sentence handed down in the "Dolors Genovés case" (STC 43/2004, March 23). In it, the Constitutional Tribunal raises the following issues that must, of necessity, be taken into account by judicial bodies when it comes to tackling future conflicts of this type. In the first place, the Tribunal affirms that "scientific freedom – in regard to historical debate, which is what concerns us here – enjoys additional protection under our Constitution in comparison to that which applies to the freedoms of expression and information, because while the latter refer to contemporary events involving living persons, the former [. . .] always refers to events from the past and individuals whose legal status as persons has necessarily grown tenuous with the passage of time." Consequently, "limits cannot be imposed on scientific freedom with the breadth and intensity with which the dignity of living persons imposes limits on the exercise of the freedoms of expression and information by their contemporaries."

Having established this distinction, the Tribunal recognizes the controversial and debatable nature of historical research, as well as the historian's need to express value judgments about historical events. And this is because "the possibility for our contemporaries to form their own world view based on the evaluation of others' experiences depends on the existence of a historical science freely and methodologically founded. Without a dialogue with the value judgments of others – with those of the historian, which is what concerns us here – we would be unable to form our own value judgments.

Neither would there be space – which can only be attained through freedom – for the formation of a collective historical consciousness."

Finally, the Tribunal establishes a requirement that ought to enable constitutional protection for historical science in cases like those described in this book: "research on past events involving deceased persons, and the publication of that research, ought to prevail over the 'right to honor' of such persons when, in fact, those findings are arrived at according to the standard methodologies of historiographical science." This reference to methodological standards is especially important to this issue, given that most of the time we lack documents or other written sources that prove beyond doubt the accusations of collaboration in the Francoist repression made in the cases described here. The historian's findings in these cases are based on oral testimonies, which are vaguer than written proof. Nevertheless, this does not mean that such testimonies have less historical value; neither does it mean that possible errors of fact do not exist. As the Tribunal says: "If history could only be constructed on the basis of unquestionable facts, history, conceived as a social science, would be impossible. In their work, historians evaluate what causes explain historical events and put forth their interpretation, and [. . .] it is not the job of this Tribunal to decide which of the possible interpretations should prevail."

Let us close with the following words from the Constitutional Tribunal, which conclude the Tribunal's sentence:

> It is the citizens themselves who, in the light of the cultural and historiographical debate, form their own vision of what happened, which can change in the future [. . .] Historical discussion is open to participation and response in its own context and by its characteristic means, but it is not open to a judicial solution [. . .] The exercise of our jurisdiction in the guarantee of fundamental rights does not serve to pass judgment on history, and even less to change or silence its events, however much these events or the interpretations that may be applied to them turn out to be troublesome and painful for those involved or their descendants.[15]

Nevertheless, this ruling by the Constitutional Tribunal has not been applied in all the cases described in these pages: in some instances because they were tried before this sentence was issued; and in other instances because there are judges in this country who are still unclear about the binding nature of the Constitution and the interpretation of its rules by the Constitutional Tribunal. Judges like those cited in this book, who put forward without blushing – occasionally in a courtroom still adorned with the Francoist escutcheon – the following affirmations: "Civil wars leave a bloody wake or trail of deeds, sometimes heroic and other times reprehensible, that it is indispensable to bury and forget, and he misses the mark who stirs up the embers of that struggle in order to awaken resentments"; "the inopportune and unfortunate recollection of episodes that took place before and after July 18"; "it is indisputable that barbarities were committed by both sides"; "what cannot be said, because it is not protected by our constitutional system, is that a particular person was responsible for the lists of those to be shot. And I do not concern myself with judging whether or not the statement is true."

Fortunately, not all judges share this philosophy. The author of this book presents us with cases in which the judge protects the work and methodology of the historian. That said, as in many other fields, "the judicial system depends on who you get," to paraphrase Francisco Espinosa. In fact, the contents of juridical norms depend on the lenses of the one who is looking at them. The reading and interpretation of the texts of constitutions and laws is an eminently subjective undertaking in which, together with other more or less interconnected factors, the ideology of the interpreter intervenes in a decisive fashion. In this case, it is the judge, who pours all his experience, training and philosophy into his sentences. For this reason it is not enough for the Constitutional Tribunal to establish doctrines in this matter. What is required is greater effort in the training of judges in these affairs, so they do not continue obstructing the work of researchers in the development of this process of recuperation of democratic memory.

Conclusion: When the Past Is Eradicated, There Are neither Culprits nor Crimes

The author of this book also invites us to look beyond the details of each of the cases put forth. With great clarity he presents the motives behind this attempt to "shoot the messenger," motives that transcend the strictly personal, i.e. the defense of a supposed honor that is being attacked, to enter a realm that is much more political. Concretely, the attempt to paralyze as much as possible all research on anything to do with the Franco dictatorship and the repression it practiced.

Nor is it appropriate to rule out strictly personal motivations: on the one hand, family members of the participants in the Francoist repression who want to keep secret that dark episode of their lives; and on the other hand, some of the cases set forth in this book have to do with the attempt to silence personal evolutions for ulterior motives. Important public figures who went

to bed one night as Falangists and the next morning woke up with democratic convictions. In either case, their claims come up against freedom of
information and the historian's freedom of creation and scientific production. As the author of this book makes clear, the Constitution protects this
search for truthful knowledge of history. This is the sense in which the judicial system does, in fact, enter the realm of the historian's work: to protect
the results of his or her free and methodologically founded investigation
from the attacks that third parties – bothered by the said results – could
launch. It is regrettable that this protection arrives too late for some of the
persons whose vicissitudes in dealing with the courts and the mass media
are recounted in these pages. It is unlikely they can be compensated for the
harm they have suffered, although it must certainly be a consolation to
know that the judicial system protects those who are now continuing the
struggle they initiated.

But, as previously stated, this attempt to silence the voices that name
the participants in the repression goes beyond the strictly personal or
familial, and beyond the protection of honor in the classic sense of the term.
From my perspective, there is a sentence by Francisco Espinosa that summa-
rizes this intent perfectly: "When the past is eradicated, there are neither
culprits nor crimes." The filing of lawsuits attempts to thwart historical
research with the aim of preventing more details about the repression from
coming to the light of the day. It is one more element in that strategy of
amnesia and impunity that the Transition installed in the political and
institutional life of Spain. It is a question now of discrediting the historians'
work through the disqualification of sources and oral testimonies.

It is well known that for the study of the repression that took place
during Francoism oral sources are of supreme importance. The repressors
tried to leave no written evidence of their activities, as proven by the very
numerous cases in which the victims' names were not even inscribed in the
Civil Death Registry. Added to that is the lamentable treatment given the
question of the archives since the arrival of democracy: many were brazenly
destroyed by the culprits themselves and others are still closed to historians.
Because of the unavailability or inaccessibility of written evidence, the oral
testimonies of those affected, of the family members of the victims and of
other witnesses, are the principal sources for the historian. Without their
contributions, the historical memory demanded by our democracy will be
impossible to construct.

For this reason, if the use of these sources and testimonies were
proscribed – as seems to be the primary objective of one of the judges
portrayed in this book – it would be a decisive blow to the historians who
specialize in the study of the Francoist military coup and its extermination

plan. It would mean the definitive enshrinement of that impunity against which every society that claims to be democratic must struggle. Nevertheless, at least with regard to this question – but not others – impunity has not won out altogether. The Constitutional Tribunal "validated" the historian's use of these sources and oral testimonies, a validation that will have to be borne in mind not only in future conflicts that could arise, but also in cases that are presently awaiting resolution.

Finally, this book also reveals paradoxical phenomena, like the intertwining of both motivations – the personal and the political – in some of the public figures in these accounts. Figures who maintain supposedly different postures depending upon whether or not they are personally affected, which leads them to engage in erratic displays of political tight-rope walking. One example – described in this book – is the case of Jorge Trías Sagnier. On the one hand, he was Violeta Friedman's lawyer, and plaintiff in the lawsuit against Dolors Genovés's documentary which purportedly violated the honor of his father.[16] On the other hand, during an interview that appeared in the newspaper *ABC* on January 31, 2005, he made the following declaration: "The memory of Violeta will always be with us. The histories of the Spanish republicans or of the Palestinians in Israel [*sic*] may be considered tragic, but they pale beside the Holocaust and its survivors."

It seems fairly plausible that what led him to make a political statement with such profound implications was his desire to justify his father's dark past. Perhaps not. In any event, it hardly matters anymore. What it represents is a lamentable attempt to establish a sort of "hierarchy of horrors," in which the suffering of Spanish republicans and Palestinians are ranked lower than that of the Jews. The findings of historians contradict this self-serving opinion, and that is why there are attempts to impede their research through lawsuits and other forms of pressure. Historians, including Francisco Espinosa himself, demonstrate in their works that the differences are not that great – at least qualitatively – and that, consequently, the crimes of the Franco dictatorship, as well as the propaganda that celebrates its culprits, should be given exactly the same treatment as that which has been given and continues to be given the Nazi regime's propagandists.

In conclusion, there are various reasons this book should be considered required reading. I will stress only two of them. In the first place because, by highlighting some aspects the Transition left open and unresolved, it emphatically contradicts those who sing the praises of that Transition. The author reminds us that the Transition armor-plated the "right to honor" of Spanish fascism, leaving its memory intact, while it forgot the "right to honor" and restitution of the victims of the long and terrible military dictatorship. In the second place, this book offers solid legal arguments to put a stop to the lawsuits and trials against historians – some of them still in progress – who, with absolute respect for the methodological principles that should guide historiographical endeavors, continue dedicating their time and energy to rescue the victims of the Francoist repression from oblivion and silence. Historians who, by their labors, contribute in a decisive manner to building a democratic memory that is respectful of human rights.

We owe that to the persons whose personal and family tragedies are described in these pages.

Rafael Escudero Alday
Professor of Judicial Philosophy
Universidad Carlos III de Madrid

Notes

1   A succinct exposition of these arguments can be found in an article by Rodolfo Martín Villa entitled "Carta a los Reyes Magos" (A Letter to the Three Kings), published in the newspaper *El País* on January 3, 2009. There, this Falangist who held several public offices during the dictatorship until he became civil governor and provincial chief of the Movement in Barcelona (1974), then Interior minister with the UCD (Union of the Democratic Center), high Commissioner for *Prestige* with PP (Popular Party) and, presently, president of the Sogecable corporation, launches – in between allegations in favor of the Transition – affirmations such as the following: "some of the victims of the Francoist repression had previously been assassins themselves"; "if criminal proceedings were initiated to investigate the responsibilities of the Military Juntas formed by those who participated in the coup or in the first governments of the Franco regime, it would be necessary to do the same for the responsibilities incurred by Republican leaders"; "let us not continue the unedifying spectacle of those death notices published in the newspapers by one side or the other that we have been seeing recently and which are not intended to extol the victims but rather to identify the perpetrators"; "besides being a resistance movement, there was above all, during the last stages of the maquis, more than a little banditry"; "you [referring to Spanish communists] were always in the anti-Francoist movement, although not always, like some of us, in the prodemocracy movement."

2   During the heated parliamentary debate preceding the approval of what is known as the Law of Historical Memory there were arguments put forth by those who – confronting the silence and amnesia imposed by the Transition – advocated the establishment of public policies regarding the historical memory of Spain. The course of that debate can be followed in J. A. Martín Pallín and Escudero, R., eds., *Derecho y memoria histórica* (Madrid: Trotta, 2008), 9–18.

3 Vicenç Navarro, *Bienestar insuficiente, democracia incompleta* (Barcelona: Anagrama, 2002), 25.

4 See this conclusion to Santos Juliá's article "¿Una memoria antifascista?," published in the newspaper *El País*, April 26, 2008.

5 It is the lack of awareness of this political aspect – or activist aspect, if you prefer – of the concept of historical memory that leads a historian like Stanley G. Payne to make the following statement: "'Historical memory' is neither history nor memory. What is called 'collective' or 'historical memory' is no such thing, but rather a version, or versions, created by publicists, patriots, political activists, journalists or even by some historians with ulterior motives. It is essentially a question of myths or legends created about the past. They may have some element of empirical truth or none at all. Memory is individual and subjective; it is never 'historical' or 'collective' as such. History, on the other hand, is not based on subjective individual memories, but on the intellectual examination of empirical data that has survived from the past" (interview published in the newspaper *ABC*, December 17, 2006).

6 In this sense, see Andrea Greppi, "Objeciones y comentarios: Democracia y antifascismo," in *Claves de Razón Práctica*, n° 184, July–August 2008.

7 All of which prevents, for example, the inclusion under protection of the Law of Historical Memory of those persons who made up the side of the army in rebellion. This was the case for the Moroccans who joined the Francoist troops, regarding whom – in response to the petition of the Moroccan Center for a Common Memory and Future – there was no obligation to recognize the character of victims deserving the protection of the aforementioned law. See their webpage: www.memoirecommune.org.

8 An opposing thesis is the one put forth by Santos Juliá, who describes historical memory as the projection "backwards of a general amnesty that would allow us to look forward." See his article "Año de la memoria" (*El País*, December 31, 2006), where he added the following: "That complex history [. . .] is what the government, with its continual tendency to reinvent the wheel, failed to take into account when it embarked on the elaboration of a law called, during its first stages, law of historical memory. And what is historical memory in a country mortally divided by a war in which brothers – and I mean biological brothers, no metaphors here – took up arms against brothers? When a country splits apart, a shared memory can only be constructed on the decision to relegate the past to oblivion: that is the meaning of the general amnesty, as Indalecio Prieto and José María Gil-Robles already understood since the first years of the postwar."

9 For a detailed analysis of the contents of this right see José María Sauca, "El derecho ciudadano a la memoria histórica: concepto y contenido," in J. A. Martín Pallín and Escudero, R., eds., *Derecho y memoria histórica, op. cit.*, 89–102.

10 The truth is that more than a year after this law went into effect its provisions

are being implemented very slowly. For a summary description of this exasperating process of applying the law see Rafael Escudero, "Un año de Ley de Memoria Histórica" (*Público*, December 26, 2006).

11 A detailed analysis of the way the Spanish Constitutional Tribunal tackles conflicts between fundamental rights, as well as appeals to the so-called court of deliberation as a way to resolve these conflicts, can be found in Luis Prieto, *Justicia constitucional y derechos fundamentales*, Madrid: Trotta, 2003, 173–216.

12 For a critical analysis of the National Tribunal's decision, see Javier Chinchón, "La actuación de la Audiencia Nacional en la investigación y juicio de los crímenes contra la humanidad cometidos en la Guerra Civil y el franquismo," *La Ley* 129/2009, n° 7102, January 29.

13 J. A. Martín Pallín, "Los muertos han aprendido a esperar," *El País*, March 20, 2009.

14 See this conclusion in Margalida Carpellà, "Desaparecidos, ¿hasta cuándo?," *El País*, September 13, 2008.

15 This sentence, whose author was the magistrate María Emilia Casas Bahamonde, received an unusual dissenting vote from the then president of the Tribunal, Manuel Jiménez de Parga, with the backing of the magistrate Roberto García-Calvo. It is important to remember, as the author of this book does so well, the personal and family circumstances of both dissenting magistrates, to the extent that these circumstances might have been deciding factors in their opinion.

16 Carlos Trías Bertrán, secretary of the Falange, testified as a witness in the initial phase of the court-martial that condemned the Catalonian politician Manuel Carrasco i Formiguera to death in Burgos. His participation in this proceeding, as well as the participation of other Catalonians residing in Burgos in 1938, led to the "Dolors Genovés case" analyzed in this book.

Acknowledgments

Arcángel Bedmar
María José Bernete
Marta Capín
Severiano Delgado
José Luis Escañuela
Lourenzo Fernández Prieto
Fabien Garrido
Dolors Genovés
Alfredo Grimaldos
Santiago Macías
Francisco Moreno Gómez
Mirta Núñez Díaz-Balart
Juan Carlos Perales
Dionisio Pereira
Hilari Raguer
Alberto Reig Tapia
Pedro G. Romero
Cándido Ruiz
Fernando Ruiz Vergara
Isidoro Sánchez Baena
Emilio Silva
María Jesús Souto

And most especially to Fernando Magán

"Judges do not resolve the problems of Memory; we are asking them to settle a debate that it is up to politicians to resolve. Judges are not going to resolve the problem of the credibility of researchers and journalists [. . .]. Therefore, what is at stake is our credibility and, consequently, the price to be paid is our humiliation. They get involved in our methodology, because that is where they can affect us and, by so doing, they can silence us. Shoot the messenger . . ."

The words of Dolors Genovés during the conference "The Repression in Galicia: The Right to Know and Freedom to Engage in Research." O Grove, September 2007

"Jurisprudence [. . .] recognizes that it cannot put historical events on trial and that tribunals have no business deciding what 'historical memory' is. In fact, the debate over the 'scientific methodology' that should be applied to historical studies is treacherous terrain [. . .] and, in any event, a courtroom is not the appropriate place for that debate, as much for the rigidity of legal procedure as for the fact that we are not in a normalized country and there are still people who are afraid to speak in the presence of a tape recorder, and even more so during a trial where the opponents are the present-day descendants or representatives of the victors, who were the cause of so much fear and so much pain. Even so, they put us before tribunals where we risk being penalized for our work researching and publishing what happened after the fascist victory in 1936, activities we carry out with meager means and without any type of remuneration."

Dionisio Pereira, "Shoot the Messenger," in Libro-Memoria de la Fundación, March 10, 2008

"The [Spanish] State should: a) consider repealing the 1977 Amnesty Law; b) take the necessary legislative measures to guarantee recognition by the national tribunals of the non-applicability of a statute of limitations to crimes against humanity; c) take measures for the creation of an independent truth commission regarding human rights violations which occurred during the Civil War and the Franco regime; and d) allow families to locate, exhume and identify the victims' remains and, where appropriate, indemnify the families."

Report by the United Nations Human Rights Committee (94th meeting, October 2008)

Introduction

The event that inspired this work was a conference held in O Grove in September 2007, entitled "The Repression in Galicia: Freedom of Information and the Right to Engage in Research." By bringing together many of those researchers affected by lawsuits related to the "right to honor,"[TN1] the conference provided a unique opportunity to look into the problem and make contact with many of this book's protagonists. Nevertheless there are prior cases I was able to follow in the press and even experience myself: that of Fernando Ruiz Vergara and his documentary *Rocío*, of Isidoro Sánchez Baena and his problems with the repression in Luque, or of Dolors Genovés and the lawsuit brought against her by the Trías family for her documentary on the assassination of Manuel Carrasco i Formiguera. There was also the case of José Casado Montado. I was familiar with his work on the living memory of the fascist repression in San Fernando, but I was unaware at the time that a lawsuit had been brought against the author.

The rest of the cases are more recent, during what has come to be called the Movement for the Recuperation of Historical Memory. In other words, during the first decade of this century. I am referring to Fabien Garrido, who was ordered to shut down his webpage by Judge Juan Carlos Carballal Paraleda, of Cambados, a figure to whom we will pay a certain amount of attention since we were able to hear him speak during the aforementioned conference; Marta Capín, sued by the family of a doctor implicated in the killing of the personnel at a psychiatric hospital; Santiago Macías and Emilio Silva, who experienced problems due to a testimony that appeared in their book; Dionisio Pereira who, for telling the story of the repression in Cerdedo, had problems with the family of a Francoist ex-mayor; and Alfredo Grimaldos, sued by the Rosón family for retelling old stories which,

TRANSLATOR'S NOTE (TN) 1. A "Right to Honor" is enshrined in the Spanish Constitution. Theoretically, it is equivalent to British and American legal protections against libel. In practice, however, the Spanish courts often use the "Right to Honor" to obstruct the work of historians writing about the Civil War and the Franco dictatorship, with total disregard for whether or not the allegedly libelous statements are true.

when originally brought to light, had occasioned other lawsuits. Other cases stand out for their peculiarities: Violeta Friedman's admirable struggle with Léon Degrelle, the Belgian Nazi given refuge by the Franco regime; the case of Antonio Martínez Borrego's family, whose reputation was tarnished —with the help of a journalist— by an individual who wanted to pass himself off as something he was not by blaming others for his sins; and the sad story of Amparo Barayón and her son Ramón, in which a lawsuit should have been brought but never materialized.

None of this is a matter of indifference to those of us engaged in researching the repression. I recall the case of Isidoro Sánchez Baena at the beginning of the 1990s and the alarm it caused those of us who delve into these matters. The criminal case of the Luque landlord, whose perpetrator's full name was given, was an early example of the denial of oral testimonies as a valid historical source. It is curious because Sánchez Baena was inspired to investigate what happened in Luque, and gather testimonies of people who lived through those events, after he read Francisco Moreno Gómez's works, and Moreno Gómez had been publishing histories of the Republic, the Civil War and the postwar in Cordoba since the early 1980s. It has to be asked why is it that Moreno Gómez did not have problems when he published his works, with their detailed accounts of the repression and with numerous oral testimonies?

According to Moreno Gómez, the Right in the 1980s did not dare to react to these publications, which were then still the exception, though newspapers in Cordoba did indeed publish some isolated criticisms from a few local characters. He also received an anonymous letter sent from Pozoblanco, accusing him of exploiting the victims' blood to line his own pockets, and one of the executioners from his home town, Diego "El Chunga," approached him and called him a liar, to which he immediately responded, "Out of respect for the victims, hold your tongue." Later, it was the Jesuit Feliciano Delgado who would attack him from the pages of the newspaper *Córdoba*, making the most of the fact that Moreno Gómez had confused him with a family member of the same name. And that was all there was to it. Not a single lawsuit for a book which, for the first time, dealt openly with the repression. So we must concur with Moreno Gómez's analysis: the Right did not yet feel sure of itself. There were witnesses still alive who could throw the past back in their faces. Protected as they were by the 1977 law of amnesty, they preferred to keep quiet.

Another pioneer researcher of the repression, Alberto Reig Tapia, tells me that his problems, in addition to publishers always wanting to simplify everything and worried about book sales, stemmed from the archives, jealous guardians of the victors' memory. Furthermore, as a result of his participation in the radio debates that followed each televised episode of the series on the Civil War coordinated by Manuel Tuñón de Lara, he was threatened with beatings and even death.

In my own case, the situation did not change in the 1990s, when I published *La Guerra Civil en Huelva* in 1996 (4th ed., 2006). The problem was the Publication Service of the Huelva Provincial Government, which delayed the book's release for three years starting in 1993 because the appendixes with lists of victims seemed "problematic" to the person in charge. Nevertheless, in spite of potential legal problems, given the exhaustive treatment of the repression, there was only one complaint. Someone from one of the towns showed up at the office of Domingo Prieto, then president of the Huelva government, complaining that his family had been implicated in criminal activity. Prieto simply told him that the information was trustworthy and that historians' findings had to be respected.

I was even more alert to trouble when I published *La justicia de Queipo* in the year 2000 (latest edition: Crítica, 2006). It was a descent into the repression's underworld in southwestern Spain as documented by the repressors themselves, with abundant names, and with the intention of describing what happened as seen from the bottom up, including the perspective of the so-called death squads. But, as luck would have it, nothing happened then either. At that time, in the year 2000, one could no longer talk of an intimidated Right. Quite the contrary. The Right was emboldened by their absolute majority in the government and would show its true face during the next four years. On the other hand, I think that if anyone contemplated suing me for bringing to light such delicate information, information that tarnished so many people's honor, they held back out of fear that, as a consequence of their own lawsuit, even more information would come to light, and what remained of their "family honor" would disappear forever into history's cesspool.

I am unaware of specific complaints and threats that affected other researchers, although there certainly must have been some. Ian Gibson and his book on the repression in Granada comes to mind, as do other pioneering works such as those from La Rioja or Soria.

The cases put forth here represent a sample – I think a significant one – of what has occurred in our country when the hidden past has been brought into the light of day, a past denied by the dictatorship and declared off limits during the transition to democracy. I am a historian and my objective is none other than to reveal a series of conflicts, isolated and generally unknown, created precisely by the refusal to admit and recognize what took place in Spain as a consequence of the military coup of July 18, 1936. I do not have legal training and, needless to say, it has not been easy to embark on these generally tempestuous legal seas, with their convoluted pronouncements that seem designed to be neither read nor understood. For that very reason it was such a pleasure to listen to presentations by legal experts like Vicente Gimeno Sendra or María Emilia Casas Bahamonde.

The earliest case discussed in this book is from 1981; the last is from May 2012. We are dealing with a phenomenon that has recurred with tiresome frequency for three decades, but especially in the last few years. The purpose of this work is to tell what happened and to whom it happened, and to try to understand why it happened in the way it did.

That said, and since the subject that concerns us here is justice, it is worth contemplating, from a historical perspective and in relation to the Franco repression, where the judicial system has stood through all this and why it has shown itself so eager at times to defend the honor of the victors. We know that from the very beginning and during the entire dictatorship, the judicial apparatus constituted one of Francoism's bulwarks, and that, like other repressive institutions, it passed intact from the dictatorship to the post-Franco democratic regime. A good example of this evolution would be the case of Antonio Pedrol Rius, an important public figure during the Transition:[TN2] president of the General Law Council, dean of the Illustrious College of Lawyers in Madrid and senator by royal appointment in 1977. Nevertheless, Rius's biographies never mention that in the wake of the 1936 coup he roamed southwestern Spain in service to the military judicial machinery created by the conspirators. A study of the Judicial Military Corps and of the lawyers who collaborated in the summary courts-martial through the judicial offices of the military governors would shed light on the origins of the Franco regime's legal system.

Starting in 1977, there were cases of exhumations related to the Franco repression in much of the country, but the judicial system did not get involved in a single case even though it was obliged by law to do so. Of course, if judges had prepared a certificate of exhumation, they would have been required to investigate who was buried in those common graves, as well as why and how long they were there. It would have been easy. There were people still alive who knew where there were human remains and witnesses who knew the circumstances of those events, but the judicial

---

TRANSLATOR'S NOTE 2. The word "transition" is spelled with lower case "t" when it refers to the process of transforming Spain from a dictatorship to a democracy. It is spelled with upper case "T" if it refers to the time period 1976–1983 during which that transformation took place.

system did nothing. Those bones and their stories did not concern the Ministry of Justice, in spite of the fact that it was the Ministry of Justice that had, at one time, taken it upon itself to conduct the "Causa General," an investigation of the victims of the "red terror."

In keeping with the politics of the 1980s and 1990s, the judicial system decided to "not look back" except, as we will see, to defend the right to honor of persons affected by the freedom of information... about the Franco repression. This is the same attitude I have criticized elsewhere, character-ized by the total absence of research into these matters by the academic world until the 1990s, along with the politics of amnesia practiced in those years by the government. Criticism of this attitude is what irritates those who sing the praises of the transition to democracy, whose prototype would be Santos Juliá, political commentator for the newspaper *El País*.[1]

When, around 1996–1997, the movements for the recuperation of Spain's democratic memory began, the judicial system still refused to acknowledge them, undoubtedly convinced that it had nothing to do with what was being debated, or simply indifferent to its own democratic past. At the beginning of the present century, the government began to realize that it could not remain on the sidelines of the social debate. Hence the process that goes from the timid and confused condemnation of Francoism in November 2002, to the commitment to draft a Law of Historical Memory in 2004 and its passage four years later, in December 2008.

The first attempt to implicate the judiciary came toward the end of 2006, when thirteen associations brought a series of cases before the Spanish National Tribunal concerning people who disappeared as a result of the 1936 military coup, with the intention that the cases be regarded as illegal detentions, forced disappearances and crimes against humanity, so that a statute of limitations would not apply. The cases would lie dormant in one of the Court's chambers for nearly two years until Judge Baltasar Garzón went public with his initial findings in September 2008.

In spite of the fact that many aspects of the document could obviously have been improved, there is no doubt that it represents the first attempt on the part of the Spanish judicial system to establish a legal definition of "July 18" and its consequences. It is the first document in which Francisco Franco and other military leaders are held responsible for organizing the rebellion, for carrying out a systematic extermination plan and for the disap-pearance of tens of thousands of persons. The document also includes a reminder that "until the present day, impunity has been the rule in the face of events that could be classified as crimes against humanity" and that what was at stake was nothing less than "a form of institutional rehabilitation in the face of the silence heretofore displayed."

This opened a path that, if it could have been followed, would undoubtedly have led to real progress, but the celebrations were short-lived. Javier Zaragoza, Director of Public Prosecution, limited himself to issuing a reminder that the events that were being debated were protected by the 1977 amnesty – it is important not to forget that, although the Law of Amnesty had been approved by Parliament, it was pre-constitutional – and that criminal legislation at that time did not allow discussion of crimes against humanity. Furthermore, the crime of rebellion was outside the jurisdiction of the National Tribunal. Zaragoza went so far as to accuse Garzón of organizing a new "causa general," a reference to the Franco regime's "red" witch-hunt. He also thought the events in question were common crimes, not political crimes. After only a few weeks the National Tribunal itself, with unusual measures that showed how seriously it regarded the matter, aborted the initiative: first by Garzón's own retraction, and then by the public prosecutor's declaration that the matter was outside Judge Garzón's sphere of authority. And with that, between the haste of a judge who had not calculated his strengths carefully enough and the obstinacy of the same Right as always, a great opportunity was quashed: that of bringing together all the scattered documentation gathered over the past three decades by various persons and collectives, and of putting together a complete report on the Franco repression, a report whose singularity and importance would have derived precisely from its having been backed by the judiciary.

With these developments, the forgotten Law of Historical Memory again took center stage. It was a weak and incomplete legal project that satisfied almost no one. All of which leaves open the possibility that cases like those described in this book will continue to occur. The path aborted by the judicial Right would eventually have led to the repeal of the 1977 Law of Amnesty, as called for in 2008 by the United Nations Human Rights Committee. The law had essentially meant "period, end of story" for Spain's transition to democracy. Let us just say that, for the time being, everything remains lashed down and firmly lashed down.[TN3]

Note

1 See his article "Amnesty as the Triumph of Memory" (*El País*, November 24, 2008). In it he says that "the substance" of the October 1976 law of amnesty

TRANSLATOR'S NOTE 3. Francisco Espinosa-Maestre's introduction ends ". . . *todo sigue atado y bien atado*" (everything remains lashed down and firmly lashed down). He is paraphrasing a famous declaration by Franco: *Todo ha quedado atado y bien atado*. (Everything has been lashed down and firmly lashed down), an expression of Franco's belief that his regime would remain intact after his death.

was "to release from prison all ETA inmates and, in exchange, to extend amnesty to the authorities, bureaucrats and police." Also that, for the same reason, "the Civil War, the dictatorship, torture and suffering were discussed, the past was brought up to date, but with the intention of finding closure on a long stage of our history. The Civil War had indeed ended, as the press noted the following day." Finally, as proof that "a tyranny of silence" had not been imposed, and for lack of better evidence, he refers us to the magazine *Interviú* and a series of articles from the end of the 1970s dedicated to the Franco repression, which makes about as much sense as demonstrating that in 1990s Spain the repression was still being discussed by giving as an example Paco Lobatón's program "Who knows where," in which, frequently, between a piece on the grandfather who went for a walk and never returned, and a piece on the girl who ran away from home in search of new horizons, a piece would be slipped in about "a man who disappeared during the Civil War." Of course it was good for their ratings. But the only thing that that program elicited from those doing research on the repression was indignation, because it represented nothing but an escape valve for a society that was not allowed to recuperate its hidden past through the proper channels.

Fernando Ruiz Vergara and his Documentary *Rocío*

The documentary *Rocío* opened in Seville in the mid-1980s at the Pathé cinema on Cuna Street, where it ran for only a few days. Those of us who saw it in the nearly empty hall were perplexed when, on several occasions that seemed eternal in the theater's darkness, the screen went black except for letters that said: "Suppressed by sentence of the Second Chamber of the High Court on April 3, 1984." We already knew from the press about the problems the movie had encountered since its first showing five years earlier at the Seville Film Festival, where it had won an award. In the meantime, its exhibition had been prohibited, first in the southwest and then throughout Andalusia.

Rocío's openings in different Spanish cities received extensive coverage in the press, in the opinion sections as much as in the sections devoted specifically to film. *Diario 16* and *La Calle* gave it favorable reviews. In *La Calle*, Fernando Lara's recommendation was "see it so you will have a better idea what kind of country we live in" (February 3, 1981). *Pueblo*, *Ya* and *El Alcázar* attacked it. Father Sobrino, considered at the time in certain quarters to be a "Jesuit film expert," said it amounted to a "manipulated and distorted documentary because of its ideological bent that smacked of an anticlerical political rally" (*Ya*, February 15, 1981).

The movie is an impressive history of the annual pilgrimage to the shrine of the Virgin of El Rocío in the countryside near Almonte. It is full of powerful visual images, mostly filmed during the years immediately following Franco's death. What stood out was that Fernando Ruiz Vergara's perspective was not the usual one. Even the same images of the *Rocío* that had been seen thousands of times acquired a very different effect, due in no small measure to the music. Especially interesting were the interviews. It is worth recalling, for example, the one devoted to justifying the "transformations" suffered by the image of the virgin, the unforgettable explanation by Hernández Díaz, Art History professor at the University of Seville and, paradoxically, one of those in charge of cataloguing, in 1936, the damages done to the artistic treasures of the Seville diocese during the five years of the Republic. His explanation of the origin of the problem was especially striking, drawing attention to the "events of 1932" in Almonte and their intimate relation to the repression in 1936.[TN1] The reading of the names and nicknames, accompanied in many cases by a portrait, of the Almonte residents who were assassinated as a result of the July 18 military coup was extremely moving. This was followed by the off camera voice of José Luis Gómez, an actor who was born in the area, stating that one hundred people were killed in Almonte: ninety-nine men and one woman. It was the first time we had seen anything like it in a movie theater.

All this was very interesting to me for a specific reason. At the time I was trying to gain access to the archive of Seville's San Fernando Cemetery to see if the Francoist repression was reflected there in some way. I had already come up against the university, which refused to have anything to do with the possibility of my writing a senior thesis on the military coup in Seville — nor even provide me a letter facilitating my access to certain archives — and against the bureaucrats at the cemetery, whose director insisted that "whatever they had there was none of my business." So I resorted to the Municipal Government, where a person connected to the Department of Health and whom I knew by sight from the university agreed to sign a permit that would facilitate my research.

This research on the military coup and repression in Seville would lead to a work that would not be published until 1990 when an abridged version would see the light of day in a book coordinated by the same university professor who had refused to accept it as a senior thesis twelve years prior. So it was during those times of absolute secrecy regarding the darkest aspects of the military coup — none of the pioneering research on the Francoist repression had yet been published — when Fernando Ruiz Vergara came forward to reveal the underside of the massacre carried out by the fascists in Almonte and put a name and a face to the man who, according to eyewitnesses, was most responsible: the landowner José María Reales Carrasco, who had been mayor during the dictatorship of Miguel Primo de Rivera.

A few years later, during the second half of the 1980s, when I was researching the military coup and repression in Huelva, I recalled the film *Rocío*. I recorded it when it was aired on Andalusian TV (very late at night) and was thus able to collect all the names of victims mentioned in the documentary. It is important to bear in mind that only a little more than one

TRANSLATOR'S NOTE 1. The "events of 1932" to which Francisco Espinosa-Maestre refers was an anti-Republican uprising in Almonte orchestrated by the local Right. The uprising was justified by the removal from the Town Hall meeting room of a decorative ceramic tile depicting the Virgin.

fourth of those shot in Almonte were inscribed in the Civil Death Registry and that Ruiz Vergara's film provided several dozen names. In the late 1980s, in order to complete the list of victims, I tried to locate Fernando Ruiz Vergara in Huelva and Almonte, but all I could find out was that he was living in Portugal. When I published *La Guerra Civil en Huelva* in 1996 I mentioned him and his contribution, and I hoped he would contact me, but he never did. I had to wait more than twenty years from the time I saw his film in the mid-1980s until I made his acquaintance, through a series of coincidences during a trip he took to Seville. That was when I finally heard the story behind *Rocío*.

As already stated, it was first shown in 1980 at the Seville Film Festival and, throughout the following year, it was distributed everywhere in Spain except Andalusia, where it could not be seen until 1985. Experience shows us that fact is stranger than fiction, its perpetual plagiarist. And I say this because, incredible as it seems, Reales Carrasco's children filed a lawsuit against *Rocío* on the morning of February 23, 1981, a few hours before Lieutenant Colonel Antonio Tejero Molina of the Civil Guard took over the Spanish parliament and held its members hostage in an attempted military coup. The lawsuit was against Fernando Ruiz Vergara, Ana Vila, who wrote the script, and Pedro Gómez Clavijo, the Almonte resident who gave his testimony in the film, denouncing the part played by the ex-mayor in the repression. Gómez Clavijo had previously used a clever stratagem to show Ruiz Vergara who belonged to the "death squad" during the summer of 1936. The two men had gone to a well-attended burial in Almonte at the end of the 1970s. During the ceremony, Gómez Clavijo had strolled among the attendees, pausing next to each one of the culprits, while Ruiz Vergara took their pictures. Nevertheless, none of this came out in the film.

The sentence handed down by the Seville Provincial Court in September 1982 describes the movie in detail, emphasizing the most egregious moments, according to the plaintiffs, José María Reales Carrasco's six children:

A) "off camera voice" "with the military uprising on July 18, the monarchists, *requetés*,[TN2] and Falangists take the initiative, arrest and kill

---

TRANSLATOR'S NOTE 2. Requeté is the name for members of the Carlist militias. Carlism dates back to the nineteenth-century supporters of Carlos María Isidro Benito de Borbón-Parma (1788–1855), pretender to the Spanish throne after the death of his brother Fernando VII in 1833. The Carlists in the Spanish civil war were ultraconservative Catholics who believed in the divine right of kings. They were as violent as the Falangists.

without trial all those who in one way or another had demonstrated their support for the Republic or had stood out for their revolutionary ideals." **B)** "Clavijo's voice", "every night this gang comes to the jail with a list of individuals to take out to the highway and assassinate in the headlights of a truck." **C)** "off camera voice." "In Almonte they killed . . . ." There follows a list of men and others totaling one hundred persons. Ninety-nine men and one woman, accompanied by photographs of cadavers. **D)** "Clavijo's voice", "the leader of the gang of criminals was . . ." (here the voice stops and there appears in the film the same photograph of Sr. Reales Carrasco that appeared before when he was presented as the founder of the Rocío Confraternity of Jeréz de la Frontera; which appears seven minutes before, but this time with his eyes hidden by a black rectangle and he appears in seventy-nine stills in which he is identifiable in spite of the aforementioned covering up of his eyes), and **E)** "Clavijo's voice continues": "may he rest in peace, for I would have given him a longer life . . . because that gentleman, when they took away the men, the workers, those who fought for freedom, bread and work, he told that gang of criminals "don't start yet, leave mine to me and riding on a horse with a club in hand he beat them to death; [. . .]" [the original is a literal transcription; punctuation errors are not corrected in this translation].

The prosecutor spoke of an "ongoing crime of libel." Everything became questionable except the reality of one hundred assassinations in Almonte following its occupation, a matter no one brought up. What was not allowed was to associate this repression with the person Reales, presented by someone who lived through those events, as "the leader of the gang of criminals" who ravaged the town after the triumph of the military coup. And not because such a thing was true or false, a question that never came up, but for other reasons that were explained, as we will see, in the sentence handed down by the High Court. In the first of many "considering that"s in the document – needless to say these documents are not created to be read, much less understood – there is a striking slip (italicized):

[. . .] because the phrase "the leader of this Gang of Criminals, followed by the projection of a photograph of Sr. Reales Carrasco, father of the plaintiffs in close relation and forming a homogeneous whole [*sic*] with which in factual account [*sic*] is contained relative to the existence of a gang, to the actions it carried out, *highly probable to be true*, and with what follows expressive of a conduct that although it does not say it refers to said gentleman it goes immediately to the aforementioned photograph which although the eyes are covered is recognizable as his photograph implies necessarily the intention to dishonor [. . .]."

A later correction added "re" to the word "probable," converting "probable" into "reprobable," (in English, "reprehensible").

In September 1982, the Seville Provincial Court asked for one year sentences and fines of twenty thousand pesetas for Fernando Ruiz Vergara and Ana Vila, and a sentence of four years and two months imprisonment and another fine of twenty thousand pesetas for Pedro Gómez Clavijo, who was then seventy-three years old. As if that were not enough, they ordered the accused to reimburse the plaintiffs with six million pesetas for "moral harm inflicted." Furthermore, the Court decreed the prohibition of exhibiting the movie in Spain as long as "it contained the second reference to D. José María Reales related to the assassinations in question . . ." The crimes that resulted in such severe sentences were slanderous allegations and libel.

According to an item found in the press by the historian Ángel del Río, Gómez Clavijo's attorney, Antonio Mate, made the following statement:

> Naturally, Pedro Gómez Clavijo never saw José Mª Reales riding a horse and killing people with a club, because it would mean that he was either part of the gang or one of the dead. But he knows it to be true and described it that way because he is of an age to know it, just like those seventeen elderly gentlemen who came here yesterday without having been called as witnesses and stood in the doorway of this courtroom to confirm my client's testimony; but that evidence was not admitted because, according to the tribunal, this courtroom is not equipped to show the film in which Pedro Gómez appears as the narrator of these events. Here it is not Pedro that is on trial but rather oral testimony as a historical source, although I fear that those Almonte residents are no longer going to tell us many of the things they know for the same reason that Pedro Gómez has fallen silent: the fear that has caused him to refute his own image.

The prosecutor, Bernardo Botello, responded sarcastically that Gómez Clavijo had at last become "a historical source."[1]

The prosecution accepted Gómez Clavijo's four year prison sentence but asked that his fine be raised to one hundred thousand pesetas, and for Fernando Ruiz and Ana Vila he requested six years in prison and fines of two hundred thousand pesetas besides paying all legal expenses, including those of the prosecution. According to the prosecution, the reimbursement to the Reales family should be twenty-five million pesetas, which the family promised to donate to the Rocío Foundational Confraternity. It also demanded the definitive confiscation of all the existent negatives and copies of the movie.

To avoid problems Fernando Ruiz assumed total responsibility before the law, which meant Ana Vila and Pedro Clavijo were absolved. Vila had to say that Ruiz Vergara was the only one responsible for the film, which was not true, and Clavijo was obligated to lie by saying that he was never warned that his interviews would be used in the documentary. Finally, the Seville Provincial Court sentenced him to two months and one day in prison and a fifty thousand peseta fine.

Then they appealed to the High Court, which handed down its ruling in February 1984. Luis Vivas Marzal,[2] the spokesperson for the court, first rejected, "for impossibility of evidence," Reales's responsibility in the events that occurred in Almonte. Vivas Marzal emphasized that although the film was about the "Rocío" pilgrimage,

> There soon arises an inopportune and unfortunate recollecting of episodes that took place before and after July 18, in which one of the two sides in the conflict is ridiculed, forgetting that civil wars, fratricidal struggles that they are, leave a bloody wake or trail of deeds, sometimes heroic and other times reprehensible, that it is indispensable to bury and forget if one wants the survivors and future generations to live in peace, harmony and reconciliation, and he misses the mark who stirs up the embers of that struggle in order to awaken animosities, hatreds and resentments put to rest by the passage of time, without the aforesaid preventing rigorously historical and impartial accounts not intended for general consumption that pay homage to the adage *De omnibus aut veritas aut nihil* ("Either the truth or nothing") with an exclusively critical and scientific finality and an objective and testimonial nuance.

The prosecution attempted to include in the proceedings the declarations of six witnesses who tried to vouch for the "lofty qualities devoted [*sic*] to the deceased Señor R. and his irreproachable conduct throughout his life, the which is manifestly superfluous [*sic*], and, on the other hand, the impossibility of his perpetrating the deeds of [*sic*] which he was attributed in the cinematographic movie *Rocío* which, on the one hand, was incumbent on the accused, who, incidentally, have not been able to accredit the certainty of those deeds, and on the other hand, the impossibility of evidence with said proofs, given that nothing prevented the Señor R. in question from being incarcerated from July 20, 1936 until the 29th of said month and year, and, later, from belonging to the cavalry unit 'Volunteers of Huelva,' and, in spite of it, to have been able to perpetrate the deeds attributed to him in the aforementioned movie, we proceed by virtue of the preceding arguments to the rejection of the appeal . . ." The testimonies of the six witnesses for the prosecution were unnecessary. In the end, the High Court rejected the appeal and the sentence handed down by the Seville Provincial Court was upheld.

We can imagine the rest of the story, but it must be told. Fernando Ruiz Vergara's private and professional life was ruined; Pedro Gómez Clavijo, who broke into tears in the Seville Provincial Court when he heard he was facing four years in prison and a hundred thousand peseta fine, spent the last days of his life an embittered man; and *Rocío* became an accursed film. When it has been shown from time to time on television, not only is it still censored, the cuts that used to reveal this censorship with references to the decree that suppressed those parts of the film have disappeared. Whoever has seen it on Canal Sur does not realize that something is amiss. The censors have achieved their final objective: to function without showing their hand.[3]

We should bear in mind that all this happened between February 1981 and February 1984, when, according to what they tell us, the worst phase of the Transition (the five-year period 1976–1982) was over, the attempted military coup of February 23, 1981 had been quashed and Spain was a full-fledged democracy with the most spectacular Socialist majority in its history.

In April 2005, for the "II Conference on Historical Memory and Justice: The Repression in Huelva and the Mining Region," which took place in the El Monte auditorium in Huelva, there was a tribute to Fernando Ruiz Vergara and *Rocío*, which was screened during one of the sessions. It confirmed the fact that the censorial fervor was still alive. The tribute was criticized by the Reales family itself, by the Rocío Confraternity – "Almonte was not amused," we were reminded by José Joaquín Gil, president of the Confraternity – and even by the Andalusian Party, which demanded that the movie not be shown, since, "in their judgment, it linked the Rocío pilgrimage to the Franco dictatorship." For its Andalusian supplement on March 29 and April 1, *El Mundo* collected the opinion "of several residents of Almonte" that "it is not the most opportune time or context to show the movie." *El Mundo* was informed by the Rocío Confraternity that "they will not allow the image of the Rocío pilgrimage to be tarnished." The newspaper reminded its readers that the film's projection in its entirety could "wound the sensibilities of those family members who, in 1981, brought a lawsuit against the producer for slanderous allegations." The family, basing its claim on the fact that the sentence was still in effect, demanded that the copy to be screened be the censured one. In spite of the pressure exerted, the El Monte employees in charge of the conference kept the program as originally planned, but the copy of the film that was eventually shown was the one in which José María Reales's image was concealed and the words about his role in the repression omitted.[4]

Notes

1 The quote is from *El Correo de Andalucía*, June 17, 1982. I cited it from Ángel del Río Sánchez, *Otras víctimas de la transición. Persecución y censura del filme "Rocío" de Fernando Ruiz Vergara*, forthcoming publication.

2 Vivas Marzal, high office holder in the magistracy and a man of openly Francoist ideology, was known, among other things, as the spokesman who confirmed the Court's finding in the case of the woman sentenced "for perpetrating a crime of public scandal" to one month and one day in prison and a 20,000 peseta fine for practicing nudism on a beach in northern Spain and refusing to put her clothes on when the police ordered her to do so. This occurred in the same year, 1984.

3 The copy in distribution now retains the evidence of censorship by the author's express wish: http://hamacaonline.net/obra.php?id=496

4 Fernando Ruiz Vergara (Seville, 1942) died on October 12, 2011, in Escalos de Baixo (Portugal). He had been scarred for life by *Rocío*. He never regretted having made it nor did he feel sorry about its consequences, in spite of having been warned at the time by Reales's descendants as well as by friends and acquaintances who did not understand his decision to get involved in the turbid affair of the fascist repression in Almonte. He was conscious of the fact that it was part of the history of the Rocío pilgrimage and decided to include it. As a result, he fell prey to a judicial system that did the bidding of the Reales family and his life took a drastic turn, forcing him to leave the country and return to Portugal, where he had been before and where he could eke out a meager living. He never complained. On the contrary, he felt at home there and had a deep appreciation for the character and lifestyle of the Portuguese. In fact, knowing him, it seems to me he could not have lived anywhere else.

During the first decade of the twenty-first century, the flourishing of the movement for historical memory brought with it the vindication of *Rocío*, the first Spanish documentary to openly confront the Francoist repression. It came a little late for Ruiz Vergara but, in spite of the fact that what he would have liked was to embark on some new project, he knew how to adapt to circumstances and let himself be carried along by the well-deserved tributes to him in various Spanish and Portuguese cities.

We who were his friends organized the first homage in Huelva in 2005, on the occasion of the Conference of the Andalusian Association for Historical Memory and Justice. We pressured the Ministry of Justice of the Andalusian

Regional Government to see if anything could be done about the sentence handed down in the 1980s, but our efforts led nowhere. We also tried to interest some national newspaper in offering a video of the documentary *Rocío* as a supplement to its weekend edition, for the obvious interest there was in that accursed film, and so that the producer would finally be compensated economically for a work that until then had brought him nothing but headaches. But that was not possible either. In the end, it looks as though there will be a book which, in addition to various texts about him, will contain the documentary, the interview with him by the anthropologist Dulce Simoes and a documentary about *Rocío* by José Luis Tirado, a project Fernando Ruiz Vergara knew about and in which he collaborated. This will be the definitive homage to his work and the commemoration he deserved.

Violeta Friedman versus Léon Degrelle

Léon Degrelle was a well-known Belgian Nazi, founder of that movement in his country, war criminal and a member of the Waffen SS. He settled in Spain in 1945. Although he lived under an assumed name, it was known that he was residing there ever since 1955 when a journalist recognized him at a meeting of veterans of the Blue Division, the military unit sent by Franco to serve on the Russian front during World War II. Franco protected him and he was helped by his friends: Girón, Arias Navarro, Blas Piñar and the Count of Mayalde (Escrivá de Romaní, former ambassador in Berlin and mayor of Madrid). This enabled Degrelle to live in luxury in Spain, collecting art and writing pro-Nazi pamphlets. Belgium's request for extradition was ignored. Nevertheless, although the statute of limitations had run out on his sentence, Belgium declared him *persona non grata* and banned him from entering the country. When he died, in 1994, Belgium even prevented the return of his ashes.

It was some statements he made in 1985 on a nightly news program on TVE that led to this case. In these statements Degrelle criticized – he used the word profanation – the examination that had been carried out in Brazil on the remains of the Nazi doctor Joseph Mengele in order to verify his identity. "Is there anything you regret, señor Degrelle?" the journalist asked. "I only regret that Hitler lost the war," the Nazi replied. Indignant at the spectacle, Violeta Friedman called TVE, where they defended the interview for its journalistic interest. She also wrote a letter to the newspaper *El País* (July 17, 1985). Degrelle replied, reaffirming his ideas and once again denying the Holocaust. And he was saying this to a woman whose family (parents, grandparents and a great-grandmother) and friends had disappeared at Auschwitz. Degrelle not only denied the existence of the gas chambers, he affirmed that Mengele was "a normal doctor." He also expounded at length during an interview published in the magazine *Tiempo* (July 29, 1985), in which he even said, "We need a leader; let us hope the

AUTHOR'S NOTE. The first part of this chapter is a summary of the final chapters in Violeta Friedman's book *Mis memorias* (Barcelona: Planeta, 2005).

right man for the job appears, the one who could save Europe. [. . .] But there is no one around anymore like the *Führer*." When Violeta Friedman requested equal space in Julián Lago's magazine so she could respond to the Nazi's ideas, they paid no attention: Degrelle was news; Friedman was not.

It was then that she decided to turn to the courts, even though she was aware of the legal vacuum that existed in Spanish jurisprudence with respect to her situation. In her lawsuit, she requested that Degrelle be prevented from making statements like those he had made and that she be compensated for moral harm suffered. Her case was taken on by Jorge Trías Sagnier, honorary president of the Madrid Jewish Community and lawyer for Max Mazín, who was the leader of the Spanish chapter of the Jewish organization B'nai B'rith. Jorge Trías refused to charge her for his services. The trial, which took place in June 1986, ruled in favor of Degrelle in accordance with the right to freedom of expression granted him by the Constitution. Friedman, whom Degrelle had not even mentioned according to the judges, "lacked legal grounds for filing a lawsuit." She then appealed to the Madrid Territorial Court.

The second trial took place in February 1988. This time Violeta Friedman was accosted by members of CEDADE, who had gathered at the entrance to the courthouse.[TN1] The Civil Guard not only failed to protect her, they even roughed her up. A headline in *El País* completely missed the mark: "The Appeal of the Acquittal of the Nazi Degrelle Pits Violeta Friedman against Extremist Groups" (February 4, 1988). On top of that, throughout the trial Degrelle's relatives and supporters were allowed to demonstrate inside the courtroom, and press coverage favored the Nazi. The outcome was the same: Degrelle had exercised his right to freedom of expression. The third step was the High Court which, in December 1988, ruled in favor of the Belgian Nazi.

In Spain there was one final recourse, the Constitutional Tribunal, which accepted the case and resolved it three years later, in November 1991. The finding (sentence 214/1991) was favorable for Violeta Friedman, compensating for the long delay. The previous sentences were nullified and Violeta Friedman's "right to honor" was recognized, indicating that freedom of expression has limitations vis-à-vis the "right to honor" and human dignity.

This finding had legal consequences that were enshrined in the Penal Code. The denial, trivialization, or justification of events classified as genocide and attempts to rehabilitate or constitute regimes or institutions that

---

TRANSLATOR'S NOTE 1. CEDADE (acronym for Círculo Español de Amigos de Europa or "Spanish Circle of Friends of Europe") was a Spanish neo-Nazi group. Léon Degrelle was a prominent member.

supported such practices were defined as crimes. Nevertheless, the paragraph that outlawed the distribution or exhibition of symbols or propaganda that represented or defended events considered to be genocide mysteriously disappeared from the final text.

Violeta Friedman was very satisfied with the result, especially the Constitutional Tribunal's sentence, although she considered the legislative text insufficient, because the omission of the paragraph mentioned above allowed "incitement to racial hatred and violence," unlike what was customary in other European countries. This omission was finally rectified in April 1995. Friedman died five years later, satisfied by the results of her long six-year struggle.

It is appropriate to mention that, besides the lawyer Trías Sagnier, Friedman had three other factors in her favor: economic support from B'nai B'rith, led by the aforementioned Max Mazín; the fact that the spokesperson for the sentence was Vicente Gimeno Sendra; and the presence on the Constitutional Tribunal of Francisco Tomás y Valiente and Francisco Rubio Llorente, the first as president and the second as vice president. Given the predominantly conservative nature of the judiciary in Spain, the participation of these men was crucial. It is also worth recalling that Degrelle's attorney was Juan Servando Balaguer Pareño, married to one of Degrelle's daughters and with a past in accord with the circumstances. He had belonged to the paramilitary forces that joined the coup at its outset in July 1936. Among other operations, he participated in the occupation of several towns in the Huelva mining region. Later he settled in Constantina where he worked as a dentist. He was a leader of Fuerza Joven (Young Force) and Fuerza Nueva (New Force).[TN2]

This is how, in 2005, Trías Sagnier recalled those times:

> On the sixtieth anniversary of the liberation of the death camps, almost no one remembers Violeta. The turmoil of her life took her from us a few years ago, but I have vivid memories of her, of her burial in the Madrid Jewish cemetery, of her daughter Patricia and of her Spanish grandchildren. I also remember Max Mazín back then, and Alberto Benasuly and the then ambassador Ben-Ami, who encouraged and supported me during the preparations for a problematical legal battle in defense of the memory of victims, personified by Violeta, a memory trampled with impunity during

TRANSLATOR'S NOTE 2. Fuerza Joven (Young Force) was a youth group associated with Fuerza Nueva (New Force). Fuerza Nueva was an extreme right-wing group founded in the mid-1960s. During the Transition, it constituted itself as a political party dedicated to Francoist ideology and the spirit of July 18, 1936.

an interview on TVE in 1985 with Léon Degrelle, ex general in the Waffen SS and founder of the Belgian Nazi Party. And how could I now forget, on this anniversary, the minister Enrique Múgica, the attorney general for the State and Francisco Tomás y Valiente, then president of the Constitutional Tribunal which, in the end, granted Violeta the protection of a civil lawsuit – not a criminal lawsuit as it is sometimes erroneously called – that I lodged in her name, declaring that her honor had been violated. Thanks to the sentence handed down in 1991 by the Constitutional Tribunal, whose spokesperson was the magistrate Vicente Gimeno Sendra, things began to change, and the Socialist Government began to take seriously the outbreaks of xenophobia and anti-Semitism that some of us had been warning about for a long time. In 1995 the Penal Code was modified and repugnant declarations, such as those made by Degrelle, are now criminally prosecuted. The histories of the Spanish republicans or of the Palestinians in Israel may be considered tragic, but they pale beside the Holocaust and its survivors. (*ABC*, January 31, 2005)

The way Trías Sagnier's concludes his article is extraordinarily striking for its strained quality. Perhaps the unexpected turn his article takes in the last sentence was prompted – in addition to the evident pro-Israeli attitude – by another, very different, case described in a later chapter in which Trías Sagnier was one of the plaintiffs.

The sentence handed down by the tribunal is a model of expository clarity, and it is worth drawing attention to several aspects. The key was the limitations placed on the right to freedom of expression which, as we know, is a matter that still provokes controversy and debate, always centered on the same conflict. The sentence emphasized that Degrelle, by exercising what he understood to be his "freedom of expression," denied and ridiculed the horrors suffered by Violeta Friedman's family members, "attributing to them a mendacity that disqualified them from public esteem and respect." The sentence respected Degrelle's freedom of expression and ideology, establishing that his opinions "can only be understood for what they are: subjective and self-serving opinions about historical events." Nevertheless, it considered his judgments to be offensive with respect to Jews, whom he discredited as liars who falsely presented themselves as victims, for which reason he was regarded as racist and anti-Semitic.

The sentence also proposed that unlimited rights do not exist and that, consequently, neither freedom of expression nor freedom of ideology can protect expressions of a racist or xenophobic character when they affect the right to honor and human dignity. The ruling nullified the three previous sentences and recognized Violeta Friedman's "right to honor." Degrelle was sentenced to desist from "making similar declarations."[1] The magazine *Tiempo* had to publish the literal text of the sentence, at the plaintiff's expense. Likewise, TVE's channel one was obliged to broadcast it during the second edition of its newscast. And, lastly, Degrelle had to indemnify Violeta Friedman "for the moral harm he has caused her," sending the money to the Association of Spanish Citizens who suffered persecution in Nazi concentration camps and death camps.

Note

1 The magazine *Sàpiens* (Number 69, July 2008) has an article on Léon Degrelle, pp. 22–31, entitled "Operació Degrelle: el segrest imposible" (Operation Degrelle: The Impossible Sequestration), signed by Jordi Finestres, Carlos Collado and Josep María Solé i Sabaté. In spite of the fact that it alludes to various aspects of the Belgian Nazi's life, and although some of the information could lead one to believe they had consulted Violeta Friedman's memoir, there is not a single reference in the article to her memoir or to Degrelle's defeat in his legal battle with her.

Isidoro Sánchez Baena and the Repression in Luque

In 1991 the municipal government of Luque (Cordoba) organized a conference on the history of the town. Isidoro Sánchez Baena, a native of Luque,
was a schoolteacher and researcher on the Civil War, residing in Málaga. He
was invited by the mayor to participate. A few months later the conference's
proceedings appeared in a book entitled *Luque: Estudios Históricos*, published
by the municipal government and distributed door to door to the town's
residents free of charge. It was also mailed to natives of the town residing
elsewhere. It contained six high quality studies that covered the town's
history from the Middle Ages to the twentieth century. Sánchez Baena's
article, "The Civil War in Luque," was on pages 157 to 178. It was an objective account of what happened in Luque after the military coup and dealt
with the victims on both sides: the forty-one leftists as well as the ten
right-wingers who were killed. He recognized at the outset that, influenced
by Francisco Moreno Gómez's work on the Civil War in Cordoba, published
in the mid-1980s, he had not only utilized the municipal archive but also
oral testimonies.

It was in fact an oral testimony that led him to write the following:

> The Falangist militias arrived at the country estate called *El Brillante*;
> apparently it had been abandoned during the first days after the coup.
> Realizing that some birds in the corral had recently been cared for, the
> patrol made a search of the property. They found a man up in a nearby olive
> tree and, without a word being said, a member of the patrol, Juan López
> Rodríguez, fired off a shot that took his life. The dead man was Manuel
> Pérez Gálvez, the estate's caretaker "de puerta abierta" [unpaid but with
> room and board]. (p. 175)

Although Sánchez Baena had also alluded to this incident during his presentation at the conference, without naming the Falangist, it was the
publication of this story that motivated López Rodríguez, who was still
alive, to file a lawsuit. The trial began in October 1991 and was not over
until March 1994, causing the defendant to suffer through numerous court

appearances, preventive confiscations and worries. In mid-December Judge Blanca Pozón Jiménez ordered the confiscation of the printing plates and the remaining copies of the book.

On Sunday, December 22, *El País* echoed what had happened in Luque in an article signed by Alejandro V. García entitled "Who killed Manuel Pérez? The Civil War still hovers over the Cordoban town of Luque." In it, one could read:

> "At first he said he did not care what it said in the book," explains Asunción, the daughter of *El Tano* [Juan López's nickname], "but my brother Alfonso insisted he refute it, since my father had nothing to do with what happened." The accused man's wife interjects, "I would grab the man who blamed him and tear him to pieces. [. . .] My man was in the Falange and was a member of the patrol. Two men died that day, the one from the estate and another from Baena who was leading a burro loaded with roots. My husband saw who shot the caretaker. He even spoke with the dead man's children and told them that he was not the one and he told them the name of the man who did it."

According to the same article, the Falangist's family considered various solutions before filing the lawsuit: for example, to hand out a photocopy of a retraction by Isidoro Sánchez Baena to all the town's residents, or for a guard to go door to door tearing out the offending page. The sentence handed down by the court states that, "in spite of offers from the author and the municipal government itself to rectify and correct the information where necessary, the plaintiff has not accepted the solutions he was offered." The defendant, as in similar cases, refused to identify his sources, but he said it was a person who had been at the estate *El Brillante* on the day of the incident. Regarding Juan López Rodríguez, the author added that, since the Falangist had very common surnames and he had not identified him by his nickname, he did not think the matter would have such serious repercussions. At one point, the journalist wrote:

> The town's residents with dead family members on both sides of the conflict nevertheless confirm the version in the book and recall the war with a disturbing freshness. "Of course what the book says is true! Go ask around and find out who pals around with Juan López. I say hello to him but that is all. I have the book in my house but I have not read it. You know why? Because among the first names that appear on the list of people shot by the militiamen is my father's."

Meanwhile, the socialist mayor, Telesforo Flores, declared: "I told them that we have all forgotten the war."

When the case got to the Cordoba Provincial Court, the prosecutor characterized what had happened as criminal libel and asked that the defendant be sentenced to six months and one day in prison, a fine of one hundred thousand pesetas and compensation for damages to Juan López Rodríguez in the amount of one million pesetas, in addition to payment of legal fees and incidental expenses. The accused and his attorney, the Cordoban lawyer Filomeno Aparicio Lobo, who requested acquittal for his client, were surprised by the severity of the sentence requested by the prosecutor. Then, the plaintiff's side saw their opportunity and raised the bar, asking for two years, four months and a day in prison for Sánchez Baena, a fine of four hundred thousand pesetas and five million pesetas in compensation.

In the basic juridical principles one could read that the jurisprudence of the Constitutional Tribunal had already established the prevalence of the right to freedom of information over the right to honor whenever certain requisites are met. The Constitutional Tribunal distinguished between freedom of information "that has as its objective thoughts, ideas and opinions, a broad concept that should include beliefs and value judgments, and freedom of expression that deals with events that could be considered news, which is limited by the requirement of verity as a precondition for its exercise." The Constitutional Tribunal even understood as inherent and inevitable to free debate that within the information there might be erroneous or mistaken data.

The sentence handed down did not perceive "consciousness of the story's falsity" on the part of the author of the offending statement, even considering that it could be a question of a circumstantial error within the text. Neither did it find *animus difamandi* in the author, which is to say "malicious intent to attribute to the plaintiff a crime he did not commit in order to discredit him. . . ." At one point in the sentence, one reads:

> The author's information says that the plaintiff fired the shot; the plaintiff denies it. An accurate description of these events could be one or the other, something in between or not; but what cannot be said is that the account of the event constitutes a crime as classified in the Penal Code.

The sentence considered that Sánchez Baena had been nothing more than a transmitter of historical information about something that occurred fifty-five years prior, for which reason no proof could be demanded of him other than that of veracity. Without going into more detail, it also alluded to the applicability of a statute of limitations regarding the alleged crime.

The sentence also alluded to a precedent we have already dealt with: the case of Fernando Ruiz Vergara and that memorable phrase by Vivas Marzal who said: "There soon arises an inopportune and unfortunate recollecting of episodes that took place before and after July 18, 1936 in which one of the two sides in the conflict is ridiculed, forgetting that civil wars . . ."

On May 25, 1993, Isidoro Sánchez Baena was acquitted of the crime of libel in the Cordoba Provincial Court by the magistrates Juan R. Verdugo Gómez de la Torre, Antonio Jiménez Velasco and Gonzalo Mendoza Esteban, who acted as spokesperson. Juan López Rodríguez's lawyer appealed but eventually, in March 1994, the High Court upheld the acquittal from the year before.

José Casado Montado
A Memoir of the Terror in San Fernando

> The breach between the wounded town and the authorities widened. We withdrew; we isolated ourselves. When we could eat our daily plate of ground wheat kernels or corn flour gruel, we would eat, in subjugation, our misfortunes and destitution . . .
>
> JOSÉ CASADO MONTADO
> *Trigo tronzado*, p. 98.

In 1992 José Casado Montado published his work *Trigo tronzado. Crónicas silenciadas y comentarios* (Cádiz: Self-published).[TN1] It is the personal testimony of a man whose family was hard hit by the repression, a powerful testimony from the perspective of the vanquished by someone who lived through those years. Casado divides the book into a series of chapters that start with the first executions by firing squad in San Fernando and end with the twenty-sixth and last group to be killed, providing dates, names, and other details about the hundred and twenty-one persons who were assassinated day after day from July 21 until November 4, 1936, and the thirteen who fell when the war was over after enduring the farce of military trials in 1940 and 1941. With the exception of Manuel Temblador López's book *Recuerdos de un libertario andaluz* (Barcelona: Self-published, 1980), we are in the presence of the first work on the fascist repression in the province of Cadiz. But the author's courage in bringing to light those events landed him in the courthouse.

We have not been able to locate the document summarizing the indictment and verdict, although we know the case was eventually dismissed. Throughout his testimony, Casado provided the names of people involved in the assassinations. For example, when he narrates the death of the mayor, Dr. Cayetano Roldán, he tells how Pepito Acosta shoved him and how the mayor responded: "You are going to take my life from me, I who delivered you from your mother's womb. Alright, do it, but please do not touch my

---

TRANSLATOR'S NOTE 1. The book's title in English would be *Ground Wheat Kernels: Silenced Chronicles and Commentaries*.

sons because they are innocent." And Acosta replied, "But we have already killed the three of them!" Sure enough, the mayor's three sons had been assassinated two months before, something he was not aware of because he had been locked up since July and, in all likelihood, no one had wanted to tell him.

Below is the text that most likely gave rise to the lawsuit:

> Among those showoffs with their shoulder belts and pistols was Pepito Acosta and his friends Fernández, Sánchez del Campa "Marquess of the Cauliflowers," a cocky and repulsive type, a criminal. There was Sufo, who was also a member of the national police force, a man of uncommon cruelty, and the vile C. Bueno, who became famous for kicking the victims of the firing squad even after they had received the *coup de grâce*, a man of sinister repute in the town of Isla. They were accompanied by the useless, pigheaded and criminal murderer Cardoso, who came to our house to arrest my father and voluntarily shot many exemplary men from Isla. Another odious type was Correa, who ran the inn called La Carraca, a schizophrenic and a criminal. M. Ortiz, intractable and sexually deranged, was also with them. He too shot many honest and decent family men and later took justice into his own hands when he hanged himself. Fossi, crazy when riding his motorcycle and crazy when shooting people, after killing many of his acquaintances from Isla, ended up dismembered in a highway accident. There was also Luis Milena, an engineer with a street named after him, and with an important position in the S.E. de C.N.,[TN2] whose members told the Falangists which of the workers from the shops under its jurisdiction should be killed. He lived in a chalet on the road out of Isla.

José Casado Montado, who passed away years later, was remembered during a tribute organized by the associations for historical memory of the Bay of Cadiz in December 2007.

TRANSLATOR'S NOTE 2. S.E. de C.N. is the "Sociedad Española de Construcción Naval" (Spanish Society for Naval Construction).

Dolors Genovés and *Sumaríssim 477*
The Value of Archives

[...] in the context of the Civil War, a tragedy whose effects have shaped "the harsh reality of history."[1]

The case of Dolors Genovés has special connotations because of its influence and, given the dimensions it took on, would be enough to fill a book all by itself. Her documentary film *Sumaríssim 477* deals with the life of the Catalonian politician, and founder of *Unió Democràtica de Catalunya*,[TN1] Manuel Carrasco i Formiguera, who was subjected to a court-martial by the Francoists and sentenced to death for the crime of supporting military rebellion. Nothing would have happened if the life of this man had been narrated with the information available in the early 1990s. We would simply have been shown, once again, the brutality of Spanish fascism, which did not hesitate to assassinate a politically moderate, democratic, Catholic and pro-Catalonian man like Carrasco i Formiguera. The problem arose because, contrary to what was customary, the filmmaker and the historian Hilari Raguer were allowed to consult and photocopy the trial transcript.[2] One would imagine that the Burgos military judge who granted them this access trusted their "prudence," which is to say, no inconvenient truth would be made public. Nevertheless, this prudence came up against the obligation to shed light on events that would enrich and clarify the Catalonian politician's final days.

The court-martial did indeed take place in Burgos, one of the "capitals of the Crusade,"[TN2] but the tribunal took into account the testimonies of several Catalonians living in that Castilian city. And not just any

TRANSLATOR'S NOTE 1. Unió Democràtica de Catalunya, founded in 1931, still exists today. It is pro-Catalonian and Christian.

TRANSLATOR'S NOTE 2. "Crusade" here refers to the "crusade," as it was called by the rebel generals, against the "godless" Republic.

Catalonians, but prominent figures such as José Ribas Seba, leader of the Catalonian Falange; José María Fontana, member of the Falange; Antonio Martínez Tomás, Josep Bru Soler and Diego Ramírez Pastor, all journalists; Carlos Trías Bertrán, a lawyer and secretary of the Falange; Josep Lluc Bonastre and Enrique Janés de Durán, both lawyers. Naturally, the court-martial took down their testimonies word for word.

The program was broadcast by TV-3 on November 27, 1994. The lawsuit was filed by all of Trías Bertrán's children: Inés, Miguel, María Teresa, Fernando, Jorge, Carlos, Ana Josefa and Eugenio Trías Sagnier, represented by the fifth child, Jorge, a lawyer whom we have already seen defending the honor of Violeta Friedman against the Belgian Nazi Léon Degrelle. There was also a formal complaint filed by José Ribas Sanpons, director of the magazine *Ajoblanco* and son of the Falangist leader Ribas Sebas. His lawsuit was dismissed in June 2004 by the High Court after having run the legal gauntlet with mixed results: the Court of First Instance backed Dolors Genovés's work and, two years later, the Barcelona Court ruled in favor of Ribas. The Constitutional Tribunal has still not ruled on the Ribas case as this English edition goes to press (December 2012). Dolors Genovés thinks that the Tribunal may have decided it is senseless to rule on the case since it has already done so in the Trías case.[3]

The lawsuit filed by the Trías family, which is the one we will be discussing here, passed through various stages. The first was the formal complaint for infringement of the "right to honor" in the thirteenth Court of First Instance in Barcelona in December 1996; a year later, the lodging of an appeal before the Barcelona Provincial Court; then an appeal for protection before the chamber for civil litigation of the High Court in March 1999; and, eventually, it ended up in the Constitutional Tribunal. Ten years in all. Once again, it pitted two fundamental rights against each other: on the one hand, the right to honor and, on the other, the right to freely express opinions, ideas and thoughts and to freely communicate and receive truthful information through any and all media.

In the film *Sumaríssim 477* there were two allusions to Trías Bertrán. In the first, with images of the transcript as a backdrop, an off-camera voice reads his testimony:

I, Carlos Trías Bertrán, from Barcelona, declare that I know Manuel Carrasco Formiguera and that, along with the *Estat Català*,[TN3] he

---

TRANSLATOR'S NOTE 3. Estàt Catalá was a Catalonian nationalist Party founded by Francesc Macià in 1922. Its goal was Catalonian independence.

attempted to found an independent Catalonian Republic, under the protection of a foreign power.

In the second allusion, the voice says:

> The Tribunal will condemn Carrasco based exclusively on the testimony of eight Catalonians residing in Burgos. They will appear voluntarily before the examining magistrate. [There follows the names and professions of the eight.] They will show no compassion; Carrasco was a red and a separatist. The defense [Eloy Alonso] will consider their testimonies to be phantasmal, resentful, serving to spread rumors.

Finally, over a black background there appears:

> All the witnesses for the prosecution who are going to testify against Carrasco would hold high posts in the Administration and in the Francoist press beginning in 1940.

Toward the end of 1996, the Court of First Instance ruled in favor of the lawsuit, considering that the way the events were narrated led the public to "a negative and unfavorable opinion of Sr. Trías Bertrán, detrimental to his honor and that of his children, since it presented him and the seven other witnesses for the prosecution as the determining factor in Carrasco's death by firing squad." The verdict considered that an illegitimate attack against Carlos Trías's honor had taken place and required TV-3 and Dolors Genovés to publish copies of the sentencing document, remove the aforementioned phrases and images from the film, indemnify the plaintiffs with a symbolic five pesetas and pay court costs. Likewise, one year later, the Barcelona Provincial Court rejected the defendants' appeal and confirmed the sentence because it considered that the broadcast information lacked truthfulness and objectivity. A further appeal, this time requesting annulment of the sentence, took the case to the High Court, whose First Chamber agreed in March 1999 to reject the Trías's lawsuit. Let us examine its reasoning.

The High Court, in a ruling whose spokesperson was the magistrate Xavier O'Callaghan Muñoz, proposed that, contrary to the prior sentences, which delved into historical events, "the events that should be the starting point for arriving at the factual basis of the lawsuit [. . .], are simpler than what was understood to be the case in those prior sentences." After a brief exposition of the events – the participation of Carlos Trías as a witness for the prosecution in Carrasco i Formiguera's trial and the phrases that were the object of the lawsuit – the High Court indicated that "the reportage presented on TV-3 is a typical example of the *freedom of information* affirmed in article 20.I.d of the Spanish Constitution, which freedom is not necessarily separate from the *freedom of expression*, recognized by the same article 20.I.a but rather these two freedoms are often intermingled and, according to the type of reportage, for example one with a political content, are necessarily intermingled"; in other words, that freedom of expression, which is unlimited, refers to opinions and freedom of information, which requires veracity and public relevance, refers to events. The right to honor is recognized as a fundamental right but "if the requirements of veracity and public relevance of the events are met, the right to honor is no longer protected in the face of freedom of information intermingled with freedom of expression."

The function of the courtroom – the spokesperson pointed out – was not to put history on trial, but to apply the Law. Therefore the High Court should make clear that, although Trías Bertrán said what he said knowing, as a lawyer, the consequences of what he said, this matter was not what was being debated. On the other hand, the High Court considered it to be objectively true that Trías Bertrán and the other witnesses held high posts in the Administration and in the Francoist press beginning in 1940. For Dolors Genovés to associate this fact with their conduct as witnesses for the prosecution was a value judgment but it was also truthful. It is interesting that the High Court's spokesperson made clear to the Trías family that if it could not be said that Carrasco i Formiguera was sentenced to death "exclusively" because of the witnesses' testimonies, neither was it reasonable to say, as they did, that it was "because of other evidence" (evidence of what?). The High Court protected this and other value judgments such as the voluntary participation of the witnesses, their lack of compassion and the allusion to their successful careers during the dictatorship. For all these reasons, the High Court concluded its findings with the affirmation that there was neither defamation nor illegitimate interference with the honor of the Trías family's father and that the documentary, which narrated true and relevant historical events, was an expression of the right to freedom of information and that the value judgments that accompanied the truthful narration of the events "are part of the scientific freedom of historians." Besides the spokesperson, the ruling was signed by the magistrates Ignacio Sierra Gil de la Cuesta, Jesús Marina Martínez-Pardo, José Almagro Nosete and Antonio Gullón Ballesteros.

After this setback, the Trías family appealed to the Constitutional Tribunal for protection from the High Court's ruling. Their appeal was accepted in 1999. They insisted that their father's testimony said nothing that was not previously known because of the "reports of denunciations" sent by the Catalonian Falange and Requeté [TN4] and that, consequently, the documentary was "an unnecessary attack on their father's honor." They criticized the way the documentary was dramatized, leading the viewer to believe that testimonies like that of their father were the key to Carrasco i Formiguera's death. They maintained that, on the contrary, it was the documents about Carrasco that led to the outcome of the court-martial and that the declaration that all the witnesses held high posts was nothing "but a setup motivated by defamatory intentions toward the person of their father." They also accused Dolors Genovés of not providing evidence for her accusations in spite of having access to the trial proceedings and to the archive of Carrasco i Formiguera's defense attorney, and accused her of acting simultaneously as journalist and historian. According to the Trías family, "the Constitution does not guarantee the right to hurl insults" and the documentary, which they called a cumulation of blatant falsehoods and gratuitous opinions, had no other intention but to defame their father.

For her part, Genovés pointed out something that the Trías family seemed to have forgotten: the peculiarities of Francoist military justice. In effect, the family was proposing a defense of their father's honor as if Carrasco i Formiguera's trial had been a legal act with all types of procedural guarantees. The family even talked about evidence. It was necessary to remind them that Carrasco was being tried for his ideology and his political career, not for anything a democratic society would consider criminal. It seems clear that Trías's children, undoubtedly conscious of what those courts-martial were like and what they represent, wished to distance their father from such an unpropitious scenario for a discussion about honor. Of course, what cannot be disputed is that Trías Bertrán served as a witness for the prosecution in Carrasco i Formiguera's court-martial. Imagine for a moment what would have happened if the allusion to Trías had been based on oral testimony instead of the transcription of Carrasco's court-martial.

After a series of procedures, the Constitutional Tribunal's ruling would have to wait until January 2004. Its spokesperson was María Emilia Casas Bahamonde. It is a text which to this reader, little versed as I am in juridical matters although I am a long-suffering dabbler in other legal texts, seems exemplary, as much for its form as for its content. And if heretofore I have had recourse to it in order to present the background material, now it will be necessary to devote some space to the ruling's nucleus: the juridical principles.

One by one, the plaintiff's arguments are set forth: Carrasco i Formiguera's death sentence was based principally on his own documents;

TRANSLATOR'S NOTE 4. Carlists. See translator's note 2, p. 10.

Trías was not a witness for the prosecution since he only testified during the preliminary proceedings, and the accusation that he lacked compassion makes the way he is depicted even worse, if that is possible. Then the defendant's arguments are set forth: Trías's participation in the court-martial was proven by the transcription of his testimony, and the documentary's purpose was to inform the public. After that, the Attorney General's office requested the dismissal of the appeal for protection, since there was no doubt about the veracity of the information broadcast, which indeed had never been questioned by anyone. Seen in this light, the matter came down to the purported transcendence of the value judgments, the excessive weight given to the declarations of witnesses and the reference to a lack of compassion. Nevertheless, all these things, as much for the Constitutional Tribunal as for the High Court, were nothing more than manifestations of the freedom of expression; in other words, the critical judgment that the conduct of the Catalonian witnesses deserved from the filmmaker.

There was never any doubt, then, that what was narrated in the documentary was true. Thus, the Constitutional Tribunal's ruling followed the same line of reasoning as that of the High Court by affirming that, even beyond the right to freedom of expression and freedom of information, it was appropriate to allude also to the scientific freedom of historians. The Tibunal pointed out that:

> it is not a question then of examining the reportage under discussion as if it were a chronicle about a judicial proceeding from our own times, as the plaintiffs and the sentences handed down by the courts of first and second instance would have it. [. . .] What is being debated here is the way in which information has been transmitted regarding an event from our recent history, as well as various persons' participation in that historical event, and the opinions about that participation which, in the course of divulging that information, were expressed by the journalist who prepared the script of the televised reportage [. . .].

The spokesperson said that the event in question "had to do, tragically, with the nation's public life, and not with an intimate biography of its protagonists" and that "assessments of and judgments about historical events, and not just about the present or the recent past, are as inevitable as they are necessary, regardless of the unlikelihood that they result in consensus or unanimity." The scientific reconstruction of the past has to do with methodology and not with a purported purity "that discards all moral or ideological perspective when presenting the past." And here is a passage that belongs in an anthology:

the possibility for our contemporaries to form their own world view based on the evaluation of others' experiences depends on the existence of a historical science freely and methodologically founded. Without a dialogue with the value judgments of others – with those of the historian, which is what concerns us here – we would be unable to form our own value judgments. Neither would there be space – which can only be attained through freedom – for the formation of a collective historical consciousness.

What was at play, the spokesperson insisted, was whether or not the information made public about Trías Bertrán was detrimental to his honor. In keeping with the preceding statements, it was also pointed out that besides being a journalist, Dolors Genovés was a historian and that her research had been carried out over several months, which proved that, besides narrating a series of events, she had also wanted to offer "a historiographical evaluation of the same." Consequently, the preparation of the documentary had to be contemplated within the context of the freedom of scientific production and creation and it should be emphasized that the "uncertainty consubstantial to historical debate represents what is most valuable, respectable and worthy of protection in that debate because of the essential role it plays in the formation of a historical consciousness suitable to the dignity of the citizens of a free and democratic society." The spokesperson also recalled a prior ruling in which it was said that "freedom of expression includes the freedom to err and any other attitude regarding this enters the realm of dogmatism. . . The affirmation of absolute truth, conceptually different from veracity as a requirement of information, is the permanent temptation of those who yearn for prior censorship."

For all these reasons, the investigation of past events should prevail over the "right to honor" of those who took part in them "as long as it truly conforms to the characteristic means and practices of historiographical science." Thus, the documentary *Sumaríssim 477* was the fruit of a long and conscientious investigation and its objective was to inform about a historical event:

> If history could only be constructed on the basis of unquestionable facts, historiography, conceived as a social science, would become impossible. In their field of study, historians evaluate what were the causes that explain historical events and propose their interpretation [. . .] it is not the task of this Tribunal to decide, by action or omission, what interpretation or which interpretations from among the possible interpretations should be imposed. It is the citizens themselves who, in the light of the cultural and

historiographical debate, form their own vision of what happened, which can change in the future.

Last of all, the Tribunal's ruling pointed out that the figure of Trías Bertrán was not the main focus of the documentary and that there was no doubt about the veracity of the information disclosed. Thus there was no intent to humiliate but simply to exercise scientific freedom and therefore it was fitting to declare that no injury whatever had been done to the aforementioned Sr. Trías Bertrán's honor. And herewith the last passage prior to the verdict of not guilty:

> Without a doubt, Sr. Trías Bertrán's children [. . .] can shed light on what, in their judgment, was their father's participation in the prosecution of Sr. Carrasco i Formiguera, explaining the motives which, in their opinion, led him to become involved in the same and, in so doing, contribute to the enrichment of the historical debate, but such a project cannot lead them to prevent the documentary from being broadcast.

The Tribunal's ruling had an unusual dissenting vote from the tribunal's president Manuel Jiménez de Parga Cabrera, some of whose family members have, on occasion, been associated with the Francoist repression in Granada. This dissenting vote was seconded by Roberto García-Calvo, Francoist ex-governor of Almería during the time when Carlos Arias Navarro was the head of government in the final days of the Franco dictatorship. Jiménez de Parga did not agree with the ruling nor with the way some of the juridical principles had been applied and proposed defining with precision what was understood as a "historical event." He considered that "an event that affected the honor of the father of living persons must be considered capable of affecting the family honor of the children of the man accused in the reportage, as well as a violation of his own honor." He said that even when dealing with a "historical event" it would be appropriate to distinguish between the narration of the facts and the expression of opinions and the veracity of the narration. According to Jiménez de Parga, "The limitations to the right to information or, if you prefer, scientific freedom have not been taken into account."

Jiménez de Parga pointed out that the Constitution differentiated between freedom of expression (the right to freely disseminate thoughts and opinions) and freedom of information (the right to freely communicate truthful information), rights which were not always easy to define. The most striking thing in his dissent was when he cited an article by the historian Josep Benet in *La Vanguardia* (April 9, 1995) – who wrote: "The film's script is abysmal and, above all, lacking in rigor" – in order to argue that certain elements of the reportage (the witnesses' willingness to testify and the exclusivity of the testimonies as the foundation for the death sentence) did not meet the requirement of veracity. To support his argument he then cited the biography of Carrasco i Formiguera written by the historian Hilari Raguer and concluded: "The televised documentary *Sumaríssim 477* lacks [the] soundness constitutionally required for any reporting of facts. [. . .] And since those facts seriously threaten the honor of don Carlos Trías Bertrán and his children, I consider that they should be granted protection."

APPENDIX I

CARLOS TRÍAS BERTRÁN'S TESTIMONY

On the same date {Burgos; March 17, 1937} the previously subpoenaed person named above appears before this court and informed of the object of this testimony promises to tell the truth to the best of his knowledge and as questioned and to that end said: – he was named as previously expressed, of legal age, native of Barcelona, Lawyer and presently residing in Burgos.

APPROPRIATELY INTERROGATED BY H.H. (His Honor) SAID: – That from a political perspective he knows Manuel Carrasco Formiguera, who for years had belonged to the party "Liga Regionalista,"[TN5] in which party he held leadership posts, and was a city councilor representing the said party. During the Dictatorship [TN6] he left the said party because he regarded it as insufficiently pro-Catalonian and founded together with other elements the party "Acción Catalana,"[TN7] which was involved in all the revolutionary acts and endeavors carried out in Spain and especially in Catalonia from the middle of the Dictatorship to the advent of the Republic. As a representative of the said party he signed and attended the so-called Pact of San Sebastián, in the summer of 1930, as a result of the said commitment, he signed the revolutionary manifesto that was issued in Barcelona during the frustrated revolution of December 1930 (the Jaca insurrection), whose

TRANSLATOR'S NOTE 5. The Liga Regionalista (Lliga Regionalista in Catalán) had a Pro-Catalonian, conservative and monarchic ideology.

TRANSLATOR'S NOTE 6. The dictatorship of Miguel Primo de Rivera (1923–1930).

TRANSLATOR'S NOTE 7. Acción Catalana (Acció Catalana in Catalán) was a pro-Catalonian political movement created in 1922.

manifesto he signed with the most prominent subversive elements operating at that time, among them Aguadé (Mayor of Barcelona during the Republic and presently minister in the Red government in Valencia), Compannis, Maurín, etc.

With the proclamation of the Republic, he was involved in the preparations for its advent as well as its conduct after the proclamation when he was named Counselor of Agriculture, first of the Catalonian Republic, and after this was transformed into the Generalidad of Catalonia following the visit by the Republican ministers Nicolau D'Olver, Marcelino Domingo and Fernando de los Ríos, he remained at his post. A short while after the proclamation of the Republic, and while still serving as Counselor of Agriculture, he was named President of the Cotton Industry Committee. He resigned from that post due to disagreements over religious matters but he continued serving as deputy of his own party until he left the said party in October 1931 because of the discussion and approval of article 26 of the Constitution.[TN8] When the Statute of Catalonia was discussed in the Parliament, he advocated such an ample autonomy that it would in fact have meant the total independence of Catalonia. Prior to that discussion and in the summer of 1931 during the campaign for the plebiscite on the said Statute, he was one of the most active propagandists and delivered a speech (he believes it was in Gerona) in which he glossed the lyrics of the separatist hymn "Els Segadors" and declared that, with the Statute that his party proposed, Catalonia would again have its ancient and absolute independence. Toward the end of 1931 or during the first half of 1932, he left "Acción Catalana" and, together with elements of the said party and others who had broken away from "Comunión Tradicionalista,"[TN9] founded "Unión Democrática de Cataluña," a party that, ideologically, is a Catalonian equivalent of the Basque Nationalist Party and, as such, advocated the total separation of Catalonia and the formation of an independent State. In the said party he was named Leader or Supreme President and with the same party was involved and collaborated actively, first during the preparation, attending numerous meetings of the Catalonian Interior Ministry directed by Dencas in preparation for the

TRANSLATOR'S NOTE 8. Article 26 of the Constitution provided for the separation of Church and State.

TRANSLATOR'S NOTE 9. Comunión Tradicionalista is a Carlist political organization with a conservative Catholic and monarchic ideology.

TRANSLATOR'S NOTE 10 (OVERLEAF). This is a reference to the so-called October Revolution of 1934, a general strike against the conservative Republican government headed by Alejandro Lerroux.

October 6 subversion.^{TN10 (PREVIOUS PAGE)} By virtue of the post he held he took part in numerous political rallies held by his party and intervened actively and leaderly [*sic*] in all the assemblies held by the said party. During the February 16 elections,^{TN11} the party did not run any candidates or ally itself with any other party, although it did recommend to its members that they vote for the separatist elements among the candidates who were running. In spite of this neutral attitude Trías Bertrán believes that, after the victory of the Popular Front, Carrasco i Formiguera's former Leader and friend Luis Nicolau D'Olver (Leader of Acción Catalana), called him with the objective of discussing the political solution that would emerge as a consequence of the Popular Front victory, although Trías Bertrán does not know the outcome of the said call. When the National Movement began,^{TN12} he immediately joined the side of the Red elements of the Popular Front and served as Technical Advisor to the Treasury Department of the Catalonian government, intervening (according to what the witness has heard) in the drafting of all the laws and decrees passed by the said Department; in that capacity he was involved along with Joaquín Bosch in the seizure of the Barcelona branch of the Bank of Spain, since the said Bosch was designated as the Catalonian government's Commissioner in the bank. Beyond these activities, the witness cannot provide concrete testimony as to where the aforementioned Carrasco directed his activities, although he has heard that he was involved together with other elements with separatist affiliations, especially with the Estat Català party, in activities designed to remove anarchist elements from power and create an independent Catalonian Republic under the protection of a foreign power; these particulars have been recently confirmed, according to reports from abroad, and apparently Companys^{TN13} recently and in view of the defeats suffered by the military forces of the Reds, is again nurturing such a plan.

Trías Bertrán indicates that José Lluch Bonastre and José María Fontana, presently residing in Burgos, could also provide information on the activities and personality of Carrasco.

Having nothing more to say, having read this document he affirms and ratifies it, signing along with H.H. to which I as Secretary bear witness.⁴

TRANSLATOR'S NOTE 11. This is a reference to the elections of 1936 that brought the Popular Front government to power.

TRANSLATOR'S NOTE 12. This is a reference to the military coup of July 18, 1936.

TRANSLATOR'S NOTE 13. Lluis Companys y Jover (previously referred to in Triás Bertrán's testimony as "Compannis") was president of the Catalonian government from 1934 until the end of the Civil War.

APPENDIX II

Dolors Genovés's Letter in Response to Javier Tusell, Not Sent to *El País*

We owe the discovery of the mechanism that functions in the degenerate consciousness to Nietzsche: he called it *"ressentiment."* We have had months of *Sumarrísim "ressentiment"* and at the rate we are going we will soon celebrate the first anniversary of 477 martyrology. According to Ortega y Gasset, the resentful person suffers from *"capitis diminutio"* (literally, a diminished head) and he goes on to say: "We live surrounded by people who lack self-esteem, and they are almost always right." He said this in 1917, another year of great confusion.

The reader must be asking him or herself – if in fact he or she still has the strength after the tedium that so much disguised theological debate must have caused – "Why bring up Nietzsche and Ortega now in a discussion of *Sumarrísim 477?*" Until now in the "children of Falangists" dispute – never a debate or discussion – the rancorous souls (sometimes determined to rescue their father's honor and other times, the majority, in need of an untainted curriculum) have dominated the entire celestial sphere.

All of a sudden Javier Tusell appears on the scene with his "change of opinion." A miracle: the "expert" speaks and his sermon coincides seamlessly with the allegations in defense of the "children." There is not a single new idea, nor a single new reproach, not one doubt, nor any argument. He is carrying out an assignment. Tusell is the friend, part of a clique with shared interests, a teammate in this dirty low-budget fight. Even Tusell admits it, while attempting to deny it: "The exclusive motive for my change of opinion resides in the fact that I have now become acquainted with the declarations of those who were witnesses at the trial."[TN14]

The word "exclusive" here is surprisingly revealing. Is Tusell perhaps insinuating that besides the appropriate loyalties – to clan, tribe or party – there may be other motives more embarrassing to confess? And the word "acquainted." With which of the two trials has Tusell become acquainted: the one in 1937 or the one in 1995? The historian Tusell explains his "change of opinion" as follows: "Outside pressure can be decisive and human beings are very often condemned to gestures and postures that do not corre-

TRANSLATOR'S NOTE 14. The historian Javier Tusell originally sent Dolors Genovés a note of support but then, pressured by the Trías Sagnier family, joined them in their attack.

spond to what they would have done under normal circumstances." I hope his friends are grateful for the gesture.

One must say in Javier Tusell's favor that, in spite of the pressures, on two occasions he refused to appear as a witness for the plaintiffs, though it is necessary to add that his attendance at the trials coincided with the summer university courses of the Christian Democrats of the Unió Democràtica de Catalunya party, to which the illustrious historian was invited, and it was rather inelegant of him to combine both activities. We were speaking of gestures. In the end, Tusell has succumbed voluntarily and has fabricated a declaration, not to benefit what he pompously calls "historical truth," but simply as a feinting maneuver in order to show up at last – having resolved the scheduling conflicts of his summer appearances – at the trial carrying his "change of opinion" under his arm.

Tusell has been handed a manipulated selection of texts on a silver platter along with a calling card from the "children." And with that crowd in tow he intends to judge others and preach morality and ethics. Even so he needs to justify himself and recognize that "I would not like it if my father had made those types of declarations before a military judge in the middle of a civil war." So where do we stand? Were they innocuous declarations – as the children claim – or, on the other hand, are they declarations knowingly intended to legitimize Carrasco i Formiguera's inexorable death sentence? Let us not forget, Carrasco did not commit suicide, he was executed. Tusell continues justifying himself and now resorts to science fiction: "Imagine," he says, "if the declarations had been different or had not existed: the results would have been the same." Is Tusell trying to tell us that the declarations could have been somewhat less substantive, more compassionate? It is true that Carrasco was doomed from the start – an idea insistently repeated in the documentary – and for that very same reason the declarations of the witnesses (well aware of what the final verdict would be) acquire dimensions that not even a civil war could justify.

Franco was not alone in that savagery, even though some would prefer to forget that. He relied on many "volunteers" – and I am not referring only to those who were fighting in the trenches without the possibility of some mother with influence rescuing them by having them given a less dangerous assignment in, for example, Burgos. Even Tusell recognizes that there was a certain "degree" of voluntarism among the witnesses: "I am in no way convinced that there was absolute voluntarism." How much voluntarism does there have to be in order to appear before a judge?

Let us finish by enumerating his last allegations. What follows is simply "immoral," a term Tusell employs profusely in his "change of opinion" (the historian has mutated into a preacher). From the pulpit he accuses

Sumaríssim 477: "It does not respect so obvious a reality, from a historical point of view, as the fact that in a civil war at times one is unable to make choices." And with that, problem solved.

Well Carrasco made a choice and I am not referring to his own personal situation but specifically to the situation a certain Tusell lived through in Bilbao in January 1937. Matías Tusell Vilaclara found himself under arrest, suspected of being a "fascist or Carlist," which is how Tusell Vilaclara himself described the charges in a letter he sent to the Christian Democrat leader on December 31, 1936, in which he asked for Carrasco's help. It is a document Javier Tusell can consult in the transcript of trial 477–37 folio 79.

Manuel Carrasco i Formiguera made a "choice" to intercede and appeal to Telesforo Monzón – Interior Minister in the Basque Executive – and in spite of the "delicate situation" and "outside pressures" which also weighed on Carrasco, he wrote to Monzón citing the long-time friendship between Carrasco and the family of the detainee and, specifically, his friend from the Liga Catalanista party, Xavier Tusell Gost. Yes, there are gestures that reveal what type of man one is. It is at the end of his "change of opinion" when the true nature of the unpleasant assignment that weighs on Tusell is revealed. Not history, not the defense of honor, not well-intentioned sermons. The resentful children, along with their calling card, construct the thesis that "explains everything": 1. In *Sumaríssim 477* there are biased attitudes influenced by ideology and, 2. A deliberate attempt to divide Catalonia in two, nationalists and non-nationalists. And Tusell takes the bait. Otherwise, how do we explain the fact that his keen sense of smell did not detect that suspicious odor when he first saw the documentary?

The children, their friends, and their friends' friends have founded a club and, to the slogan "they are going to find out who they are dealing with," they camouflage their Falangist papas and disguise themselves as warriors in another crusade. Let no one be fooled. What is happening with *Sumaríssim 477* is about something other than the dead or history, the history of 1937. It is about what has been happening in Spain during the past year (1995).[TN15]

Mª DOLORS GENOVÉS, *Journalist and historian*

TRANSLATOR'S NOTE 15. No date appears with this letter but, according to Dolors Genovés, it was written toward the end of 1995, one year into her ten-year ordeal. It was not sent to *El País* or to any other newspaper because, as a good journalist, she was aware that it would be more beneficial to whatever newspaper published it than to her, increasing the sales of the edition in which it appeared and, at the time the letter was written, she was being crucified in the media. She never sent it to Javier Tusell either. This information was provided to me by Francisco Espinosa-Maestre.

Notes

1 "The harsh reality of history" is a phrase taken from point 4 of the juridical principles, which refers to case STC 28/1982, May 26, FJ 2. It is the dismissal of an appeal by a former Republican soldier who requested that his rights be recognized according to decrees passed in 1936 and 1937. In the sentence, whose spokesperson was Rubio Llorente, it says: "At the end of the Civil War, whose juridical implication was a break with the previous body of laws, the new legal system incorporated as valid only those norms that were in effect in the territories that had been wrested from Republican control, whose dispositions were not granted any other consideration than that of mere artifacts, not only lacking any force but even susceptible to being considered criminal. This is the harsh reality of history which cannot be ignored or evaded.

2 In fact, both of them were already acquainted with the most important parts of the transcript, since the Carrasco i Formiguera family was able to photocopy it when Narcís Serra was the Minister of Defense.

3 The Barcelona Court ruled in favor of Ribas in 1998, accepting the claim that *Sumaríssim 477* "distorted reality." At issue was the statement that "from the reading of the trial transcript the veracity of the categorical claim by the documentary that Carrasco i Formiguera was condemned to death based exclusively on the testimonies of eight Catalonians residing in Burgos cannot be inferred" and also that "the attempt to create a historical vision in which his death was due to the personal envies, antipathies and intrigues of a group of Catalonians is to distort and prostitute history as the collective memory of a people" (see *El Mundo*, May 12, 1998). Ribas said: "It is not a question of defending my father, but of defending the memory of Catalonia"; he also stated that Dolors Genovés could have consulted his father's archive, which "would have allowed her to act with the impartiality and serenity that our history and our condition of being Catalonians deserve." He added: "José Ribas Seva, my father, taught me from when I was a child that the civil war had been a catastrophe for everyone, and that there were neither victors nor vanquished. He taught me that we all lost and that the important thing was to rebuild Catalonia" (*La Vanguardia*, March 19, 1995).

   María Dolors Cruells also turned to the justice system: her father, Manuel Cruells was erroneously mentioned as the director of the *Diari de Barcelona* and as the anonymous author of an article published in the said newspaper which called for "Carrasco's head." Dolors Genovés had taken the reference to Cruells as director of the newspaper from a book when, in fact, the director was Marcel·lí Perelló.

4 I am indebted to Dolors Genovés for this document. Except for a few details that I thought worthy to add, I have respected the original wording.

Amparo Barayón
The History of a Slander

> In the city of Zamora, at eleven o'clock on the eleventh day of October, nineteen thirty-six, in the presence of D. Agustín Pérez Piorna, Municipal Judge, and D. Mario Aparicio de Santiago, Secretary, the death of Dª Amparo Barayón Miguel, 29 years of age, native of Zamora, is registered [...]. SHE PASSED AWAY _____, on _____, eleventh day of the present month at _____ and _____ minutes, as a result of _____ as determined by _____ and medical examination, and her cadaver will be buried in the Municipal cemetery of this city. (From the Death Certificate)

In May 1982, only months after the death of the novelist Ramón J. Sender, who had died in January of that year, the magazine *Interviú* published an article entitled "This is how they killed Ramón J. Sender's wife," signed by Heriberto Quesada. Without a doubt, it is one of the best articles in the series the magazine published on the fascist repression, as much for the quality of the writing as for the meticulous research that went into its three pages. It is a fine example of investigative journalism, as opposed to other cases where the most absolute sensationalism prevails.

Shortly thereafter, in July, Ramón Sender Barayón, son of Ramón J. Sender and Amparo Barayón Miguel, decided to travel to Spain in search of traces of his mother, murdered in Zamora in October 1936. Ramón's, as well as his sister Andrea's, peculiar relationship with their father precluded satisfactory answers to their many questions and doubts. The trip resulted in the 1990 publication, by Plaza & Janés, of a book entitled *Muerte en Zamora*. On the cover there was a photograph of Sender in the foreground and another of Amparo in the background, along with the question "What were the circumstances of the death by firing squad of Ramón J. Sender's wife?" The book had been published a year earlier by the University of New Mexico Press, with the title *A Death in Zamora* and was translated into Spanish by Mercedes Esteban-Maes Kemp, a resident of Cornwallis (England) and cousin of the book's author. In it, Ramón Sender Barayón related, almost in the style of a travel journal, the story of his quest and its results. It is likely that Ramón and Amparo's son came across Quesada's article during his trip, since some of the people he contacted must certainly have brought it to his attention. But although he made liberal use of it for his book, he mentions it only once, without naming the author or including it in his bibliography.

The book reads like a novel, but the terrible part is that the story he tells, his mother's murder, was real. After the military coup Ramón J. Sender thought his wife and their two children would be safer in Zamora, where she was born, than in Madrid, but Zamora fell immediately into the hands of the rebels with nightmarish results. Although their origin is somewhat murky, Amparo Barayón's problems began the day she came to an appointment related to her application for a passport. With her daughter in her arms, she made a complaint, critical of the new governor, about the death of her brother Antonio, assassinated that very day. Shortly thereafter she was arrested and incarcerated. She would remain in prison until she was taken out and shot.

One of the testimonies cited by Ramón Sender in his book was from Pilar Fidalgo Carasa, the author of a text entitled "A Young Mother in Franco's prisons," published in the newspaper *El Socialista* in May 1937, and in London and Paris after the Spanish civil war. The quote from Fidalgo, who had also just given birth to a daughter, is the origin of the defamation that concerns us here:

> Because I continued hemorrhaging, I constantly begged the warden for help. Finally she brought the prison doctor Pedro Almendral who came merely as a matter of form. Upon seeing my suffering, he commented that "the best cure for the wife of that scoundrel Almoína is death." He prescribed nothing – neither for myself or my baby.[1]

What we know is that Amparo Barayón, arrested on August 28, 1936, was killed on October 11 in one of those dark and dirty intrigues made possible by the military coup. Amparo was a catholic and tried to confess but the priest, as he would later tell one of her sisters, refused to absolve her because she was not married in the Church. Besides Amparo and her brother Antonio, another brother, Saturnino, councilman for the Republican Left party, would also be killed. Both brothers used to run the Café Iberia, which was regarded as something like the unofficial Republican meeting hall in Zamora. The family always believed that Amparo's killer was the lawyer Segundo Viloria, an ex-suitor of hers who, it seems, ended his life in a lunatic asylum and about whom we have evidence of his participation in the death squads operating in Zamora after the coup (see Appendix II).

The Spanish edition of *A Death in Zamora*, translated by one of the author's cousins, had a striking peculiarity: a series of "E. N."s, Editor's Notes, which could more accurately have been called "Notes against the Author." They are corrections and commentaries, mostly absurd, a good sample of which would be the one that corrects a quote from Pilar Fidalgo which states: "In the province of Zamora more than six thousand people were killed, six hundred of whom were women" (p. 164). The footnote says:

> The Nationalist historian – but one of the most impartial – Ramón Salas Larrazábal, in his book *Pérdidas de la guerra* (Barcelona: December, 1977), referring to Zamora writes . . .

In 1990, when the Spanish edition of *A Death in Zamora* was published, it was already well known that Salas Larrazábal's work, edited by Planeta in 1977 and whose "exact figures" were endorsed by Hugh Thomas in his monumental edition the same year of *La Guerra Civil española* published by Urbión, represented the last Francoist operation to whitewash the regime's great foundational massacre. Nevertheless, the key to our story lies elsewhere. *A Death in Zamora*, which exposed the maliciousness of Zamora's conservative middle class and told part of what it had done, did not sit well in those circles, unaccustomed as they were to hearing the truth. No one responded openly, thinking perhaps that it would have made things worse, since there were still people alive who had provided their testimonies to Ramón Sender Barayón. They decided to bide their time. For example, someone who knew of Sender's book and had seen Pilar Fidalgo's reference to Dr. Almendral swore vengeance, but would wait fourteen years for the opportune moment.

On July 13, 2004, *La Opinión de Zamora* included an interview by Begoña Galache with Ana Isabel Almendral Oppermann on the occasion of her donation of an oil painting and a photograph to the Provincial Government – called "works of art" by the newspaper – with portraits of her father and grandfather, doctors associated with that Institution. The following was the second question:

> "He was a doctor at the jail. What was that experience like for him?"
> "That's right. He worked in the jail. In fact, it was my grandfather who took care of Ramón J. Sender's wife in the prison. The writer's son, in a book he wrote while in the United States, says that his mother was ill in the jail, that nobody attended to her, and that a doctor who stopped by said that, in the final analysis, with what little remained of her life it was better

to leave her where she was. But it was not like that. My grandfather did not let her die on her own. On the contrary, he helped her. She was terribly ill from syphilis and my grandfather said that with what little remained of her life it was better to take her to the infirmary. This was many years ago, but there is a lot of confusion in the book *Muerte en Zamora* and I want to dot the i's and cross the t's. It really struck me the way some of the facts are distorted.

Someone at the newspaper, probably conscious of the implications of the declaration and aware of what he was doing, gave the article the strange headline "My Grandfather Did Not Let Sender's Wife Die When She Was in Jail." Consequently, the motive for the interview, the donated "works of art" was relegated to the background. What mattered was the defamation: Amparo Barayón, according to the prison doctor's granddaughter, had syphilis. The journalist and the newspaper saw no problem in backing her up. But Almendral, intentionally or not, was confused. In his book, Ramón Sender Barayón never once alluded to the treatment his mother received from the doctor. What he did do, among other things, was transcribe Pilar Fidalgo Carasa's testimony and those of other people and present the Right in Zamora with a mirror-image of the reality of the "Glorious National Uprising" in a small provincial capital where not a single right-winger had suffered any harm before the military coup. What Almendral could not forgive was that Sender had identified the role her grandfather played after the 1936 coup and, albeit quoting someone else, had placed in his mouth the words "the best cure for the wife [Pilar Fidalgo] of that scoundrel Almoína [her husband, a prominent socialist militant from Benavente] is death." And she found no better way to attack the guilty party, Amparo Barayón's son, than to come out with the statement that his mother was suffering from syphilis, as if she had died in the infirmary. It is even possible that Almendral's granddaughter knew, as Ramón Sender had been told by many people he interviewed, that Amparo went insane and that, to torment her, her captors convinced her that the person responsible for her suffering was none other than her husband.

A few months later, the news of the interview reached Amparo Barayón's family. Perhaps the first to hear of it was her niece Magdalena Maes Barayón, living in Málaga, who, years after the war and still quite young, transferred her aunt's remains from the common grave where she was buried to the Maes family pantheon. Magdalena must have contacted her daughter Mercedes Esteban Maes, the translator of *A Death in Zamora*, who was living in England, and from there the news reached Ramón Sender in the United States. It was the historian Helen Graham, a friend of Mercedes, who passed the story on to Paul Preston and to me, enabling us to be participants in and witnesses to a story that would go on for another year.

The family took up the challenge and, toward the end of January 2005, composed a letter that would be published in *La Opinión de Zamora* on February 14:

TO THE EDITOR,

On Tuesday, July 13, 2004, your newspaper published an interview with Anabel Almendral, granddaughter of the Zamora doctor Pedro Almendral, on the occasion of her donation of some family portraits to the Zamora Provincial Government. During the interview, Anabel Almendral makes several statements about Amparo Barayón Miguel, wife of the writer Ramón J. Sender. The following statements are inaccurate:

- That Ramón Sender Barayón wrote a book about his mother "when he was in the United States." Ramón has lived in the United States most of his life because of his mother's assassination and his father's exile, but when he wrote *A Death in Zamora* he spent many months in Spain interviewing his parents' families, as well as a great number of people who knew of his mother's death.
- That in his book *A Death in Zamora* Ramón Sender Barayón had written "that his mother was ill in the jail, that nobody attended to her, and that a doctor who passed by there saw her and said that in the final analysis, with what little remained of her life, it was better to leave her where she was." The quote in the book is not from Amparo Barayón, but from Pilar Fidalgo Carasa, Amparo's fellow prisoner who, in her testimony "A Young Mother in Franco's Prisons" (London: United Editorial Limited, 1939, p. 6), affirmed that "... the prison doctor Pedro Almendral [who] came merely as a matter of form. Upon seeing my suffering, he commented that "the best cure for the wife of that scoundrel Almoína is death. He prescribed nothing for me" (quoted by Ramón Sender Barayón in *Muerte en Zamora*, Plaza & Janés, 1990, p. 160). Let us clarify here that Pilar Fidalgo Carasa was an eyewitness to these events.
- That Amparo Barayón Miguel "was terribly ill with syphilis." According to the testimonies of her surviving family members, Amparo Barayón was in good health when she entered the prison. She had a daughter only months old and a boy just a few years old, both of them healthy. Her husband, Ramón J. Sender, died in his eighties of old age after a lifetime of heavy smoking. Her children,

Ramón and Andrea, are now both in their seventies and, naturally, free of syphilis.

We are aware that it has taken us seven months to respond to the many errors contained in the aforementioned interview. Among many other misfortunes, Amparo Barayón Miguel's assassination was the cause of the family's dispersal. We all live far from each other and news takes time getting around. Nevertheless, and in spite of the intervening months, it seems to us we have a right to refute the declarations published in your newspaper.

We await your prompt reply and publication in your newspaper of the text of this letter in its entirety.

Our attentive greetings,[2]

The response took only three days to appear, but it was not from the granddaughter of the prison doctor, but from Miguel Ángel Mateos Rodríguez, secondary school teacher, councilman representing ADEIZA (Association of Zamora Independents), and Zamora's official chronicler. He called on Ana Isabel Almendral, "esteemed academic professional" (professor of Philology at the University of Castilla-La Mancha), to prove the part about syphilis or admit her mistake; he defended her grandfather with the story of his difficulties during the Popular Front government, in addition to describing him as a man concerned, shortly thereafter, for the lives of his companions; and, in passing, he attacked Ramón Sender's book, calling it historical fiction. Naturally, he did not mention Pilar Fidalgo. Nor did he concern himself with the obstacles Sender Barayón faced in the 1980s while investigating his mother's death. The attack against Ramón Sender's book was echoed by other habitual contributors to *La Opinión de Zamora*, who followed the same line, defending Dr. Almendral. The book had attacked "one of their own and the decent people of Zamora," who had not forgiven Sender, came to the doctor's defense. The "esteemed academic professional" and her slanderous swipe at the memory of Amparo Barayón had faded into the background or, at most, was interpreted as an understandable overreaction given the harm Amparo's son had done to her family as well as to other well-known Zamora families whose members appear throughout the book, some as assassins, others as accomplices or instigators and, finally, others as mere passive spectators.

On March 14, a new letter from the family, signed by Mercedes Esteban Maes, was published in *La Opinión de Zamora*:

I have not reacted immediately to the two articles expressing opinions of our response to Anabel Almendral's declarations published in July 2004 in *La Opinión de Zamora*. I was waiting for Dr. Almendral to retract her statement and apologize for tarnishing the memory of my great aunt, Amparo Barayón Miguel, as the Zamora historian Miguel Ángel Mateos had requested (*La Opinión de Zamora*, February 17, 2005). This has not happened. Obviously, silence implies confirmation.

Let me start from the beginning and refresh the reader's memory. On July 13, 2004, *La Opinión de Zamora* published an interview with Anabel Almendral in which she asserted that her grandfather, Dr. Pedro Almendral, "treated Ramón J. Sender's wife in prison because she was terribly ill from syphilis." She also attacked Ramón Sender Barayón's book, *Muerte en Zamora*, in which the son of Ramón J. Sender and Amparo Barayón investigates his mother's death in October 1936, alleging that "there is a lot of confusion in the book." At the same time, she displays her own confusion when she says that: "In his book, the writer's son says that his mother was ill in the jail, that nobody attended to her, and that a doctor who stopped by said that, in the final analysis, with what little remained of her life it was better to leave her where she was." As is made clear in *A Death in Zamora*, this incident comes from Pilar Fidalgo Carasa's testimony, a historical document published in London in 1939, which contains the declarations of a woman who was Amparo Barayón's fellow prisoner and an eyewitness to the events she narrates. The protagonist of the incident is not Amparo Barayón, but Pilar Fidalgo Carasa, who affirmed that "...Dr. Pedro Almendral came purely for form's sake. When he saw how I was suffering, he commented that 'the best cure for the wife of that scoundrel Almoína is death' and he did not prescribe me anything." "A Young Mother in Franco's Prisons" (London: United Editorial Limited, 1939), p. 6. Quoted by Ramón Sender Barayón in *Muerte en Zamora* (Plaza & Janés, 1990), p. 160.

In our letter of February 14, 2005, we offered irrefutable evidence against Almendral's declaration that Amparo Barayón was ill from syphilis. We also corrected other errors in Almendral's interview.

On February 17, 2005, an article by the Zamora historian Miguel Ángel Mateos appeared in which he provided documentary evidence that confirmed the baseless nature of Almendral's insulting declaration regarding the state of Amparo Barayón's health. He also asked Anabel Almendral to admit her mistake, since an "esteemed academic professional should not lower herself to fueling false rumors worthy of gossip circles." Although his article had no effect on Anabel Almendral, whose silence continues to imply confirmation, we are grateful for his support.

That said, I need to respond to the second part of Mateos's article, where he attacks Ramón Sender Barayón's book *Muerte en Zamora*, alleging that it is a work of "historical fiction" based on "unsupported, imagined and erratic information from dubious and weak oral sources." *Muerte en Zamora* is not a historical novel: it is a second generation testimony comparable to works published by and about the children of survivors and victims of the holocaust. In many cases, the testimonies collected by Ramón in his book are first-hand accounts. My mother, Magdalena Maes Barayón, Amparo's niece, assures me that her memory of those events is as clear today as they were almost seventy years ago. I would not call her a "dubious source." There is also Pilar Fidalgo Carasa's testimony in "A Young Mother in Franco's Prisons," a very important historical document from the perspective of any historian worthy of the name.

Let us give an example: Mateos says in his article that Ramón Sender Barayón makes accusations against his own uncle Miguel Sevilla (among many others) "based on unsupported, imagined and erratic information from dubious and weak oral sources, far removed from the events being narrated." In "A Young Mother in Franco's Prisons," Pilar Fidalgo Carasa testifies that when Amparo Barayón knew they were going to kill her because they had wrested her daughter Andrea from her arms, "she wrote a farewell letter to Sender which I kept for a long time but had to tear into pieces and eat because of the continual searches to which we were subjected. In this letter she delivered her children to his care and held Sevilla responsible for her death" (p. 28). My mother, Magdalena Maes Barayón, clearly remembers Miguel Sevilla arriving at the Barayón's café, where the family was gathered, saying, "Tonight they are going to kill Amparo." It seems to me neither fair nor rigorous for Mateos to call these sources weak or dubious.

Because of Mateos's allusions to the need for a "trained and, of course, impartial historian," I think it appropriate to make clear that the letter we wrote to *La Opinión de Zamora* in response to Almendral's statements, and to which Mateos responded in his article, was not only signed by Amparo Barayón and Ramón J. Sender's children, Ramón and Andrea, and by me, her niece, with a degree in History and twenty years experience as a university professor in Great Britain, but by nine other signatories whose names were not published, I imagine for lack of space. Besides various family members, including Magdalena Maes Barayón, the letter was signed by Francisco Espinosa-Maestre, a historian specializing in the repression; Helen Graham, Professor of Contemporary History at Royal Holloway, University of London, United Kingdom, a specialist on the Spanish Civil War and the early Franco regime; and Paul Preston, Professor of History at the London School of Economics and author of some of the most important works on the Spanish Civil War. We are all in agreement about the importance of *A Death in Zamora* as a historical document containing testimonies by survivors of the war, as well as the experiences and quest of a man from whom the war stole not only his mother but his homeland.

And here it is fitting to include a plea to Miguel Ángel Mateos: the documents he cites in his article were not accessible when Ramón carried out his research in 1983. We beg you to inform us where we can obtain those sources, of incalculable value to the Barayón family.

I also feel obliged to comment on the final paragraphs of Mateos's article. With the intention of exonerating Dr. Almendral, if he had indeed been the original source of the insulting rumor about Amparo's syphilis, Mateos affirms that Almendral's life "had been placed in serious danger" following an incident that occurred in May 1936. In another article, published on February 21, 2005, R. Gamazo repeats this defense of Dr. Almendral. Gamazo, after commenting about "testimonies that only a trained and, of course, impartial historian can evaluate and interpret" (see our credentials above), relates an anecdote, referring no doubt to the same incident in which Dr. Almendral's life may have been in danger in May 1936.

It is regrettable that Dr. Almendral was in some sort of danger, just as the excesses committed in the province of Zamora before the war are regrettable. But it is more important to remember that what is in play here is not what could have happened to Dr. Almendral, but what in fact did happen to Amparo Barayón Miguel, whose memory has been attacked by Dr. Almendral's granddaughter. It is not surprising that Dr. Almendral survived. According to the Francoist historian Ramón Salas Larrazábal in his book *Pérdidas de la guerra*, the leftist repression was non-existent in the province of Zamora while there were one thousand two hundred and forty-six victims of the right-wing repression. We will have to wait for the results of a more serious investigation. The truth, as Mateos says, citing Ricardo de la Cierva, is unlikely or impossible to achieve, but what is certain is that Amparo Barayón was assassinated in Zamora and the responsible parties are those who were brought to power by the military coup in July 1936.

MERCEDES ESTEBAN MAES

The debate goes on when, on March 29, *La Opinión de Zamora*'s correspondent in Benavente, Isabel Reguillón, writes an interesting article entitled "Chronicle from a Jail in 1936." Her point of reference is the testimony of Pilar Fidalgo, Benavente's schoolteacher arrested on October 6 and transported to Zamora because she was married to José Almoína, secretary of the Socialist Organization. Reguillón narrates the fate of some of the residents of Benavente in October 1936 and repeats Pilar's allusions to Amparo Barayón and other women.

When Reguillón's article appeared, there was another curious phenomenon under way. During March and April, the local chronicler Miguel Ángel Mateos was writing a series of seven long articles entitled "*Death in Zamora*, the Tragedy of Amparo Barayón." It is obvious that the newspaper was on the chronicler's side. His articles were published on the best days and printed on the most favorable pages, while the writings of the Barayón family and others were relegated to the letters section and appeared on less important days. Mateos rails against Pilar Fidalgo and Ramón Sender, and devotes many sections to justifying and whitewashing the conduct of priests, fascists and others who supported the military coup, all the while employing a liberal discourse which, nonetheless, does not conceal the author's ideology. He even attempts to dismiss certain charges against Amparo Barayón's ex-suitor, the lawyer Segundo Viloria: "I do not claim to justify what can in no way be justified: the irresponsible attitude and activities of Viloria throughout the Civil War. I am not yet ready to reveal who was responsible for Amparo Barayón's death by firing squad. I will do that in the part of this series to be published by *La Opinión de Zamora* at the appropriate time. I do not want to be so explicit nor reopen old wounds [...] What I can affirm is that Viloria neither took charge of, nor directed, nor participated in the assassination of Amparo Barayón. There is irrefutable evidence of other executions he carried out. But not this one. I realize that stories require suspense as well as action" (*La Opinión de Zamora*, April 6, 2005). Here we can see how the newspaper exploits the sensationalism of the "Amparo Barayón affair" and how the chronicler takes advantage of the pulpit provided him by the newspaper to advertise the forthcoming episodes of his series. He has achieved his objective: center stage no longer belongs to Amparo Barayón but to the chronicler himself and the revelations he promises to mete out in small doses.

On occasion, for example April 8, the newspaper simultaneously publishes a letter from Mercedes Esteban Maes and an article, the sixth, by Mateos in which he alludes to the same letter. First Mercedes Esteban's letter:

To MR. MATEOS:

I have read with surprise, even astonishment, M. A. Mateos's dismissals of Pilar Fidalgo's testimony and Ramón Sender Barayón's book. He dismisses Pilar Fidalgo's memories by citing documents that she was unable to consult for obvious reasons. What a great mistake it was on the part of

Pilar Fidalgo to speak of six thousand victims of the fascist repression in Zamora when there were only four thousand! Besides the fact that this type of cheap attack is unworthy of someone who thinks of himself as an impartial historian, Mr. Mateos seems to forget that if a person living in exile misstates someone's second surname, it does not in any way disqualify what she says about the brutality she observed while imprisoned. Mr. Mateos's certainty in denying the possibility that a female prisoner was raped displays not only a lack of imagination but complete ignorance of how things were in the prisons run by the so-called Nationalists. With regard to Ramón Sender Barayón's book, Mr. Mateos dismisses the author because his sources were oral testimonies and yet, when it comes to secrets he himself has been told, oral sources seem perfectly acceptable. Mr. Mateos boasts of his vast knowledge, but one must ask why he did not help Ramón Sender when he was carrying out his research for *A Death in Zamora*. If that was impossible for some reason, why did he not speak up when the book was published? Instead of "holding those cartridges in reserve," as he said, it is high time for him to stop showing his superiority over his victims (Pilar Fidalgo and Ramón Sender) and tell us once and for all who were responsible for the assassinations of Amparo Barayón, her brothers, and several thousand more people in the province of Zamora. And he ought to apply the same rigor to the documents generated by those who carried out the military coup and see if he can convince us of the legality of so many "courts-martial," "death sentences," and "executions." Ah, and one more thing. He should not forget to give us the exact number of people assassinated since he has demonstrated his superiority to Pilar Fidalgo regarding that question.

Mercedes Esteban Maes

In April 2005, given the direction the affair was taking, Amparo Barayón's family looked into the possibility of taking legal action against Almendral's granddaughter. They were told that, according to article 18 of the Constitution, it would be considered in the context of the right to honor, either as a criminal lawsuit after taking legal action for the crime of libel, or as a civil lawsuit seeking protection of the right to honor through a Grand Jury, which is the normal procedure, initiated by filing a suit signed by a barrister and a solicitor. But in spite of the fact that this would be the ideal solution and what they wanted, the family did not feel they were capable of going through with it: their geographical dispersion – especially in the case of Amparo's children who were thousands of miles away – and the fact that they could not rely on a single family member in Zamora dissuaded them from pursuing this course.

What Amparo's children did do, thinking it might have some effect, was to send a letter to Dalmiro Gavilán, editor in chief of the newspaper's opinion section, in which they asked him to act as intermediary between them and Almendral Opperman, whom they asked for a retraction. They even sent her a model:

To Srta. Anabel Almendral:
It seems to us that there should be a civilized way to resolve this matter without having to take some sort of legal action. We understand, of course, that it may be possible you heard this story about syphilis from your grand-father or some other family member and are simply repeating what they told you one day.

Nevertheless, since there is no truth to this defamation and since it is a serious offense to the memory of our mother, who died guiltless at the hands of hired assassins, we must ask you with all sincerity to make a public retraction. This retraction should consist of the following text and be published in *La Opinión de Zamora*:

"After further reflection and having become aware of new information about Amparo Barayón Miguel's situation during her incarceration in Zamora in 1936, I have decided to reconsider my words published in La Opinión de Zamora *in July 2004, regarding any possible illness suffered by Amparo Barayón Miguel. Given the harsh conditions under which the incarcerated women were living, it is possible that my grandfather, Dr. Almendral, may have either misdiagnosed Amparo Barayón or confused her with someone else.*

I understand that Amparo could in no way have been suffering from the last stages of a disease as infectious as syphilis without her children manifesting some sort of symptoms. Bearing in mind that they never showed the said symptoms at that time, nor during the entire course of their lives (according to their own testi-monies and those of acquaintances), and having looked through the testimonies of several women who were incarcerated with their mother – cited in her son's book – I realize that my information was incorrect. I pass on my sincerest apologies to the Barayón and Sender families for allowing such a declaration to appear in a pub-lic newspaper, and I hope that, with this correction, the matter can be considered resolved."

Signed: Anabel Almendral

This declaration will serve to satisfy Amparo's family, which honors a brave woman who was illegally arrested, incarcerated under terrible conditions and assassinated simply for being the wife of a well-known radical writer. Her children hope you can publish this retraction so they will not be compelled to take other public measures that will only serve to revive memories that are painful for all of us. Peace and justice is our primary objective.

SIGNED BY RAMÓN AND BENEDICTA [ANDREA SENDER BARAYÓN]

AS DIRECT DESCENDANTS

Naturally, nothing came of it. Ana Isabel Almendral had said what she wanted to say, disappeared from Zamora and did not make any more public statements on the matter. It is the newspaper and the chronicler who exploit the situation, each for their own interests, while Amparo Barayón's family and their friends seek compensation and the restoration of Amparo's honor. All to no avail. On the contrary: the chronicler Mateos takes advantage of the situation to attack Ramón Sender's book and those who told him what had happened in Zamora. Each of Mateos's articles constitutes a warning that he is the one who knows the most about the matter and the only one with the right to speak out. His message, confused but smooth-spoken, is aimed at the same social sector portrayed in Sender's book: do not worry, they cannot prove anything, I have the documents and I will not share them; besides, I will be the one who provides the definitive version in my articles and books. Later, during a conference held in 2006, Miguel Ángel Mateos *will disclose* "the party materially responsible for Amparo Barayón's assassination." His talk, reported in the press, is not to be missed.

Basically, what was said by the "expert," as the journalist Jesús Hernández defined him in his article in *La Opinión de Zamora* on December 23, was that Amparo Barayón was free to leave Zamora but did not do so, and that she may have "spread rumors," which "perhaps weighed heavily against her." He denied that she was a "dangerous communist," as she was called in a report from the military governor (a document that underscores the governor's character and the style of those who carried out the coup and which allows the chronicler to present himself as the victim's defendant); she was thought to be a "spy" and "in the service of the government in Madrid," which Mateos also denies in a show of clairvoyance; "her assassination was due to decisions that went beyond what was strictly determinative (sic) by the civil governor himself" (?); and finally, the great secret: Amparo Barayón's killer was a certain Martín Mariscal, a sergeant in the Falangist militia. It turns out that Mateos has discovered the document recording Amparo's removal from prison on the night of her assassination with the signature of Mariscal as the one in charge of taking her to the cemetery.

What Miguel Ángel Mateos seems to have forgotten is that the Falangists were merely carrying out the orders of their superiors. What does it matter whether it was Mariscal or anyone else who fired the shot? Besides, Mariscal surely did not operate all by himself. Who told the chronicler that Viloria was not in the group? Maybe Mr. Mateos has the names of the members of the firing squads operating in Zamora in those days. But the story does not end here. Having rescued the family honor of those he wanted to protect, the local chronicler describes the killer's fate. "He had problems in Zamora because of his behavior," we are told. The problem was that he began to charge money in exchange for saving people from the firing squads. Then he fled Zamora and enlisted in the Legion in Toledo where, according to Mateos, another Zamora native heard him recount his activities in Zamora. "It is a fact," Mateos adds, "that he shot most of Zamora's prominent victims," including Amparo Barayón. Word of Mariscal's boasts reached the Legion lieutenant and the Legion imposed justice on him. So the killer paid for his crime and the Zamora bourgeoisie was off the hook. The problem of the repression in Zamora was solved.

And what an evil person Amparo's killer was! According to Mateos, this Mariscal was strong, violent, gruff, profane, bloodthirsty, lacking any ideology – although he adds that "he was in the hard right-wing of the Falange" – and had an itchy trigger finger, in other word, "a bloodthirsty psychopath" and "a pervert of limited intelligence" who "used his strength and his Falangist blue shirt to commit outrageous abuses." Evidently, it is easier to divert attention toward an individual like Mariscal than to point a finger directly at those who were actually responsible for the great massacre carried out in Zamora. Finally, Mateos used the conference to refute a claim that, until then, no one had made: in Dr. Almendral's report "there is nothing about Amparo suffering from any type of disease." This refutation demonstrates that the Zamora chronicler had forgotten that it was not the prison doctor who had defamed Amparo Barayón; it was his granddaughter, in revenge for the book by Amparo's son Ramón.

Afterwards, silence reigned again: Ana Isabel Almendral Oppermann with the affront to her honor avenged, and the Barayón family without hope of restoring theirs. In the middle, *La Opinión de Zamora* and the city's chronicler, undoubtedly satisfied, not so much for having carried out their duty to keep the public informed as for having rescued the Zamora right-wing and its sacred legacy.[3]

APPENDIX I

Death in Zamora: The Tragedy of Amparo Barayón[4]

In *La Opinión de Zamora* (February 14, 2005), with understandable delay and bluntness, Amparo Barayón's children responded to Anabel Almendral, that "Amparo was not suffering from syphilis," providing personal information and evidence that deserve the utmost respect and consideration.

Almendral's claim (July 13, 2004) surprised me, although I took it with a grain of salt. Having gone through the relevant documents, which are abundant, I had not read anything to support her claim. In the various reports about Amparo that came to light, all of them hostile since they were intended to justify her assassination (October 11, 1936), not a word is said, nor any comment made, about syphilis. If there had been any truth to Almendral's claim, the chief commissioner of investigation and surveillance – M. P. – who did not mince his words when it came to describing the conduct, affiliations and suspicious activities of political detainees, would, I think, have reported it to the commanding military judge – Juan Losada.[TN1] For example, in a report referring to Amparo Barayón on March 4, 1937, M. P. writes "that said individual female (sic) was considered a dangerous communist, [. . .] that her husband Ramón Sender (he should have written Ramón J. Sender), a journalist with the *El Sol* company (it was a newspaper) [. . .] travelled from San Rafael to Madrid on July 18 to cash some checks, [. . .] that Amparo, along with her children and a servant, came to Zamora and lodged with her brothers, who were also considered dangerous extremists [. . .]," etc., etc. It is no small feat to commit so many errors in so few words. War propaganda.

In other reports he calls her "an anarchist, a red, a dangerous revolutionary and extremist, a spy, an agent of Moscow and of the International Red Aid society," and other anathemas in vogue at the time to disqualify the accused.

But neither in the records of the provincial jail – see her prison file – in which the civil governor Hernández Cortés writes: "Be so kind as to admit and hold at the disposition of my authority in the establishment under your supervision Amparo Barayón Miguel, twenty-nine years of age, single (obviously only in the eyes of the church in the Nationalist zone where civil

TRANSLATOR'S NOTE 1. Miguel Ángel Mateos is selective in concealing the identity of the people he mentions in this article. He uses initials – M. P. – for the chief commissioner of investigation and surveillance but the full name – Juan Losada – for the commanding military judge.

marriages were not recognized), black hair, also black eyebrows, regular nose and mouth, round face, healthy in appearance and coloration, tall of stature, by profession: employee of the Ministry of Agriculture residing in Madrid, Menéndez Pelayo St., 41 . . ."

Neither in the report from the jail's infirmary, where files were kept, nor in the chaplain's report have we found the faintest clue. Amparo Barayón was so degradingly slandered and vilified that I think if they had been aware of the alleged illness, it would have been reflected in the reports in order to further tarnish the memory of this poor and unhappy woman, who was known to be an enthusiastic catechist at the church of San Juan. Anabel Almendral's allegation could be considered a slanderous rumor but would never, in the eyes of the law, rise to the level of libel, as Amparo Barayón's children write in their response. Anabel's information must have come from oral sources connected to the Almendrals' family and professional circles, but it does not seem to be backed up by any clinical, official or unofficial documents.

If there is any proof, let us see it and, if not, it seems only fair to retract the statement. Even if it were true, no harm would be done by such a retraction. The worst part is that it is not true. Idle chatter over drinks at a bar or the confessions of a repentant Mary Magdalene need to be examined carefully and fact-checked. If not, an esteemed academic professional should not lower herself to fueling false rumors worthy of gossip circles. Otherwise, she lowers herself to the same level as Ramón J. Sender Barayón when he makes accusations against his own uncle Miguel Sevilla, against Hernández Comes – whom he repeatedly and erroneously calls Claomarchirant (sic) on several occasions – against Segundo Viloria, against many members of the Barayón family, against his own father, and against many others, based on unsupported, imagined and erratic information from dubious and weak oral sources far removed from the events he is narrating, even if it is unreasonable to doubt the good intentions of those he interviewed. Consequently, if *Muerte en Zamora* is intended as historical fiction, the product of the author's fantasies and inventiveness, he is quite at liberty to write it. Its merit would depend upon his eloquence. But if what is intended is to narrate and preserve for posterity real events involving specific people to whom he attributes explicit responsibility for certain actions, and especially in relation to such a complex, subjective and contentious matter as the Spanish Civil War, the most exhaustive, contextualized and profoundly analyzed information possible is required.

I understand Ramón J. Sender Barayón. He needs an explanation and cannot understand the tragic and, from any perspective, unjust death of his innocent and grief-stricken mother. But I cannot approve most of what is written in his book, because it does not conform to the events as known and documented, either orally or in writing.

I also understand Dr. Pedro Almendral if in fact it was he who passed on the unfounded rumor – he could not have been the source – that Amparo Barayón "was terribly ill from syphilis." Anabel's grandfather was an old-style liberal and a follower of Santiago Alba Bonifaz.[TN2] He was almost lynched outside the San Martín Workers' Center when he was falsely accused of negligence in the death of "El Pelao" in May 1936. They had forgotten that "El Pelao" had been treated, with due diligence and competence, by Dacio Crespo, according to the medical report. Almendral was also accused of carelessness in his treatment of a worker affiliated with the Socialist Party at the Zamora Clinic.

If Dr. Félix Valbuena Artolozábal had not hastened to protect him, Almendral's life would have been in serious danger. There are documents to prove it. After the coup, Almendral advised the famous humanitarian doctor Felipe Anciones to flee Zamora and go into hiding because he was about to be arrested. Later, Almendral begged the governor to spare Anciones's life. Given the outcome, Pedro Almendral did not seem to have much influence with those brought to power by the coup. Being an old-style Albist liberal, he did not have the best of credentials for interceding on behalf of anyone.

Nevertheless, until Anabel Almendral provides evidence, I cannot approve her unfortunate and highly debatable assertions about something that happened almost seventy years ago, assertions that do not rise above the level of idle gossip.

The best way to understand and comprehend our controversial uncivil war today is to study it rigorously until the existent documentation is exhausted. Hiding one's head in the sand, refusing to speak or write about it, as some would prefer, only serves to encourage rumors, slander and errors which, in my opinion, are harmful to many families' reputations. As

TRANSLATOR'S NOTE 2. Miguel Ángel Mateos calls Dr. Pedro Almendral a "viejo liberal albista." Francisco Espinosa-Maestre informs me that "albista" refers to the doctor's association with the Zamoran lawyer and liberal politician Santiago Alba Bonifaz, who held high posts, including some ministries, during the monarchy, and joined the Radical Republican Party during the Republic. According to Espinosa-Maestre, M. A. Mateos is showing off his knowledge of local history. No doubt he is, but he is also attempting to depict Pedro Almendral as a pro-democratic moderate caught between the extreme Left and extreme Right during the Spanish civil war. In fact, by the 1930s, the Radical Republican Party had become very conservative, despite its name. Many of its members embraced the military coup. Dr. Pedro Almendral seems to have been among them.

Ricardo de la Cierva said, "To think we can arrive at the truth strikes us as unlikely, and the whole truth, impossible."[TN3]

MIGUEL ÁNGEL MATEOS
(*La Opinión de Zamora*, February 17, 2005)

TRUTHS LARGE AND SMALL

I have read with great interest the seven articles written by Miguel Ángel Mateos about the repression in Zamora in general and about the cases of Amparo Barayón and Pilar Fidalgo in particular. As might be expected of the city's official chronicler, the articles contain many details that would otherwise never have seen the light of day. For that, we owe him our thanks.

Nevertheless, there are aspects of his articles that seem to me unworthy of both Miguel Ángel Mateos and of *La Opinión de Zamora*. I am referring to the venom with which he tries to discredit the book by Ramón Sender Barayón and the sarcasm he uses to diminish the value of Pilar Fidalgo's testimony, which he does by mocking her ignorance of documents that have become available only half a century after the events she describes. With regard to the book by Ramón Sender Barayón, and referring to a previous letter published in *La Opinión*, he writes "I imagine that its signatories, the historians who have written in favor of the book, especially Professor Preston, have not read it. I am sure they have signed like those who used to sign manifestos without having read them."

Well, I have read the book. I am not in the habit of signing in the dark. I also happen to know that the historians Helen Graham and Francisco Espinosa-Maestre have read it. I know because I have discussed it in detail with both of them. It is possible, even probable, that the book by Sender Barayón might contain minor errors of detail. The nuances and corrections made by Señor Mateos in this regard are certainly valuable. However, this does not detract from the reality that, by placing on the agenda his mother's death, Pilar Fidalgo's imprisonment and mistreatment, and the many assassinations that took place during the repression in Zamora, Sender Barayòn has done a great service to the history of the period. There are truths large and small. In other words, it is possible to recount a big overarching truth

TRANSLATOR'S NOTE 3. M. A. Mateos ends the first of his eight articles with a quote from Ricardo de la Cierva y Hoces, author of numerous books in defense of the 1936 military coup. In the 1960s, de la Cierva headed the Cabinet on Historical Studies, part of the Ministry of Information and Tourism, and directed the BOB, Bulletin of Bibliographical Orientation, which published scathing critiques of the works of foreign historians whose books on the Spanish civil war were being translated into Spanish and smuggled into Franco's Spain.

without necessarily having all the minute details correct. In fact, the valuable information being published by Señor Mateos is appearing only now because he has decided to reply to Sender Barayón's book, and has done so only after a delay of nearly fifteen years. It is almost as if Señor Mateos feels offended that Sender Barayón had dared to trespass onto what, as the official chronicler, he regards as his private reserve.

Throughout his articles, Señor Mateos has manifested a commitment to precision, even to the point of demanding it of those who have not had the same opportunities he has had to examine more recently available sources. Given this obsession with exactitude, it is difficult not to be startled by the sheer anti-historical nature of Señor Mateos's statement that "If the military coup had not failed and there had not been a war, there would certainly have been no repression and no firing squads. Thus, it is only after July 25, when the armed conflict started, that there are the first executions, committed either by uncontrollable elements or elements remotely controlled from afar."

Can this possibly mean that Señor Mateos is unaware of the secret instructions issued in April 1936 by the director of the military conspiracy, General Emilio Mola, and which were published in 1939? Mola stated "It has to be borne in mind that the action has to be violent in the extreme so as to subdue as soon as possible the enemy which is strong and well-organized. It goes without saying that all leaders of political parties, societies and trade unions not part of the movement will be imprisoned and exemplary punishment carried out on them in order to choke off any rebellion or strikes." Is it possible that Señor Mateos does not know that there was a fierce repression in Valladolid, in Seville, in Huelva, in Cádiz and many other provinces before July 25? Is it possible that Señor Mateos is unaware of what happened in Ceuta and Melilla, immediately after the coup?

I said earlier that there are truths large and small and, by the same token, there are errors large and small. So let us overlook the fact that Señor Mateos refers to Señora Mercedes Esteban Maes as "el Señor Esteban Maes Barayón" or that he refers to the "book" by Pilar Fidalgo when no such book exists, but only fewer than twenty pages based on statements by her, published in the French press and in a short English pamphlet. It is necessary to show some understanding when reading things and to judge them with sensitivity, recognizing what is of value in each book or article. For that reason, it is possible to see beyond his mistakes and the gratuitous sarcasm of his tone and recognize the merit in his work.

PAUL PRESTON
(*La Opinión de Zamora*, April 10, 2005)

Extra-judicial Deaths

Here in the United States, writers who receive negative reviews are told: "Count the number of words they write about you and thank them." Bearing this in mind, I ought to thank Mr. M. A. Mateos profusely for his series of long articles. Regarding the historical errors he points out, I sincerely wish he had been able to help me during the two trips I took to Zamora in the 1980s to investigate the events that led to my mother's assassination.

I am not a historian, and when I travelled to Zamora I hardly understood Spanish, although I could rely on the help of my wife Judith, who did speak it. The only documents I had access to were my mother's birth certificate and baptismal record, and a fraudulent death certificate. Since the only sources at my disposal were the interviews I conducted with people who, during almost forty years, had been unable to talk for fear of losing their own freedom – or even their lives – I think my attempt to tell my mother's story deserves some recognition. If it has served no other purpose, my book is at least a reminder to the citizens of Zamora that they ought to acknowledge the thousands of extra-judicial deaths that took place, tacitly approved by those in power. In his attempt to correct my errors, it is possible that Mr. Mateos has done us all a favor by drawing our attention to the documents now available for consultation, and by awakening the public's conscience to the fact that, to date, nothing has been done in Zamora to publicly commemorate the many women who were brutally incarcerated and dragged out in the darkness of night to be shot in such a cruel fashion that it would be inappropriate to describe it here. Although Mr. Mateos alludes to similar assassinations that took place in the Republican zone, I do not believe that excuses the enormity of the extra-judicial deaths that took place in the areas occupied by those who carried out the coup, especially in Zamora.

Personally, I always feel grateful whenever Amparo's story is told with ever greater truth. I will always be grateful to Pilar Fidalgo Carasa for her testimony. Any errors to be found in her declarations to the Spanish Consul should be attributed to the brutal treatment from which she had just escaped.

RAMÓN SENDER BARAYÓN
(*La Opinión de Zamora*, April 10, 2005)

About Amparo Barayón's Assassination

For the past several weeks I have been following what M. A. Mateos is doing with his articles. It is worth recalling the beginning of the affair: last summer Dr. Almendral's granddaughter took advantage of an interview in this newspaper to launch an inappropriate attack on the memory of Amparo Barayón, assassinated along with two of her brothers in 1936. In order to spread the false rumor that Amparo was suffering from syphilis, the doctor's granddaughter had to distort and misrepresent Pilar Fidalgo's recollections of her imprisonment. And it was when Amparo Barayón's family reacted to this slander that Mateos entered the fray. At first he pretended he was not taking sides and, to prove his impartiality, proposed that if Anabel Almendral could not back up her claim, she should make a retraction. But from the person in question, not a word.

Then, as if he were on the same relay team as Almendral, he takes up the baton and begins ridiculing Pilar Fidalgo's testimony and Ramón Sender Barayón's book. With the crudest devices as his only recourse, Mateos attacks them both. The trick he employs consists of presenting their testimonies as if they were works of history. For Mateos, Pilar Fidalgo's personal recollections of her passage through the Zamora prison are worthless and the same goes for Ramón Sender's inquiries into his mother's final days. They are a series of errors and falsehoods. He is the one who knows, his sources are all valid and, furthermore, he has all the information. For several weeks now, article after article, he goes on utilizing memory in the service of righteousness, unlike everyone else.

The last thing he has told us is that the guilty party in Amparo Barayón's death is Ramón J. Sender for sending her to the slaughterhouse. This was to be expected. But he takes it even further. However often he calls her that "exquisite, unhappy woman," that "innocent, suffering mother," or that "good and worthy lady," as if writing a melodrama, he is not at all credible and the suspicion floats through his writing that she herself was responsible for her tragedy when she insulted the civil governor brought to power by the coup. After all, what did she have to complain about? All they had done was murder her brother. In fact, other than attacking Fidalgo and Sender's writings, the only thing Mateos has accomplished since he entered the fray, despite his obfuscations and dissimulations, is to blame Ramón J. Sender for his wife's assassination and exonerate fascists, paramilitary forces, hired killers and priests at the service of the military coup. His conclusion is that if the coup had triumphed everywhere, there would not have been a repression. That must be why, wherever it succeeded, the top priority was respect for life. Like in

Zamora. As someone has said, history, conveniently utilized, can become the most powerful narcotic of our times.

FRANCISCO ESPINOSA-MAESTRE
(*La Opinión de Zamora*, April 13, 2005)

TO THE HISTORIAN MATEOS

We must recognize the importance of stressing the time period during which the action of a drama takes place. This is true for all types of dramas, but especially for the crimes committed during our Civil War. As if following a serialized novel, I have anxiously awaited each of your articles in this newspaper, which would bring me closer to the *dénouement*, no less tragic for being known beforehand. These are legitimate strategies used by schoolteachers to hold their students' attention. But here such devices were not necessary, because "our war" has marked us with fiery scars and, when evoked, summons images, situations and characters vaguely remembered that form a part of our collective memory. We even share last names with some of them. The whole drama is cloaked in a panicky vertigo where one perceives the horror of the hunted prey and the snuffing out of lives as hidden hatreds are unleashed and scores are settled in the shadow of cemetery walls. It is praiseworthy that there are professionals who deal with the spoils of death. For that reason, we owe them our admiration. But, oh, the investigation of death at close quarters demands the utmost respect!

That is why I have taken it upon myself to write this note because, in my opinion, Mr. Mateos's history of Zamora reveals a lack of historical rigor when he makes assertions, that are not supported by facts as they should be and are written in a style of devastating certainty, about the direct participation of one of my relatives in Consuelo Barayón's death.[TN4] Since the work was published, I have held my tongue for years, in spite of the convictions and opinions of some historians that such a condemnation does not conform to the truth. Now, with the publication of Miguel Ángel Mateos's articles in *La Opinión de Zamora*, my suspicion that the blunt assertions in his history of Zamora are untrue is confirmed. It is the typical plotting of a drama, with good guys and bad guys, and roles assigned by the new demiurge, who interprets events to suit his purposes. Is it not frivolous to issue blunt assertions that fall apart under the first serious scrutiny? It makes one

TRANSLATOR'S NOTE 4. This letter is a defense of the honor of one of the writer's ancestors. He has not taken the trouble to check the first name of Amparo Barayón.

doubt his scientific rigor. Because how can events be reinterpreted in this way without providing the necessary evidence?

He skims superficially over reality, picking the characters he needs and assigning each of them a role. Is it not arrogant, and an attack on public harmony, to air controversial issues and emit verdicts of guilt to third parties who had nothing to do with that tragedy? But, as has been pointed out by other readers of this newspaper, we can expect no less from someone who continually disparages the assertions of those who do not share his opinions. As if that were not enough, M. A. Mateos takes the liberty of interpreting the behavior of a person close to me with apparent benevolence, along the line of "good lad who kept bad counsel, etc." Leave it alone and stop stirring up dirt.

ANTONIO VILORIA
(*La Opinión de Zamora*, April 16, 2005)

A FAMILY'S SENSIBILITIES (REFLECTIONS FOR DON MIGUEL ÁNGEL MATEOS)

I am sitting at my word processor with a book in my hand, *Muerte en Zamora*. I have opened it to the central pages and gaze at the photograph of the Maes Barayón family. I am the little one to the left, the one who looks like he wants to put his finger up his nose. I am looking at my grandmother Magdalena and, now that I have reread the book, I understand why she was always so sad. Mr. Mateos, as Mr. Preston put it so well, there are truths large and small.

I am going to tell you how I became aware of the existence of the writer Ramón J. Sender. It was at my school run by missionaries of the Claretan order on the day we studied this author in our literature class. Srta. Lourdes, who knew my family, called on me to tell my classmates about him. I could not say anything because I knew nothing about him. With this anecdote I want to tell you that there are families that have suffered so much that they do not want to involve even their closest relatives in that suffering. They only want to forget.

Muerte en Zamora is a book of great sensibility, a son's homage to the mother he barely knew. It is a book that does not deserve your detailed clarifications. I do not know History but I see my father's eyes in the photograph and, this morning, I do not like the way they look. We all know that in any war, people who lose their sons, daughters, brothers, sisters, or spouses suffer, and suffering does not differentiate between winners and losers but, if such a thing is possible, the suffering of the losers is greater.

Believe me Mr. Mateos when I say that the history in seven installments that you have published in this newspaper has done nothing but reawaken memories in people with no desire to remember. I ask you, please, save this harsh and objective History, with its detailed clarification, told –pardon the expression– in such a pedantic fashion, for your classroom. Without a doubt, your pupils will be the winners.

FERNANDO MAES ARJONA BARAYÓN
Castellanos de Moriscos, Salamanca
(*La Opinión de Zamora*, April 19, 2005)

A LITTLE SERIOUSNESS, MR. MATEOS

I have read with great interest the controversy provoked by the inopportune declarations about Amparo Barayón by one of Dr. Almendral's descendants. Since Amparo Barayón is dead and could not defend herself, her family has come forward to defend her from the attacks on her personal dignity, a totally proper response. We all know, even you, that Amparo Barayón was assassinated. She did not die from an illness. The proper thing would have been for Dr. Almendral's descendant to retract what she said and apologize; she did not do so and we are not going to oblige her to. Let her be. The regrettable part is that you, a sensible person, are determined to find errors in the book that Sender Barayón wrote about his mother and, day after day, turn out articles on the same subject so incessantly that it has become tiresome.

You say that Sender Barayón got information for his book *Muerte en Zamora* by interviewing people whose responses may have been somewhat influenced by the personal situation of someone interviewed in your book *La República en Zamora*, volume I, page 695, section 4, Oral Sources, where you list a series of people you interviewed. If you use interviews as a source of information, why is it that Sender Barayón is not allowed to do the same? You are not being serious don Miguel Ángel. You have other sources of information which, by the way, are less reliable than personal interviews. You know as well as I do that a good part of the documentation related to the Civil War is falsified. Besides, perhaps – I do not know – Sender Barayón did not have access to documentary sources and therefore got his information from people. It is wrong to censure him for that.

I do not doubt your merits as a historian and I admire your capacity for work, but I advise you to be humble enough to accept the opinions of other historians, some of whom are specialists in the Spanish Civil War, like those who signed one of the letters from the Sender Barayón family. Take my word for it, don Miguel Ángel Mateos Rodríguez, only God is omniscient. We poor mortals only possess some part of the truth. We will only arrive at the whole truth if each of us contributes that small part we possess. To claim that my truth alone is valid and disqualify others' share of the truth is pride and I remind you that God rejects the proud.

Saturnina Lorenzo García

Toro

(*La Opinión de Zamora*, April 20, 2005)

APPENDIX II

Sergeant Venom's Patrol in Villalpando

Toward the end of August 1936, while Lieutenant Colonel José Redondo, Commander Gervasio Fernández Noaín and Captain Juan Rodríguez Guillén were at the Civil Guard barracks in Zamora, a delegation arrived from Villalpando consisting of, among others, the mayor (Maximiliano Peláez Blanco?), the doctor, Tonanzos, and the judge, Juan Esteban Romera. The purpose of their visit was to request that the Civil Guard corporal, whose last name was San Román, be relieved of duty "because he was afraid and, according to them, did not dare to operate energetically in the events unfolding in the town." According to the captain's declarations months later, the judge was the principal spokesman during the meeting. Besides reminding them that the corporal could not be held responsible since there was a line officer there, Lieutenant Colonel Redondo asked them to submit their complaint in writing, which the members of the delegation refused to do.

What we know is that a few days later the Zamora civil governor ordered the governmental delegate to pay a visit to Villalpando with his patrol. This delegate was Sergeant Luis Valera Nieves, better known as "Sergeant Venom," whose duties since July 18 until mid-October 1936, were "to arrest individuals who had stood out for their opposition to the aforementioned Movement and for their extremist ideas, and to adopt and carry out with respect to those individuals whatever measures he deemed advisable and fitting."

The day "Sergeant Venom" approached Villalpando, his patrol consisted of the lawyer Segundo Viloria, Julio Gómez, Carlos Gómez and the requeté Domingo Gómez.[TN5 (OVERLEAF)] The objective, since according to the aforementioned complaint, "there were leftist elements in said town who were considered undesirables and that it was necessary to remove them from the town," was the following:

To arrest the individuals of said town who had stood out as extremists and opponents of the Movement, with orders to the effect that all those who had taken up arms against the Civil Guard or armed forces be left dead in the cemetery of the aforementioned town.

So the patrol arrived that morning in the town, where it was met by the mayor, the judge and the other members of the delegation, who put themselves at the patrol's disposal and proceeded to draw up a list of those who should be arrested. Those on the list were taken to the barracks that afternoon, in the presence of Corporal San Román and the line officer. As they were arriving, "Sergeant Venom" made inquiries to find out if they should be taken to Zamora or directly to the cemetery wall. It was precisely when the two groups of prisoners were halfway formed that the judge, Esteban, who was standing guard at the barracks door, came in and said "that he could not consent to any of those arrested being taken to Zamora or executed because that would lead to an uprising of all the townsfolk against said judge and the other local authorities, who would be blamed for said arrests and executions."

Then, Sergeant Valera telephoned the civil governor, who, apprised of the situation, ordered that "only the most rebellious be taken and that the rest be set free." Meanwhile, Judge Esteban, somewhat out of control, called Corporal San Román a coward and a liar in the presence of the mayor, Valera, the line officer, and Viloria. In his report, Valera maintained that the judge's behavior "was not due to the judge's antipatriotic sentiments or directed at the National Movement but, on the contrary, due only to said gentleman's kindness, his desire to avoid bloodshed in the town, and the fact that he and other members of the town's authorities would be blamed for what happened because it was they who went to the provincial government to report on those who were under arrest." Valera also recalled that, during that day, the judge "was very adamant about carrying out the aforementioned arrests and executions of persons who deserved it." For which reason he says it is possible that the judge's change of mind was influenced by the

TRANSLATOR'S NOTE 5 (PREVIOUS PAGE). Requeté is the name for members of the Carlist militias. Carlism dates back to the nineteenth-century supporters of Carlos María Isidro Benito de Borbón-Parma (1788–1855), pretender to the Spanish throne after the death of his brother Fernando VII in 1833. The Carlists in the Spanish civil war were ultraconservative Catholics who believed in the divine right of kings. They were as violent as the Falangists.

But the important thing to notice here is the presence in this "death squad" of the lawyer Segundo Viloria, ex-suitor of Amparo Barayón and, according to members of her family, the man who shot her.

fact that, when the moment arrived to take the prisoners away, the area around the barracks was so crowded with people that the Civil Guard had to clear the nearest stretch of highway.

These statements about the incident in Villalpando are from the investigation to remove Judge Juan Esteban Romera from his post. They are statements by Captain Juan Rodríguez Guillén and Sergeant Juan Valera Nieves, taken down on November 16, 1936.[5]

Notes

1 Ramón Sender Barayón, *Muerte en Zamora* (Barcelona: Plaza & Janés, 1990), 160; *A Death in Zamora* (Albuquerque: University of New Mexico Press, 1989), 134.

2 The letter is signed by Ramón and Andrea Sender Barayón; Magdalena Maes Barayón; Mercedes, Ignacio and Mónica Esteban Maes, and Ana Marín Esteban.

3 According to Cándido Ruiz, who investigated the Republic and the military coup in Zamora, in 2008 the municipal government accepted a proposal from the Zamora Republican Circle to rename several streets to honor people associated with the Republic who were assassinated following the military coup. Among the new street names was "Barayón Brothers," for Amparo's brothers Antonio and Saturnino. Nevertheless, the local press never mentioned who these two men were and how they died.

4 Miguel Ángel Mateos published eight articles on the subject from February to April 2005. I only include the first. Those interested can find the rest in the newspaper's archives.

5 I owe this document to the kindness of Mónica Lanero Táboas. Agapito Modroño Alonso's book *Víctimas de la represión en Villalpando, 1936–1939* (Benavente, Ed. El Autor, 2005) does not contain any reference to these events. During the controversy caused by the declarations of Almendral's granddaughter, Modroño takes Miguel Ángel Mateos's side and speaks of "jealousies among historians."

Antonio Martínez Borrego and the Impostor Gila Boza

The policies of silence and oblivion put into practice during the Transition bore fruit in the following decades. It is only possible to understand the strange stories of the impostors Enric Marco and Antonio Pastor in the context of this total void regarding the past. They each pretended to be what they were not: Enric Marco in Catalonia and Antonio Pastor in Andalusia. Enric Marco, recipient of the Cross of St. George (2001), president of the principal Spanish association of deportees, the Friends of Mauthausen, had invented a past for himself as an inmate at the Flossenburg concentration camp "in order to call attention to himself and, by so doing, to be better able to promote awareness of the victims' suffering," according to his own declaration. For his part, Antonio Pastor, recipient of the Medal of Andalusia (2002), was considered a "survivor of the Nazi camps" by the Andalusian press[1] and was featured in a program entitled "Mauthausen, Live to Tell the Tale" on Canal Sur. He showed documents purportedly proving his passage through Mauthausen, documents that no one had taken the trouble to read. It turned out he had never been a deportee, had never been at Mauthausen, and had never fought in the French resistance. Each of these impostors took advantage of the lack of rigorous research on Spanish deportees to the Nazi camps. "In France he would never have become the president of an association," several deportees said after the 'Marco case' became known" (*El País*, May 15, 2005).

Benito Bermejo and Sandra Checa were the first historians to investigate the affair in depth and bring it into the light of day, showing the impostors for what they were. It was Bermejo and Checa who had to make a formal complaint. Adding insult to injury, the historians were criticized by those who should have been the most grateful: the Friends of Mauthausen themselves, Marco's fellow anarchists – Marco was secretary general of the CNT[TN1] – the journalists who had been incapable of questioning a single declaration by the deportee impostors and had not even taken the trouble

TRANSLATOR'S NOTE 1. Confederación Nacional del Trabajo (National Confederation of Labor) is an anarcho-syndicalist union.

to read the papers they had been shown, the documentary filmmakers who had made undocumented documentaries, etc. The "Marco-Pastor scandal" revealed a terrible reality: thirty years into the transition to democracy, those responsible for the violence that desolated the country since July 18, 1936 could continue to conceal their past and present themselves as innocents: the true victims, in this case exiles and deportees, could be supplanted by persons who had snatched their own past from them. This terrible reality was the result of the policies put in place during the Transition by the parties that came to power, whatever their ideologies. Obviously, this reality would have been impossible if the government had encouraged the investigation of the fates of the thousands of Spaniards who ended up in Nazi concentration camps.

The case that concerns us here represents a further turning of the screw. The backdrop is, once again, the desire for undeserved attention and the confidence that nothing will happen if one lies. In 2005 Oberon published *La hoz y las flechas: un comunista en Falange (The Sickle and the Arrows: A communist in the Falange)*,[TN2] by the journalist Mercedes de Pablos Candón. On December 15, an article about the publication appeared in the Andalusian supplement of *El País*, signed by Santiago Belausteguigoitia and with a photograph of the author. A reading of the book, which is ludicrous from beginning to end, prompted José María García Márquez, leading expert on the Francoist repression in the province of Seville and perhaps the researcher best acquainted with the documents available at the Archive of the Second Territorial Military Tribunal, and me to send a letter to the Andalusian supplement of *El País* on December 19:

RE THE SICKLE AND THE ARROWS

Just a few days ago there was an article in this newspaper about the publication of *La hoz y las flechas*, a book by Mercedes de Pablos based on the testimony of Juan Gila Boza. The author's account is based on an error: the disappearance of Gila Boza's trial transcript. Said document exists. The reason for this letter is the slanderous accusation that Antonio Martínez Borrego was the informer who caused dozens of persons to be imprisoned in 1948. It is not true. Gila Boza has forgotten that he presented his own declarations before Martínez Borrego did and that he talked a good deal

TRANSLATOR'S NOTE 2. The escutcheon of the Falange has a yoke and arrows. Thus the title of the book combines an element from the Falangist escutcheon with an element from the Communist hammer and sickle.

more. He has also forgotten that no one had asked for a death sentence for him. Furthermore, according to his own words at the trial and his prison dossier, Gila Boza, who says he was a Falangist since 1934, joined the PCE (Spanish Communist Party) in 1935 under orders from the Falange. We believe the existence of this trial transcript invalidates his testimony and we recommend a complete revision of the book. It is possible that what we have here is not a "Communist mole" who infiltrated the Falange but rather a recipient of the Medallion of the Old Guard of the Falange[TN3] who infiltrated the PCE beginning in 1935 and carried out espionage assignments during the war. This would make Juan Gila Boza's strange curriculum vitae somewhat more comprehensible.

But the newspaper, perhaps out of corporate self-interest, considered that the letter did not deserve publication. Consequently, on January 6 we sent it to *El Correo de Andalucía* and the Andalusian supplement of *El Mundo*. They both published it on January 17, with near-instantaneous results: the following day it appeared in *El País*, undoubtedly because they wanted their fellow journalist De Pablos to be able to reply at her pleasure, as she did on January 20:

COMMUNIST AND MILITANT

Juan Gila Boza is a card-carrying Communist and party militant. He has been a party member for eighty years and is still one now at the age of ninety-one. Let this blunt affirmation serve as a response to the letter published by your newspaper in which Sr. Espinosa expresses doubts about the political and personal trajectory of Juan Gila Boza, the protagonist of *La hoz y las flechas*, a book I wrote based on his testimony and corroborated by his recollections. The writer bases his letter on an error, claiming that the book analyzes a trial transcript. It is not a book about a dossier but about a person. The difference is not subtle; it is substantive. To doubt the veracity of Juan's life is somewhat more serious than a professional error or a lack of truth. It is perverse and immoral. All of us who have read Juan's biography know, just like his party comrades know, and his friends and neighbors, and those who paid him an indemnity many years ago as a victim of Francoism, that Gila Boza still has the

TRANSLATOR'S NOTE 3. The Falange was not a mass movement until after the July 18, 1936 military coup. To be regarded as "Old Guard of the Falange" one had to have joined before the coup.

dossier from the trial that sent him to jail, but that the original has not been available in the corresponding archive, at least not when the book was published. He does have the photocopy, of course, as well as other documents that are just as valuable and support his recollections. But it is a man's memory, a man's life that is narrated in the book. What matters to me is Juan Gila Boza, his life, his dignity and the respect we all owe him. History belongs to the men and women who make it, as all of us who love histories and write them know, personal attacks, patrimonies and jealousies notwithstanding.

This response conforms to the adage "The best defense is an offense." Mercedes de Pablos's letter never even mentioned José María García Márquez, it claimed that our error was to assume that her book was an analysis of a trial transcript (on the contrary, we were encouraging her to consult it), that to doubt Gila Boza's testimony was "perverse and immoral," that Gila Boza had the dossier from the trial (what he probably had was a copy of the court's ruling) and, after defending the life and dignity of this gentleman, it ended with the assertion that our letter was motivated by personal and patrimonial matters and by jealousy. De Pablos's letter never addressed the question being debated. A few days later, January 25, *El País* published a letter from someone who seemed to be one of the journalist's fans. "I have followed the career of the remarkable journalist Mercedes de Pablos . . .," the letter began. It was obvious that for the letter's author, Selva Otero by name and one of De Pablos's faithful devotees, it was sufficient to read De Pablos's letter without having read ours. Convinced that we were the same enemy as always, Francoist reactionaries, Selva Otero came to the defense of "the rigor and sensitivity of a brave woman" and took up arms against us – though she admitted she had never heard of us – saying we were two of those "who could not bear those 224 pages in which Mercedes had made short work of us."

A few days before, on January 22, García Márquez and I had sent another letter to *El País* in response to the one published by De Pablos. At first, the letter received the same treatment as had our first letter until, after a complaint to the public editor and another to the then editor-in-chief, Jesús Cebrero, they decided to publish it on February 11:

OF MOLES AND INFORMERS

We are not going to answer M. de Pablos in the tone she has decided to adopt. All we will say is that she ought to document what she writes. Her snide remarks and disqualifications oblige us to remind her that the reason for our letter was the accusation that appears in her book that Antonio Martínez Borrego was an informer, an inadmissible accusation (in this case clearly "perverse and immoral") about which she has preferred to remain silent. What if the real informer was not Martínez Borrego? Can it be that only Gila Boza has the right to dignity and respect? There were two options available to the letter's author: turn to the archive to confirm what she had been told by comparing the trial transcript with Gila Boza's oral testimony, or continue acting as if the trial transcript did not exist and discredit the messenger with various fabrications and prejudices. It is clear that she has chosen the second and easiest option.

With respect to Gila Boza, we fail to understand why we are not allowed to doubt the veracity of his declarations, especially since we know the tricks memory can play and are acquainted with the trial transcript from 1948. For example, it is untrue that Martínez Borrego informed on all his comrades. It is also untrue that "no one was killed because of him [Gila Boza]." In fact there are a few still alive whom he denounced. Furthermore, Boza has forgotten important events that explain many things: according to the trial record, he was awarded the Medallion of the Old Guard of the Falange in 1935, the same year he was ordered by the Falange to join the PCE, but his membership in the party, no longer as a Falangist mole, did not become official until after 1944. These four "oversights" alone would require that his testimony – and De Pablos's book – be revised.

Meanwhile, fed up with the direction this affair was taking, we decided to forget about the mainstream media and turn to the Internet. On February 2, we sent the following text to various WebPages:

RE THE SICKLE AND THE ARROWS OR HOW TO END THE HISTORICAL MEMORY FAD ONCE AND FOR ALL

Experience shows that history is within the reach of anyone who knows how to practice it well. There is no such thing as good history written by historians and bad history written by everyone else. Although it is not easy to overcome certain deficiencies associated with a lack of historical knowledge, there are basically, as in almost any endeavor, works that are done well and works that do not achieve the required standard. With regard to our recent history, nevertheless, almost all of us think we have the right to our opinions. But in spite of the fact that we are dealing with events that people we know have lived through, some of whom are still alive and from whom we can gather testimonies, this task must be carried out with an adequate understanding of what we are doing. The risks and excesses of oral history are well known: it is hardly worthwhile talking to someone who lived through the Republic, the military coup, the war and the dictatorship if we do not have a minimum acquaintance with the events from 1931 to 1975. Let us say, even at the risk of exaggerating, that in oral history 50% of the work is preparatory: the elaboration of the questionnaire. The benefit to be derived from eyewitnesses will always be in proportion to our knowledge and to the quality of our questions. And if the person we are interviewing is mistaken or is lying, we must be able to detect it and, with practice, be aware of their lack of reliability. Two examples: one thing is *Recuérdalo tú y recuérdalo a otros* by Ronald Fraser (Barcelona: Crítica, 1979)[TN4] and quite another is *Historias orales de la Guerra Civil* by Alfonso Bullón de Mendoza and Álvaro de Diego (Barcelona: Ariel, 2000). Twenty years separate an oral history classic from a landmark of slapdash revisionism.

Two relatively new phenomena must be added to this initial explanation of the problem: the proliferation of persons from outside the realm of history (usually novelists and journalists) who are encouraged to publish things "about the Civil War" by the "historical memory fad" that emerged at the end of the 1990s, and the gradual development of a "round-table culture," an extended practice in the mass media exemplified by awarding "expert" status to any unlicensed individual who appears before a microphone or has a regular column in a newspaper, and treating their undocumented utterances as if they were reasoned opinions. Having said this, it must be added that there are novels that can coexist quite well with history and in that sea of "round-tables" there are also competent opinions. But unfortunately these cases are infrequent. Those who attract the most attention are people, especially in the fields of journalism and literature, who work the "Civil War" goldmine, relying on the inestimable support of the mass media. Thus a chain of relationships emerges (author + publisher + literary supplement + audiovisual media) that allows inferior products to be transformed into bestsellers. Furthermore, adding to the confusion, all this has been accompanied by the revisionist tide that emerged in response to the movement for historical memory, a trend promoted by the PP[TN5] during its second term in office.

This is the context in which M. de Pablos's book, published by Oberon,

TRANSLATOR'S NOTE 4. *Blood of Spain: The Experience of Civil War* (London: Allen Lane, 1979).

TRANSLATOR'S NOTE 5. Partido Popular, the Spanish conservative party.

should be examined. We are in the presence of a book that is the result of a combination of circumstances: a man (Gila Boza) appears at the right time with a story to tell, whether it is true or not; a journalist (M. de Pablos) and a publisher deeply involved in the aforementioned "historical memory fad" (Oberon). One does not have to be an expert on the history of Spain from 1931 to 1950 to know that *The Sickle and the Arrows* is fraught with all sorts of problems which would make it almost impossible for it to be accepted by a publisher specializing in History. But this would not be enough to actively lament and criticize its publication. After all, dozens of similar books are published every year, and it is not worth wasting even a minute to prove it (imagine the time it would take just with the books published by Torres or Eslava). What distinguishes M. de Pablos's book is that it contains a serious slander: an innocent man, Antonio Martínez Borrego, is accused of being the informer who caused the arrest of numerous people during a dragnet that took place in 1948 in the mountains north of Seville. It is understandable that the author did not consult the documentation available in the military archive concerning the trial, since she thought it did not exist; but it is inconceivable that the same author, having been informed of the existence of the trial transcript and the serious nature of her error, not only refuses to admit her mistake and apologize to Martínez Borrego's family and to her readers, but has doubled down, employing the most preposterous demagoguery. Consequently, we feel obligated to comment in more detail on why the book about Gila Boza is ridiculous from beginning to end and why we should not be surprised by the enormity of the gaffe committed. We will limit our comments to seven key points regarding the book:

1. According to the book, Gila Boza joined the PCE (Spanish Communist Party) in 1933 in Llerena (Seville) when he was eighteen years old, sponsored by Helios Gómez. This is impossible: By 1932 Helios Gómez, an artist from Seville (not Extremadura), was in Madrid and would never set foot in Seville again. Furthermore, Gila Boza and De Pablos refer to Helios Gómez as an "active Falangist." They must be confusing him with someone else. Anyone who knows anything about Helios Gómez's life knows he had nothing to do with the Falange. With respect to the date when Juan Gila joined the PCE, according to his own testimony during the 1948 trial: "in 1935, I joined the Communist Party, having been ordered to do so by the Falange, in order to uncover and disarticulate the activities of said Communists, as can be verified by documents filed in the Falange Provincial Headquarters." So his

entry into the Communist Party was neither in 1933, nor in Llerena, nor sponsored by Helios Gómez.

2. The story that Gila Boza happened to be in Madrid on March 4, 1934 and appeared in a photograph with Primo de Rivera, Onésimo Redondo and Sancho Dávila during the fusion of Falange and the JONS does not hold up under scrutiny: the formation of FE de las JONS took place in Valladolid, not Madrid.[TN6] If by chance this is an innocent mistake and refers to the founding of the Falange, which took place in the Teatro de la Comedia on October 29, 1933, there would be another problem: Onésimo Redondo did not attend that event. So it was neither on March 4, 1934, nor in Madrid, nor in the presence of Onésimo Redondo.

3. Gila Boza's memory seems to vanish into thin air when he recalls what happened between July 18 and September 9, 1936. Knowing as we do the role played by the Seville Falange during those crucial weeks, Juan Gila does not seem to know where to place himself: whether devising a plan to evacuate people, whether demanding arms at the Alameda barracks, whether dressed in his Falangist uniform with his membership card firmly in hand, whether defending the working-class neighborhood of San Julián, whether removing arms and propaganda from the working-class neighborhood of Ciudad Járdin, whether hiding leftists, whether carrying out "administrative tasks" at the Falange barracks, whether at the cemetery . . . We have no way of knowing what he really did. What we do know is what others like him did.

4. The story that Gila Boza left Seville on September 9 on a local train that took him to Azuaga presents certain problems: Azuaga had yet to be occupied by those who carried out the coup and, logically, there were no trains in service that could depart from Seville and arrive in Azuaga, tranquilly crossing the frontlines. The information in his police file seems more logical: when they lost track of him in Peñarroya he was part of one of the Falangist militia units that were formed in Seville and in which it was obligatory to enlist. But,

TRANSLATOR'S NOTE 6. Falange Española de las Juntas de Ofensiva Nacional Sindicalista (Spanish Falange of the Assemblies of the National Syndicalist Offensive) was the result of the fusion of the Spanish Falange, founded by José Antonio Primo de Rivera, with another fascist organization, the Juntas de Ofensiva Nacional Sindicalista, in which Onésimo Redondo Ortega was a prominent member. Sancho Dávila, José Antonio's cousin, was the Seville territorial chief of the Falange.

TRANSLATOR'S NOTE 7 (OVERLEAF). The Fifth Regiment was Communist.

without a doubt, one of the high points of the book is his journey from Peñarroya to Madrid and his immediate enlistment as a second lieutenant in the V Regiment,[TN7 (PREVIOUS PAGE)] based on his military experience in the Falange. This story is only surpassed by his interview with José Antonio Primo de Rivera in Valencia on October 3, 1936 when, according to Gila and De Pablos, Largo Caballero's government was already in that city. The only problem is that the said government did not relocate to Valencia until almost forty days later.[TN8] So it is anybody's guess when, where and with whom he held this interview.

5. Gila Boza's passage from the camp in Albatera to Seville, mediated by Sancho Dávila, is also surprising. An individual who had fled in September 1936, who had risen to the rank of second lieutenant in the Republican army, who had been a political commissar, Saturnino Barneto's bodyguard,[TN9] and a member of the Republican secret service. For far less, hundreds of persons found themselves facing a firing squad. But no problem, he immediately rejoins the Seville Falange under the wing of Sancho Dávila and becomes a member of the Falangist-controlled Vertical Syndicate for Transport Workers, under the orders of another of his benefactors: the Falangist Carlos McLean. Of course, if what we have here is a Falangist mole who infiltrated the PCE, as the documentation indicates, all this would be much easier to explain.

6. Gila Boza makes contact with the anti-Franco guerilla in mid-1944. "In Europe the war against Hitler has broken out," the author tells us (it began in 1939). But it is regarding the dismantling of a guerilla group in 1948 that Gila Boza displays total memory loss. According to what he says, the principle informer responsible for the group's fall was Antonio Martínez Borrego. But the truth lies elsewhere. Gila Boza was the first to testify and the one who betrayed Manuel Castro, Calixto Pérez Doñoro, Jerónimo Parra Díaz, Antonio Álvarez Díaz, Justo Murcia de Abajo, Rafael Moreno Conde, Eulalio Corral Expósito, José Rodríguez Tirado, José Gómez Caraballo, Romualdo Grande Penco and the very same Antonio Martínez Borrego. So

TRANSLATOR'S NOTE 8. The Republican government, led by Francisco Largo Caballero, was transferred from Madrid to Valencia on November 7, 1936, the night before Franco's forces attempted to take the Spanish capital.

TRANSLATOR'S NOTE 9. Saturnino Barneto was a Seville labor leader and member of the Communist Party. After the military coup he went into hiding until, in early August, he managed to escape to Madrid.

Martínez Borrego was not only innocent of the charge of betrayal, he was a victim of Gila Boza's denunciations. Another of the victims, Jerónimo Parra, whose torture is described by Gila Boza in the book, is still alive. Perhaps the author should talk to Martínez Borrego's family and to Jerónimo Parra himself. Or with another prisoner, Juan Antonio Velasco Díaz, also described in the book as deceased though he is still alive.

7. Juan Gila Boza was a nobody in the PCE as well as in the clandestine resistance in Seville in the 1940s. And his crime was none other than that of selling arms to the guerilla fighters in the mountains, arms he had purchased, along with an accomplice, from his Falangist friends. Profiting from the transaction is what earned him a twelve-year sentence, of which he served less than half. No one asked for the death penalty. There were ninety-eight guerilla fighters arrested, not two hundred, plus five killed; the men on trial were not Communists, they were anarchists from Constantina and Las Navas de la Concepción.

It is worth pointing out other errors in the book that prevent a placid reading experience: Saturnino Barneto is rebaptized Julián, San Nicolás del Puerto (Seville) is confused with San Juan del Puerto (Huelva), General Queipo de Llano's granddaughter Ana Quevedo is called Ana Nieto, Helios Gómez becomes Elio Gómez, and the Civil Guard Colonel Arturo Blanco becomes Arturo Márquez. The man who was assassinated in the Park in 1931 is not Manuel Parra but Francisco Parra Díaz;[TN10] Antonio Corpas was not killed in 1936 but in 1935; José Rodríguez Corento was not merely a Communist sympathizer but a member of its central committee. La Nava (Huelva) has nothing to do with Las Navas de la Concepción (Seville); the name of the town near Llerena is Fuente del Arco and not Fuente de Arcos or Fuentes de Arco. Luis Campos Osaba was not arrested in Málaga but in Seville, and, to finish, the protagonist's Communist brother, Ángel Gila Boza, was not shot in Paterna del Campo (Huelva) in 1940 but in Paterna (Valencia) on August 13, 1942. These are only a sample of the errors; there are many others. Someone should do a thorough revision of the book to

TRANSLATOR'S NOTE 10. This refers to an incident that took place in María Luisa Park in Seville in the wee hours of the morning of July 23, 1931. Four Communist workers, under arrest for their participation in a general strike, were being taken from Seville to the Cádiz prison. They were being transferred to a different vehicle in the park when they purportedly attempted to escape and were shot. One of them was Francisco Parra Díaz.

rectify some of the more exasperating defects: there are many towns named Mairena (which one is the author of the preface talking about?).

Furthermore, we would prefer not to go too deeply into another category of details such as the use of the word "uprising" when talking about the military coup or the reference to the "unaffected ease" displayed by General Queipo de Llano during his bombastic radio chats, citing, for example, his renaming Martínez Barrio, the Republican politician, Martínez Birria.[TN11]

By now it is appropriate to harbor serious doubts about the validity of Juan Gila Boza's testimony and M. de Pablos's book. Nevertheless, we must say that it is all the same to us if this man has decided to reinvent his life. What is unacceptable is that, with the help of a journalist, he has whitewashed his past at the expense of an innocent man like Antonio Martínez Borrego. Nor is there any justification for the fact that the author has not only believed everything this man has told her but that she has no command of events and dates, the foundation of any narrative of a historical nature. The morass of wrong dates and her ignorance regarding events come to be the book's most noteworthy feature. M. de Pablos could have written a novel using fictitious names, but she chose not to do so. She thought that the "mole's" testimony and a few touches of local color here and there would suffice. Of course, if there is a good side to the "memory" recuperated by works such as this – we should bear in mind that the book belongs to the Serie Memoria published by Oberon – it will be to end once and for all the "historical memory fad." Amen.

I imagine this article was of little benefit to the book. The author, perhaps busy with so many publicity appearances organized around *The Sickle and the Arrows* in all types of media (radio, television and the press), appearances that no doubt benefitted from her privileged position in the Andalusian political-journalistic complex, acted as if this article did not exist. We will never know for certain but, given the marketing style of the publisher, it is a safe bet that many copies of the book were sold.

Let us summarize by saying that Juan Gila Boza, a Falangist "mole" who infiltrated the PCE, was able to rewrite his biography with the help of the journalist Mercedes de Pablos and portray himself as a Communist mole who infiltrated the Falange. What we have, then, is a book that claims to be an example of "recuperation of historical memory" when, in fact, it is a consummate exercise in historical mystification. Furthermore, the journalist, believing everything Gila Boza told her, accuses an innocent man

TRANSLATOR'S NOTE 11. A "birria" means an "ugly or useless object."

already deceased, Antonio Martínez Borrego, of having been responsible for the arrest of many others in 1948, some of whom were condemned to death, when, in fact, the real informer was Gila Boza himself. Fortunately, in this case, there is a transcript of the military trial that shows he is lying, a transcript that the journalist refused to consult even when her error was pointed out to her, probably so she would not have to face what would be the next logical step: acknowledge her gaffe, apologize to Martínez Borrego's family and withdraw her book from circulation.

In 2006 Martínez Borrego's children, Alberto and Carmen Martínez Núñez, after their request for arbitration was turned down, filed a lawsuit against Mercedes de Pablos and Oberon, of the Anaya group, for the crime of "libel with publicity." Their lawyer was José Luis Escañuela Romana, then president of the Andalusian Association of Progressive Attorneys. The text of the lawsuit establishes the facts in detail with the phrases that are attributed to "Borrego," as he is usually called in the book. The children maintained that, contrary to what was said in the book, their paternal grandmother had never been a Communist and had never been in prison; and, above all, that the "frail, weak and immature Borrego" in the book never informed on twenty-five persons in exchange for one hundred thousand pesetas and admission to the Corps (he was a civil guard). On the contrary, they defended their father's integrity, stating that he was a pro-Republican civil guard and a member of the Communist Party until his death in 1987, and they recalled the privations and heartaches they suffered as a result of their father's imprisonment and reprisals against the family.

Then the plaintiffs proved that the author's account was untrue and slanderous, as shown by the transcripts of courts-martial 328 and 368 from 1948, transcripts that can be consulted in the Archive of the Second Territorial Military Tribunal in Seville, and that if De Pablos had consulted those transcripts she would have avoided writing "such a shameful and untrue account that offends the convictions of a man who, unlike Sr. Gila Boza, dedicated his life to the cause of freedom." And that, according to the transcripts, the first to testify was Gila Boza, who was the one who informed on many people in this and other testimonies. Antonio Martínez Borrego, on the other hand, did not inform on anyone. The transcripts also prove that Gila Boza was awarded the Medallion of the Old Guard of the Falange and that he trafficked in arms that he bought from Falangists for two hundred pesetas and sold to Communists for three hundred. And, above all, his trial proves that Gila Boza joined the PCE in 1935 under orders from the Falange "in order to uncover and disarticulate their activities," according to his dossier in the Provincial Falange Headquarters. A police report adds that he was a personal bodyguard of Sancho Dávila, who held a high post in the Falange.

The lawsuit also mentions the collusion within the media after the publication of the book and, regarding the peculiar attitude of *El País*, adds: "It is no coincidence that the publisher being sued belongs to the same Editorial Group as *El País*, which was acquired by PRISA in March 2000." And adds:

> The book has received ample dissemination by Canal Sur and Localia Televisión, including an interview with the author [. . .] and has been promoted by all the media companies owned by PRISA, the largest communications conglomerate in Spain, which operates in twenty-two European and American countries and reaches eighteen million people through, among other entities, Cadena Ser, Canal Plus and Digital Plus.

The lawsuit also stressed the successive reproductions of the slanderous declarations due to the controversy over the book (*El País* has an average daily readership of four hundred and seventy-five thousand) and the increased profits obtained by the publisher as a result. The lawsuit concludes by setting the civil responsibility at seventy thousand euros as compensation for damages and moral suffering, an amount which would be paid to an association dedicated to the recuperation of historical memory, and demanded that Oberon be required to withdraw the book from circulation.

Finally, in November 2011, five years after Martínez Borrego's children filed their lawsuit, the ruling was made public by the Third Criminal Court of Seville. With no small degree of astonishment, we were able to read that the journalist Mercedes de Pablos had been absolved of the crime of libel. According to Judge Francisco José Guerrero Suárez, the defendant documented her work in the archive of Comisiones Obreras, where she filed her recording of Gila Boza's story, in the Fundación "Pablo Iglesias"[TN12] and in the Municipal Newspaper and Periodical Library, "being unable to go to the Archive of the Territorial Military Tribunal, located in Seville, because the transcripts of the courts-martial 328/48 and 368/48 were filed there under the name Gabriel Santamarta and not Juan Gila." Without seeing any contradiction with this claim, the judge had no problem accepting the author's statement in the book that "the dossier has disappeared from the Seville Military Archive."

TRANSLATOR'S NOTE 12. Comisiones Obreras is the Communist labor union. The Pablo Iglesias Foundation is named for the founder of the Spanish Socialist Party.

The ruling recognized that, according to the transcript, Gila Boza, whose testimony at the trial "was fundamentally accurate," informed on several persons associated with the Communist Party, but the ruling expressed compassion towards him because he had received a harsher sentence than had Martínez Borrego, whose misfortunes are minimized (he was not tortured and he received a light sentence and according to his children he talked about it as if it had been a minor battle). For Judge Guerrero freedom of information and expression are paramount, and all that can be demanded of the author is that what she relates is relevant and veracious and that her conduct displayed diligence and was guided by good intentions, which the judge considered to have been proven. There had therefore been no evidence of an attempt to defame. The author has merely "written down the orally-transmitted remembrances of Gila Boza," the real author of the book's contents, for which reason what we have is "a book of memories taken down by an intermediary . . ." Mercedes de Pablos "cannot be considered the author of statements she has limited herself to transcribing . . ."

For Guerrero Suárez "the fact that she was unable to gain access to the contents of the trial transcripts archived in the Territorial Military Tribunal located in Seville was in no way an obstacle to the resulting book." And herein lays the key to this matter. The entire ruling is founded on a falsehood. The reality is that Mercedes de Pablos never attempted to gain access to the military archive and consult the aforementioned transcripts of the trials involving the protagonist of her book. The fact that the said transcripts were under someone else's name ("Gabriel Santamarta and forty-two others") means nothing, because Gila Boza's name can indeed be found in the general index card cabinet which refers the researcher to those transcripts. If she had gone to the archive when she should have, the archivist would have brought her the transcripts with no problem at all. But she did not go the archive, just as she did not go when she was told that the transcripts were there and that their contents profoundly affected what she had written.

Even though she wrote in her book that the transcripts did not exist, during her trial she maintained that what had prevented her from consulting the military documentation was that they were in someone else's name. And the judge believed her without corroborating her claim by making inquiries at the archive. Without this falsehood, the rest of the judge's ruling unravels: the author's conduct was neither diligent nor veracious, nor was it guided by good intentions but rather by ignorance and credulity. And just to set the record straight, her shortcoming is not so much that she believed everything Gila Boza told her, but rather that she did not consult the documentation of the courts-martial, which would have resulted in considerable modifications to the book and, above all, that once she was alerted to the problems in her book she did not attempt to solve them but instead stuck to her guns and discredited those who had put her on notice.

Nevertheless, the justice system pronounced a verdict of not guilty without a declaration of civil damages, thereby allowing the Falangist and informer Gila Boza to rewrite his life story with the help of a journalist and causing Antonio Martínez Borrego to go down in history as a traitor.

Note

1 The journalist Tereixa Constenla wrote an article about him entitled "El músico que odia a Wagner" (The Musician who Hates Wagner), which includes the following curious sentence: "Pastor relates his experiences with a certain distance, as if he were talking about things that happened to others although his narration is in the first person" (*El País* de Andalucía, March 24, 2004). Her colleague in Granada did not notice this "distancing" and tells us that during one year Pastor spent his time at Mauthausen transporting "wagons full of cadavers" (*El País* de Andalucía, October 3, 2002).

Ramón Garrido and the Democratic Memory of O Grove

In July 2006, the lawyer Raquel Santos García, on behalf of Antonio C. and María Eloísa Álvarez Corbacho,[1] requested that the content of the webpage http://bteysses.free.fr/espagne/Cuando_estallo_la_guerra.html be removed from the free.fr (France) domain, or if it could not be removed, then its contents should be blocked. The webpage was an autobiographical text by Ramón Garrido Vidal. Judge Juan Carlos Carballal's writ issued on September 1, 2006 begins with a long first paragraph in which he theorizes on the justification of the preventive measures, basing his argument on two suppositions: the appearance of proper legal practice and the foreseeable existence of the danger of procedural delay. According to the plaintiffs, the said webpage contains "an appreciable interference with the honor of their father Don Joaquín Álvarez Lores, who passed away on August 29, 1981." With respect to the latter, mayor of O Grove during the dictatorship of Miguel Primo de Rivera and again following the military coup, the webpage asserts that "it was *vox populi* that he spent his time drawing up lists of those to be 'taken for a walk,' which is to say, that he was one of those in charge of selecting the persons who, because they held ideas contrary to those that were dominant at that time, should be shot or assassinated." The judge's writ recognized that it was not possible "to analyze the content of the matter being debated for obvious procedural reasons," but at the same time admitted the legitimacy of the arguments put forward by the mayor's family who

> question the publication [. . .] on the grounds that it accuses their father of participation, more than seventy years prior, in the tragic events that happened in Spain, namely the Civil War, and more concretely, and without evidence of any sort, based solely on rumors (*vox populi* as stated in the article itself) it is affirmed that he was one of those in charge of indicating the persons who should be assassinated.

As we have seen on other occasions, there were references in the judge's writ to the fact that, while it is inappropriate to demand evidence in order to exercise the freedom of expression, because this freedom deals with personal or subjective value judgments, it is indeed appropriate to demand that there be public relevance and veracity in order to exercise the freedom of information, whose object is to relate events.[TN1] Since, in Judge Carballal's view, the demand that there be veracity must be met by providing evidence, he went on to declare that:

> no data exists that can verify the information set forth in the article, whose implications for the honor of Sr. Álvarez Lores's successors is evident, since it should not be forgotten that in the town where their father was mayor and in which his children and family members now reside practically all the residents know each other, for which reason to recall so many decades later that which in the media is now called "historical memory" in a malicious, unbridled and vengeful way or without serious and correct data that verifies what is affirmed certainly violates the honor and reputation of those persons and their families, it being equally reasonable to accept the premise of the plaintiffs' argument, according to which the seriousness of the harm done to their honor is greater, if that is possible, since access to the said webpage is easy by entering the term "civil war in O Grove" in any search engine, and there even exist direct links to the said webpage, for which reason failure to implement a block of the webpage's content would mean there would be an ongoing interference with the honor of the affected persons.

According to Carballal, failure to block the website would result in "the risk of perpetuating the moral affront that we are attempting to remedy." Therefore, the titular judge of the Cambados Court of First Instance and Preliminary Investigation N° 2 agreed that the domain free.fr should eliminate the contents of the webpage written by Ramón Garrido Vidal.

It is appropriate to say that Ramón Garrido Vidal (O Grove, 1915), a Communist sailor and the author of the document on the webpage that was eliminated, had passed away eleven years prior, in January 1995, and that the text that had motivated the lawsuit, "When the War Broke Out," was a brief memoir on political life during the Second Republic and the consequences of the July 18 military coup in O Grove. It was found by Garrido's

TRANSLATOR'S NOTE 1. For a prior discussion of the distinction between "freedom of expression" and "freedom of information" in the Spanish Constitution, see the chapter entitled "Dolors Genovés and *Sumaríssim 477*: The Value of Archives," pp. 30–31.

son after the author's death. Garrido, forced to join Franco's forces, crossed to the Republican zone in October 1937. Then, in 1939, he escaped to France and experienced the bitter life of an exile. He fought against the Nazi occupation in Brittany, leading four hundred and fifty Spaniards who had joined the resistance. He was arrested in 1942 and ended up in Dachau. After the liberation he settled in Montigny Le Bretonneux, near Paris. His son Fabien believed his autobiographical writings would be of interest to the residents of O Grove – there were plans for a tribute to Garrido and his activities as an anti-Fascist combatant – and he decided to go public with them.[2]

The section of the webpage that alluded to the ex-mayor was as follows:

> The leader of the civic guard,[TN2] or at least the one who bossed its members around, was the ex-mayor from the Primo de Rivera dictatorship, Joaquín Álvarez, nicknamed O Potro (The Colt). This character, who would be mayor again under Franco, was a real braggart with a large dollop of village thug, in other words a guard dog that barks when protected by the fence around the family garden and runs away when outside its own territory. The Colt was brave when, with a *vergajo*[TN3] in hand and accompanied by two civil guards, he used to go from tavern to tavern throwing out the sailors who were having a drink and chatting. I do not know all the mischief he was up to during the war; but what I do know is that it was *vox populi* that he and his father participated in drawing up the lists of those to be "taken for a walk." In any event, his father Don Eloy Álvarez confessed during the last moments of his life that he was never able to sleep well because of his memories of some of the people, like his former friend Ángel Cadavid, who were punished, persecuted or shot without having committed a single crime.
>
> Returning to that "character" Don Joaquín, I remember that one day – I think it was a Sunday – while I was walking up the sidewalk where Pepe Besada has his bookstore now, I saw a colorful character coming down the sidewalk on the other side of the street. He was wearing all the Falangist trappings, always a bad sign: blue shirt, leather shoulder straps and gaiters,

TRANSLATOR'S NOTE 2. The Civic Guard was a corps of volunteers, unlike the Civil Guard, which is a professional paramilitary corps. As the towns were taken by the forces of the rebellious generals, right-wingers who did not want to be associated with either the Falange or the Requeté volunteered for the Civic Guard, forming their own violent vigilante groups under the command of the Civil Guard.

TRANSLATOR'S NOTE 3. A *vergajo* is a whip fashioned from a desiccated bull's penis.

black riding breeches, shiny copper buckles and a huge pistol that must
have been a nine millimeter. When I saw it was The Colt I could not
contain myself and burst out laughing. What had I gotten myself into? He
looked at me, his face trying to turn pale, but with great difficulty because
his dark skin would not allow it. He did not say a word and headed off in
the direction of the Civil Guard barracks. Not two hours had passed when
the civic guard Pepe Troncoso filled me in on what happened. The Colt
had arrived in a rage, saying he was going to destroy me and that he would
have plenty of opportunities at night. I should clarify that at night, while
that drunkard general, Queipo de Llano, delivered his radio chats, broadcast through loudspeakers installed in the town, one could wander the
streets at will. After that, one ran the risk of a beating or even of being
shot, because the civic guard was more prone to making threats with a rifle
than with a whip.

In July 1939 I was drafted into the army. The Colt had still not had an
opportunity to give me the thrashing he had promised. It was not because
he lacked the will, judging from the following incident.

Many years later, while living in France, I had many opportunities to
return to O Grove. During one of my trips, I had to go to Pontevedra and
boarded the intercity bus in the town of Corgo. A little further up the line
– in Fonte do Galo – the bus stopped to take on more passengers. Among
them The Colt boarded through the back door. I had seen him get on.
When he noticed the empty seat beside me – without knowing it was me
because my back was turned – he approached and was about to sit down.
As soon as he realized who I was he turned and went to the back of the bus
where he remained standing – I do not know for how long because after a
while I lost interest in what he was doing. It was apparent that he had never
forgotten our encounter and it still rankled.

As we can see, this is the personal testimony of someone whose credibility
is reinforced by his life story, a fact never mentioned by the judge, and who
lived through the events he narrates. Consequently, he knew firsthand about
Álvarez's participation in the repression. Even though Ramón Garrido
commented that this participation was *vox populi* it was simply to reinforce
his statements concerning "what I do know." The fact is, and this is important to point out, that Ramón Garrido's testimony, presented either orally
or in writing, could easily have been utilized by any historian of the fascist
repression in O Grove and in that case, protected by historical methodology,
in other words, combined with other sources and signed by a historian, it
would have been perfectly valid and the judge would have had to admit its
public relevance and veracity. What Judge Carballal in fact decided, at the

Álvarez family's request, was to silence the voice of an uncomfortable witness who recalled events and names which were no doubt part of O Grove's collective memory, as in the case of the fascist ex-mayor.

In fact, and this is another peculiarity of this case, Ramón Garrido's text had already been published in 2003 by Aurora Marco, professor of Language and Literature at the University of Santiago, in a work about Ramón Paz Carvajal, a Socialist printer in Pontevedra.[3] Neither the family or the judge took action or even mentioned this fact at any time during the lawsuit to block Garrido's webpage. Apparently Aurora Marco herself did not come forward with this fact either when it could have been useful for the record.

On March 12, 2007 the Galician edition of *El País* published an article entitled "Un silencio de setenta años" (A Seventy Year Silence). The author, Óscar Iglesias, had collected some interesting opinions, like that of the historian Ramón Villares, president of the Galician Cultural Council, who said that "what is being debated is not just the degree of veracity of historical sources," but also "whether historians in Spain can use sources involving living persons." Or the judicious words of the historian Ángel Viñas: "Perpetrators as well as victims ought to be identified, whoever they may be. If we still cannot talk about the Spanish civil war seventy years later, we should turn out the lights and go home." There was also an interesting and astute declaration by the Galician historian Dionisio Pereira: "The repressors also fall into distinct categories. If I only indicate the most wretched murderers I would not have any problems."

More than a year later, on June 2, 2008, another article was published in *El País*. Written by José Andrés Rojo, it was entitled "La historia oral llega a juicio" (Oral History on Trial). Dionisio Pereira again provided a revealing statement: "The situation in this country has still not been normalized. Perhaps in Madrid, Barcelona or Vigo, but in the small towns and villages the victims' moral dignity is still not recognized." The historian Julián Casanova also participated: "Nevertheless, the war's victors were so convinced that they were the bearers of good who had put an end to evil that they left many traces of their excesses: trials without guarantees for the accused, extra-legal executions, the confiscation of the losers' property . . . They even left written clues, and that is how we have been able to appreciate the magnitude of the terror generated by the Franco dictatorship." Rojo concluded his article as follows: "Perhaps investigations based on oral testimonies do not change our view of recent history. In social terms, however, the moral reparation that the victims and their descendants declaim is the energy that encourages so many historians to seek the truth in order to close the wounds of that terrible war once and for all."[4]

In December 2006 Ramón Garrido's son Fabien wrote a letter to Judge

Carballal Paradela informing him that the writ in his father's name had been delivered to his domicile in Mantigny le Brettonneux (France) on November 23, 2006, and that Judge Carballal should have been aware of his father's demise because this information was on the very webpage that had been eliminated, and because, in addition, he was buried in O Grove. And Fabien added: "We understand, therefore, that a deceased person cannot be sued. For this reason and in case the plaintiffs had acted in bad faith, we request that the Court be informed of the demise of . . ." This letter did not elicit a reply from Judge Carballal, who, furthermore, as can be read in the appendix, boasted a year later that "no one has come forward to say I had been mistaken, no one, not a single person yet, even after a year has passed and, of course, the deadlines for filing an objection . . ." This was not the first time he had ignored Ramón Garrido's son. In fact, Fabien Garrido had never been informed of the judicial proceeding during which the decision to suppress his webpage about his father was approved. Consequently, he had been unable to offer his side of the story before Judge Carballal or to defend his father's memory, whose text is no longer available at http://bteysses.free.fr/espagne/Cuando_estallo_la_guerra.html. Presently, one can read the following statements there:

> My father Ramón GARRIDO VIDAL passed away in January 1995.
> He was juridically resuscitated in September 2006 by Judge Juan Carlos CARBALLAL PARADELA and the solicitor Raquel SANTOS GARCÍA.
> He was condemned to silence.
> At the request of MARÍA ELOÍSA ÁLVAREZ CORBACHO and ANTONIO CÁNDIDO ÁLVAREZ CORBACHO children of the Francoist mayor Joaquín ÁLVAREZ LORES
>
> *Fabien GARRIDO*

APPENDIX

JUAN CARLOS CARBALLAL PARADELA, CAMBADOS JUDGE, PARTICIPATES IN ONE OF THE DEBATES DURING THE CONFERENCE IN O GROVE ON FREEDOM OF INFORMATION AND THE RIGHT TO ENGAGE IN RESEARCH (SEPTEMBER 2007)

I believe we are in a place where ideas are debated in a reasonable and coherent fashion. I do not ask some of you to share my criteria, just as I am not going to ask some of you to accept my criteria. Since we are in a free, democratic and pluralistic society, we all defend ideas and positions in a reasoned manner, without imposing our criteria on each other. [. . .] Well then, being a judge undoubtedly carries with it a very important responsibility and we are always in the cross hairs of everyone who enters our courtroom. I believe that only those who are judges, or are close to us, know how difficult a judge's function is . . . And arriving at a decision is not at all easy. Of course I have doubts, indubitably. And indeed in a matter such as the one that finally brings me here where someone confronts me with: "See here, they are saying this about my grandfather" [. . .]

The Civil War and the consequences of the Civil War is (sic) an incontrovertible historical fact, and that barbarities were committed by both sides is equally incontrovertible. Obviously, if we analyze it from a merely quantitative point of view, forty years has provided more opportunities for barbarities than four, five or six years. Evidently. But things cannot be examined only from a quantitative point of view lest we commit errors. [. . .] I am a citizen and in my family we also suffered . . . crappy treatment. My uncle, who died a year ago, was maimed in the war when he was eighteen years old. My grandmother went hungry and, [. . .], first the reds beat her up and then the others. And of course, we all have a life and we all have a story. So I cannot resolve these matters by saying: "but look what outrageous things they did." I have to evaluate each particular case, and with respect to the particular case that I resolved, no one has come forward to say I had been mistaken, no one, not a single person yet, even after a year has passed and, of course, the deadlines for filing an objection.

In that particular case there was a manifest infringement of a family's right to honor in which, analyzing the five pages of that webpage, I assessed that for all the aspersions directed at persons, 80% were protected under freedom of expression and the right to criticize and in that right to insult with justifiable cause, as I said before. But there was one aspersion that was not protected under freedom of expression, but rather under freedom of information which, according to the arguments of the Constitutional Tribunal and the European Court of Human Rights, must meet a series of requirements, which is (sic) indubitable public relevance, and veracity, not to the extent of absolute veracity but rather that the affirmation was arrived at by an accredited scientific method. And what cannot be said, because it is not protected by our constitutional system, is that a specific person was responsible for drawing up the list of those to be shot. And I am not going to enter into an assessment of whether the affirmation is true or not. What I demand as a judge is that the affirmation be supported by sufficient historical evidence. Whether supporting that affirmation is easy or difficult is not my problem. It is the problem of the person making the affirmation. The mere affirmation of an event has to be supported. I am not the one who says so; the Constitutional Tribunal says so and the Court of Human Rights in Strasbourg says so. That is what we have to bear in mind. Everything else is theory and we could spend hours and hours debating theories.

But when a matter enters a courtroom, it is not a theory that enters. It is a practical problem that enters. And it is a matter that affects a citizen and his rights. And that is the serious part. Undoubtedly in a city with a population of five million the affecting matter is diluted by the multitude but when that affecting matter occurs in a town like O Grove, the matter, which for some people may seem of little importance, is serious because the descendants of one party and another are always sitting near each other at a café drinking coffee. And, obviously, we are not denying the right to conduct research. No. The right to conduct research is never restricted. What is demanded is that research fulfill certain requirements. It is not a question of anything goes. Because my freedom ends where yours begins. And that is a conflict. That I am in the right, certainly not, but that is why we have a democratic system, not only because I form part of the judicial system but because I believe in it profoundly and because before I was a judge I was an attorney, in other words I have been on both sides and I have attained judicial power through study, professional experience and competitive examinations. And the system of appeals, the system of guarantees works. And that is what we have to bear in mind.

[. . .] At lunch we were discussing this. He said [referring to someone present]: "I do not have faith in the judges." Well one must have faith in the judges, because undoubtedly there must be judges who are imbeciles just like there are doctors in the healthcare system who are imbeciles. But I have more faith in the judges than in the doctors, because maybe a doctor who treats me sends me to my grave but a judge is never going to send me to my grave [murmurs]. And it may be harsh to say so but the advantage we have is that if a decision is wrong there will be a superior court to review it and then we have the Constitutional Tribunal that will review it.

[. . .] We know that obviously we do not have oral witnesses because these events happened seventy years ago and I am not going to ask you to bring me a witness [murmurs and protests].

[. . .] . . . I think none of you has understood what I was trying to express. It is not a question [murmurs] of demonstrating the truth of an event. It is a question of whether the method utilized to support what is said is justified. I am not going to enter into an assessment of whether it is true or not. What we are asking for is a method, which is a different matter. And that is what I am trying to express and you are not grasping [murmurs]. We all know that the truth about things is impossible to arrive at in the majority of cases. If you, as historians, do your work well, undoubtedly, whatever you say, you are protected by the law. And I am sorry I have not convinced you, but neither, believe me, was it not (sic) my intention. Thank you.

Notes

1 Álvarez Lores's other son, Joaquín, did not participate in the filing of the complaint, although he gave moral support to his brother and sister. Joaquín Álvarez Corbacho is the Communist ex-mayor of O Grove and presently a member of the PSOE (Spanish Socialist Worker's Party).
2 See Óscar Iglesias's article "Un silencio de setenta años" (A Seventy Year Silence), *Él País* (Galician Edition), March 12, 2007.
3 Aurora Marco, *Ramiro Paz Carvajal (1891–1936): Unha vida segada pola barbarie* (Noia, A Coruña: Toxosoutos, 2008).
4 José Andrés Rojo, "La historia oral llega a jucio," *El País*, June 2, 2008.

Marta Capín and the Mass Grave in Valdediós

To the nobodies, the nonentities, the negated, those who are not, who have no face, who have no name, who do not appear in the history of the world. The nobodies who are worth less than the bullet that kills them.

Words of EDUARDO GALEANO that conclude *El Valle de Dios*, based on the poem "The Nobodies," from *Libro de los abrazos*

Marta Capín Rodríguez's story, like so many others related to "historical memory," is the story of an inherited struggle. It was her father who took the first steps to find out what had become of two uncles, his father's brothers, and then it was she who, after a long investigation, brought the search to its conclusion. It was her contacts with the ARMH (Association for the Recuperation of Historical Memory) in Gijón that led her to the mass grave in Valdediós, a story I will tell based on the written account she herself sent me and on information I obtained in the press and on the internet.

That mass grave, which contained the remains of the personnel who worked at the psychiatric hospital located near the town, was excavated in the summer of 2003. The exhumation ended the rumors spread by some people in the area who maintained that the story of the Valdediós massacre was a legend. It was then and there that the book which would recount those events was conceived: *El Valle de Dios* (Madrid: MS – CYC, 2004). The origin of the massacre has to do with the evolution of the Civil War, which led the Republican authorities to transfer the psychiatric facility from Oviedo to Valdediós, near Villaviciosa, where the monastery of the same name is presently located. On their part, the Francoists created their own psychiatric hospital in Cangas de Narcea. In October 1937 Franco's forces occupied the area around Valdediós and a battalion of brigades from Navarre settled into the hospital. Several employees were taken to Oviedo where some of them were assassinated. On October 21, a list arrived with the names of members of the hospital's staff who should not leave the hospital under any circumstances. That same night seventeen persons were assassinated, twelve of them women.

And now comes the part that led to a lawsuit. According to various testimonies, the list was signed by Dr. Quirós, ex-director of the psychiatric facility in Oviedo, expelled from his post during the Republic and later director of the center opened by the Francoists in Cangas. The reason was simple: Quirós was identified as the person responsible for drawing up the list because he wanted revenge for his disciplinary dismissal from the Oviedo hospital a few years prior. Marta Capín tried to speak to Quirós's family in order to hear their version of the events; nevertheless, all she got was a warning that if she pursued the issue she would be faced with a lawsuit. It was then that, according to what she told me in a letter, she made a decision:

> Nevertheless, I thought I should tell the whole story, not half the story as had always been the case, and that I should either be brave and accept the risks or abandon the project. It is a question of being just like them or the complete opposite [. . .] They do not frighten me. I will pay what I have to but I will always tell the truth.

In July 2005, the doctor's family – Juan, María Ignacia, María Pilar, María de los Ángeles, José Antonio, Santiago and Pedro González-Quirós Corujo – carried out their threat and requested two years imprisonment and half a million euros in damages against the author, one of her sources, Ángel Antonio Piedrafita González, and the publisher. The plaintiffs were represented by the lawyer Gerardo Turriel de Castro and the defendants by Miguel Bajo Fernández. The first trial, in September 2006, brought a verdict of not guilty, but then came the appeal, which was settled the following year.

The section of the ruling called "proven facts" from the appeal includes the following passage from the book:

> On August 3, 2003, at 11.45, Ángel Antonio Piedrafita González received a phone call at his house in Oviedo. The voice of an elderly man. A voice that did not want to identify itself in spite of Antonio's request and his repeated insistence that now we live in a democracy and that the need for anonymity is a thing of the past.
>
> "I was twenty-one years old then and belonged to the battalion that carried out the executions on that fateful night. And although I was not part of the firing squad, that nightmare has never left my mind in spite of the time that has passed. I am eighty-seven years old now and I have never been able to erase so much cruelty from my mind.
>
> "It was no coincidence that our battalion went to Valdediós. We went there purposely, under orders we received from our commander who, in

turn, had been ordered there by the High Command. The mission was to shoot certain persons who would be indicated in a written order that would arrive shortly.

"When that order arrived, it was signed by Don Pedro Quirós Isla, who I believe had been the director of the Psychiatric Hospital in Oviedo and was in charge of another facility in Cangas de Narcea at the time of these events.

"Once the commander had received the list, he ordered his deputy, who was like his lapdog, to accompany him. They went out and reconnoitered the hospital's surroundings in search of an adequate place for what was at hand.

"They decided that the ideal place was a small forest of trees and underbrush that would conceal what they had done. They did not realize that right next to the spot there was a path used daily by people coming down from the villages. I believe the place was in fact called 'The Forest.'

"No one told me about the reconnaissance, but I saw the commander and his deputy returning from the forest and I imagined the rest. So, that night of October 26 (sic) there was indeed a supper at the hospital, but no one got drunk and no women were abused, as some versions of the story would have it. There was no alcohol at the hospital except what they had for medicinal purposes nor was there anywhere to obtain it. Consequently, everyone was fully conscious of what was about to take place.

"The deputy, list in hand, was ordering all of the persons on the aforementioned list to leave the building one by one without any sort of violence. Among them was a small girl, the daughter of one of the women, who when she saw her mother leaving began crying and clinging to her, for which reason she too was ordered to leave with the group.

"No one was handcuffed. They left without a struggle, surrounded by those of us who, rifles in hand, accompanied them to the chosen site.

"It was about two o'clock in the morning. They were placed two by two next to a large tree that was there, since behind it there was a clearing, ideal for digging the mass grave. A few meters away, the commander's deputy, along with the commander, set up a machine gun.

"At that moment, one of those about to be shot, seeing there was no alternative, took off at full speed toward the exit from the forest, but with the darkness and the uneven terrain, he fell to the ground. He was the first to be killed. Immediately thereafter, the others were finished off.

"Then we members of the brigade began digging the common grave with tools that had been hidden that afternoon in the underbrush. I had not known they had hidden tools there until one of the other soldiers pointed them out to me.

"Next we began dragging all the people, some by their heads and others by their feet, and depositing them in the trench like sacks of potatoes, one on top of the other because otherwise the trench would have been too small for all of them.

"Next to the tree there was a large puddle of blood that the earth was unable to absorb. With leaves and underbrush we covered up the puddle and the overturned dirt the best we could. And then we went back to the hospital as if nothing had happened."

The other versions alluded to by this anonymous source – it is well known that silence and secrecy is a breeding ground for ignorance and morbid imaginings – spoke of a party the nurses were forced to attend and where some of them were raped. The Community Nursing Association participated in the public acts and tributes that took place as part of the exhumation. During the Association's fifth congress it decided to make known what had happened in Valdediós as a memorial to the nurses who had been killed.

The "proven facts" in the ruling by the court of appeals also included, in great detail, the book's allusions to Dr. Quirós, most of them critical, which the plaintiffs considered to be "clearly tending to predispose the reader against him."

Nevertheless, the section of the ruling devoted to juridical principles – in which we can see the influence of Judge María Emilia Casas Bahamonde's ruling in the lawsuit filed against Dolores Genovés by the Trías family – maintains that, more than slandering anyone, what was done in the book was to reconstruct "a series of events through a labor of historical research involving the consultation of archives and bibliographical sources, and the gathering of testimonies which the author limited herself to transcribing." The book, therefore, dealt with "a newsworthy event of interest for the historical reconstruction of episodes that unfortunately occurred in the course of the Civil War and which constitute the affair that serves as the basis for an account with public relevance or general interest." Later, this section of the ruling goes on to insist that

> the positions of the High Court and the Constitutional Tribunal are well known, because they have been repeated on many occasions, with respect to possible conflicts [. . .] pointing out in that regard that the constitutional requirement of veracity of information does not demand the attainment of concordance between the information divulged or the material or objective truth of the events narrated, in such a way that errors or inaccuracies that the author may have incurred be proscribed, but rather,

more exactly, the aim of the requirement of veracity is to place on the author a specific obligation of diligence in the search for the truth of the events and the verification of the information divulged, so that what is transmitted as a fact or event has been the object of prior confirmation by objective data or reliable sources of information.

Furthermore, according to the ruling it is the Constitutional Tribunal itself that, in purported conflicts between the right to honor and freedom of information, advocates on behalf of "scientific freedom," however much this may entail the "subjective participation of the author, as much in the way the sources that serve as the basis for the account are interpreted, as in the choice of what to recount and how to do it, and where the requirement of veracity does not impose the exclusion of research into the origin or cause of the events, or when dealing with these origins or causes, hypotheses or conjectures are formulated when dealing with historical events that had to do, tragically, with the public life of the nation and not with the intimate biography of the protagonists and whose immediate effects interfere with the actions of generations still living . . ." Definitively, as the Constitutional Tribunal maintains, "assessments of and judgments about historical events [. . .] are as inevitable as they are necessary, regardless of the unlikelihood that they result in consensus or unanimity."

The section of the ruling laying out juridical principles even says that "without a dialogue with the value judgments of others (with those of the historian, which is what concerns us here) we would be unable to form our own value judgments" nor would there be space for the formation of a collective historical consciousness. Also that it is precisely the debatable and polemic nature of historical research that is most valuable, respectable and worthy about it "because of the essential role it plays in the formation of a historical consciousness suitable to the dignity of the citizens of a free and democratic society."

And, as the Constitutional Tribunal itself recognizes, "if history could only be constructed on the basis of unquestionable facts, historiography, conceived as a social science, would become impossible." In the final analysis, no juridical solution can decide which historical truth should be paramount.

The second part of the section of the ruling devoted to juridical principles describes the methodology utilized by the author, maintains the validity of the eyewitnesses, and tells us that the Quirós family not only refused to talk to Marta Capín but also that none of the children appeared in court, not even the sessions proposed by the prosecution. So on September 12, 2007 the magistrate María Paz González-Tascón Suárez found Marta

Capín and Antonio Piedrafita González not guilty of the charges of libel and defamation.

Epilogue in O Grove

A few days before the verdict was known, Marta Capín attended the conference entitled "The Repression in Galicia: Freedom of Information and the Right to Engage in Research," which was held in O Grove in September 2007. While there, she, as well as I, had the opportunity to listen to Juan Carlos Carballal Paradela, the judge from Cambados who, as we have seen, shut down the webpage Fabien Garrido had dedicated to the memory of his father. During the midday meal, Marta Capín was at the same table as the judge. Here is her testimony:

> The judge was seated at my table during the meal and I mentioned my trial to him. We had a fairly intense conversation because he was defending a position that conflicted with what I believe and defend. In fact, during his talk later that afternoon he said it did not matter to him whether what we write is true or not. He told me that I was obligated to write the two versions: the one provided by my oral sources and the one the plaintiffs maintain. But I told him he was wrong, that the plaintiffs' version was what we had heard during many years and that I refused to repeat it in a book with my name on the cover. I told him it was about time we were allowed to tell the version that has been silenced for too many years, and that was when he told me, "Then you will end up in jail." And I told him that that may be so, but I would prefer going to jail rather than writing things that were untrue.
>
> Anyway . . . Someone said that my stubbornness and my defense of what I believed was because of my youth, but it is not that way. (letter dated September 26, 2007)

An Unexpected Outcome

The Quirós family filed another appeal with the Oviedo Provincial Court which, in May 2008, ruled once again in favor of Marta Capín. Let us examine the juridical principles. In the first of these, it is stated that the events narrated by the author "are not even mentioned by the plaintiffs' lawyer and this omission is conclusively because the appeal is not based on factual motives but rather juridical and technical motives." Without a doubt, the second juridical principle is the most spectacular one, since it establishes that

> [. . .] it must be borne in mind, which was not done during the prior appeal, that the principal motive for the inadmissibility of the lawsuit and for the subsequent verdict of not guilty is that the plaintiffs lack a legitimate claim, as can be inferred from what is stated in article 214. I of the Penal Code and 104, first paragraph, of the Law of Criminal Indictment, which is that a passive subject of the crime of libel must be someone who, in turn, can be the active subject of the crime of libel and, if the passive subject is deceased – as in this case – their honor, as a right inseparable from their personality, is extinguished along with their personhood (article 32 of the Civil Code), and therefore offenses inflicted on the memory of the deceased are only punishable when they also reach the personhood of his or her family members or heirs, which is not the case here, as can be inferred from the tenor of the complaint that has been lodged, for which reason it cannot be regarded as a crime of libel.

It seems then, and in saying so I recognize my ignorance in these matters, that what is established in the ruling is that the course chosen by the plaintiffs – a criminal suit – is not appropriate in this case, leaving open the possibility that the plaintiffs may decide to take their case to a civil court.

Santiago Macías and the Words of Rosa Muñoz

In the case of *Las fosas de Franco (Franco's Mass Graves)*, by Emilio Silva and Santiago Macías (Madrid: Temas de Hoy, 2003), the legal problems were caused by a testimony Macías had recorded. Gloria Olmedo Sánchez-Cabezudo did not like what Rosa Muñoz Garrido had said about Gloria's parents and filed a lawsuit against the authors, against Muñoz Garrido and against the publisher. In the Court of First Instance, the lawsuit was dismissed, but then the suit was taken up by the Toledo Provincial Court.

Rosa Muñoz Garrido, a native of Domingo Pérez (Toledo), was born in the 1950s. Her testimony is unusual because she was not an eyewitness to the events she describes. Instead, her account was the fruit of a long search for information about an uncle of hers, one of three men assassinated in June 1938. Her search ended when she located documents in the Ocaña prison – transcripts of the men's courts-martial. Rosa told the stories of Epifanio Pérez Ciruelos, Ángel Garrido Erustes and Paulino Cuesta Ciruelos, all twenty-eight years old, who were killed after each of them passed through two courts-martial. In the case of her uncle Ángel, she recalled the letters he wrote to his wife two months before his death, in which he asked his son not to harbor hatred toward anyone.

At that point in her testimony she turned her attention to Besa Olmedo Rioja, one of Domingo Pérez's largest landowners, whose death, according to Rosa Muñoz, "was what triggered the events that led to the deaths of those three men." She described him as a local political boss. On July 21, 1936 a group of persons sought him out and murdered him, after which they went first to Talavera, where they did the same to his son, Miguel Olmedo, and later to Zarralgos, where they ended the life of the Falangist leader Juan Garrido. After reading the records of the 1938 courts-martial, which included a statement by Besa Olmedo's wife, Adriana Sánchez-Cabezudo, accusing numerous persons, Rosa Muñoz provided the names of four persons who she said were responsible for the crime. None of them were the three men court-martialed and executed in 1938. The records included statements by other witnesses which, in the purest style of the fascists' judicial farces, implicated the three men, who were arrested and taken to the jail in Torrijos at the end of March 1937. Their families lost track of the men when they were transferred to Talavera, where the authorities did not provide information regarding their whereabouts. According to Rosa Muñoz, the families did not even find out that the men were court-martialed in February and March 1938, condemned to death and killed a few months later. Eventually, Rosa Muñoz learned from a municipal bureaucrat in Talavera that the men's remains were in the common grave in that town's cemetery. The wives of two of the men had died a few years earlier without knowing where their husbands were buried.

The publisher of *Las fosas de Franco* responded to the lawsuit by defending the book's public interest and the veracity of Rosa Muñoz Garrido's testimony. For her part, Rosa Muñoz maintained that there was no intention to humiliate anyone in what she had said but simply her well-founded opinion. The two authors of the book questioned the plaintiff's intentions and affirmed that they had limited themselves to reproducing Muñoz Garrido's statements without adding any opinions, assessments or comments of their own. As always in these cases, the question came down to which should prevail – the right to honor or the freedoms of expression and information.

The ruling took into account the theory of "journalistic neutrality" and asked whether it would not be more proper to verify if the statements were accurate and evaluate their public impact based on the topic's interest. Along the same lines the ruling recognized the affair's public relevance and the authors' experience in relation to the phenomenon of the "recuperation of historical memory." Then the ruling focused on the second part of the book, where Rosa Muñoz Garrido's statements about the disappearance of her uncle and her statements about Gloria Olmedo Sánchez-Cabezudo's parents appeared, and took as its reference point the transcript of military trial 555/38 concerning the disturbances in the town of Domingo Pérez.

The ruling emphasized that Rosa Muñoz – the tape with her statements, which had constituted the most important evidence in the Court of First Instance, was not considered as prime evidence – had connected the disappearance of her uncle and two other men after being court-martialed in June 1938 with Besa Olmedo, "one of Domingo Pérez's largest landowners." The ruling deduced from this that, just as it said in the book, the death of the plaintiff's father appeared to be "what triggered the events that led to the deaths of those three men." It happened, nonetheless, as has already been seen, that the three men condemned to death had received that sentence precisely because they were accused of having participated in the landowner's death and, while acknowledging the lack of procedural guarantees in the Francoist justice system, it must be said that at least those three men, unlike Olmedo, were given a trial and that therefore it was unacceptable to say that they had been "assassinated" and, on the other hand, that the landowner had been "executed."

The ruling also claimed there was a total lack of documentary evidence for the affirmation that Besa Olmedo had a "tyrannical attitude" toward the town's field workers, even to the extent of compelling some of them to abandon the locale. There was also criticism of the description of how, on the same July 21, 1936 when Olmedo was killed, the town confronted this local political boss "in the purest Fuenteovejuna[TN1] style," leading the reader to an opinion of where justice lay and who was the tyrant. In the same manner, the book considered Adriana Sánchez-Cabezudo's testimony at the court-martial about who had killed her husband to be false and also claims that she lied in her declaration to the justice of the peace when the Francoists occupied the town. Furthermore, the book took for granted that the justice of the peace, Vicente Sánchez Cabezudo, was the brother of Olmedo's wife when, in fact, he was not. For all these reasons, the information was not "untainted, objective and neutral."

The magistrate accepted the public relevance of the matter but maintained that

> this chapter would have the same interest if the aforementioned expressions had been avoided, expressions which clearly threaten the honor of two persons without documented evidence other than questioning the validity of the courts-martial and the alleged responsibility for Besa Olmedo's death of four persons whom Rosa Muñoz indicates with names and surnames, supported only by what was said there and the words that were used to reflect the special circumstances that clearly arose during the Civil War. Such a conclusion and the informative value would have been the same without leading the reader to specific conclusions but, instead, to the conclusion that there were a multitude of deaths on both sides of the conflict, some without trial and others with trials that were unjust.

TRANSLATOR'S NOTE 1. The famous play *Fuenteovejuna*, by Lope de Vega y Carpio, was written in the early 1600s. Based on a true historical event in 1476 in an Andalusian village now called Fuente Obejuna (Córdoba), the town's peasants rise up and kill the tyrannical Commander Fernán Gómez de Guzmán. Interrogated and tortured by the King's representative, the peasants answer only that Fuenteovejuna did it. The peasants appeal to King Ferdinand and Queen Isabella, who pardon them after hearing their story.

Furthermore, in spite of the fact that the testimony was Rosa Muñoz's, the lawsuit applied to everyone, since, as has been maintained elsewhere, jurisprudence has clarified the idea that responsibility extends to all, including authors and publishers, because they constitute a community of economic interests. And in spite of the fact that the problem was in the part of the book by Santiago Macías, Emilio Silva was also affected, "given that the integral contents of the book were not unknown to him." Nevertheless, although the plaintiff requested the withdrawal of the entire book, the justice system understood that the withdrawal should only affect pages 207–208. The justice system also did not accept the demand for twenty thousand euros compensation for "pain and suffering," since the said price had not been justified or quantified.

Having said all this, the verdict handed down by Judge Mercedes de Mesa García established that the contents of pages 207–208 constituted an attack on the honor of the parents of Gloria Olmedo Sánchez-Cabezudo[1] and that, therefore, the said pages should be deleted in future editions and that this verdict should be made public in the country's major newspapers, which did in fact take place during the first days of December 2007. The cost of printing these announcements would be borne by the defendants.

Another lawsuit was filed in April 2004 with the Toledo 2nd Court of First Instance against *Las fosas de Franco*; once again because of statements made by Rosa Muñoz Garrido. The lawsuit was motivated by the following passage:

[. . .] Ángel Garrido's widow was one of so many thousands of women whose heads were shaved and who were forced to ingest castor oil. Afterwards, she was exiled to Valladolid together with a sister of hers, whose husband also had nothing to do with the events that had occurred in their town. When her internal exile ended, she did not return to Domingo Pérez for fear of reprisals. Instead she settled in Toledo, where she worked for a while in a sanatorium for patients with tuberculosis [. . .] The police opened a file on one of her sons, who was seven years old, before exiling him with his mother; today he has an equestrian photograph of Franco in his house. His sons have published a book about the men who disappeared in Russia with the Blue Division.[TN2] (ON FACING PAGE) Twenty-five kilometers from their house nothing has been done about people who have disappeared and, on the other hand, Ángel Garrido's grandsons go to Russia to recover cadavers, financed of course by the Spanish government. Apparently when the Russians buried the "volunteers" in the Blue Division they used to tie a bottle to their neck with their name inside; at least they had the courtesy to do that, not like here. Many of these men have been brought back with all kinds of ostentation and pomp, with drummers even, to be buried as they deserve, although it is true that not all of them went voluntarily [. . .].[2]

The plaintiffs were Rosa Muñoz Garrido's cousins: Miguel, the son of Ángel Garrido Erustes; and Fernando and Miguel Ángel Garrido Polonio, grandsons of Ángel Garrido Erustes. The defendants were the publisher Temas de Hoy and the book's authors, Emilio Silva Barrera and Santiago Macías Pérez. There were four things in the text that gave rise to the lawsuit: the allusion to Miguel Garrido and the statement that "today he has an equestrian photograph of Franco in his house"; the phrase "twenty-five kilometers from their house nothing has been done about people who have disappeared," an allusion to Ángel Garrido Erustes; the phrase "on the other hand, they go to Russia to recover cadavers, financed of course by the Spanish government"; and finally the part that says, "Many of these men have been brought back with all kinds of ostentation and pomp, with drummers even, to be buried as they deserve." In points three and four of the ruling's juridical principles, freedom of information and the right to honor are defined according to their application in prior cases. There is also a reference to the theory of "journalistic neutrality" where the ruling states that the authors "fulfill their obligation to be veracious by making clear that what is stated in the book is the declaration of another person, who is identified."

Nevertheless, Judge Consolación del Castillo Fuentes Rosco went on in the ruling to recognize that the authors had not done all they could have done to corroborate the veracity of the facts. Indeed, Santiago Macías had been warned beforehand during a public event that the accusation that nothing had been done about the victim who was buried twenty-five kilometers from their house was not true, which was confirmed in the testimony of another of the authors' sources. Other statements, such as whether there were "all kinds of ostentation and pomp" or whether there was "an equestrian photograph of Franco," were the objects of differing opinions on the part of different sources.

TRANSLATOR'S NOTE 2 (OPPOSITE). The División Española de Voluntarios, or DEV, is better known by its nickname, the Blue Division, for the color of the Falangist shirts worn by its members. Formed in the summer of 1941, it served on the Russian front as part of the German army. Initially, its members were indeed fervent anti-communist volunteers. But by 1942 the Blue Division had suffered frightful casualties and there were not enough volunteers to replace so many dead and wounded, or those who had lost limbs to frostbite. From then on, many of the "divisionarios" were forced to "volunteer."

In any event, the judge opted for the theory of journalistic neutrality, "a theory that avoids assigning responsibility to the accused, since a tape-recording figures in the proceedings, on which Doña Rosa Muñoz Garrido, a relative of the plaintiffs, expresses to one of the accused journalists [. . .] events and commentaries which subsequently become part of the book *Las fosas de Franco* and that contain the expressions that constitute the bases for the present lawsuit." And with respect to public interest, the judge added that the public relevance of the topic was abundantly evident, "since it would be difficult to find a topic with greater relevance for a people like the Spanish public who, during forty years, were deprived of freedom and democracy and subjugated by a fascist regime." Therefore, a verdict of not guilty was handed down in December 2004. The ruling also informed the plaintiffs of the possibility of lodging an appeal with the Toledo Provincial Court.

Shortly thereafter, in 2005, the Provincial Court overturned the verdict because it did not consider the ruling to conform to the law. The Court recalled once more the allegations of the plaintiffs and observed that the Court of First Instance had only attended to one of the allegations, the one concerning the plaintiffs' neglect of the victim closest to hand. Regarding the other allegations, the Court did not think the theory of journalistic neutrality applied. The essential problem was, again, the statements made by Rosa Muñoz Garrido, who did not appear at the trial. The only thing taken into consideration was the tape-recording provided by the accused.

To state that someone has an equestrian photograph of Franco in his house "is not in itself a humiliating act," but according to the Court the veracity of the assertion must be taken into account as well as the context of the statement. In this regard, there was a testimony on file that denied the statement and another testimony, on the aforementioned tape-recording, which because it was later disallowed by the Court, lacked value. Emphasis was placed on the context, which was "offensive to the honor of the plaintiffs," since it led the reader to understand that Ángel Garrido "is an admirer of the person who killed his father." With regard to the assertion that two of the plaintiffs took no interest in their grandfather's whereabouts, the Court found it to be false and also offensive, since the assertion, while emphasizing the plaintiffs' efforts on behalf of the men who died in the Blue Division, suggests that the plaintiffs have forgotten their grandfather altogether. The Court also stressed that the purported financial support by the Spanish government for trips to Russia had not been documented and that the person who spoke of "ostentation, pomp and drummers" had never attended burials of the remains of members of the Blue Division.

In addition, the Court attempted to deny the possibility that the case could have recourse to the theory of journalistic neutrality: "It is evident that the book's authors did not seek confirmation of the veracity of the information they had about the points which motivated the lawsuit." It also denied that there was any public relevance to the recuperation of the uncle or father's remains or to the plaintiffs' ideology. Those matters were of concern only to the private lives of the individuals involved. The ruling overturned the prior verdict and declared that there had been "an illegitimate interference with the plaintiffs' honor," for which reason the accused were ordered to suppress the text in question from all subsequent editions and to publicize the ruling in two newspapers with a national circulation.

The accused attempted to reach a satisfactory conclusion to the affair by means of an appeal for annulment. This Court of Appeals found, in Emilio Silva's case, that he knew nothing about the matter until the lawsuit was filed and therefore "lacked means of authentication." Furthermore, he apologized to the plaintiffs in the courtroom saying "it was no one's intention to harm anyone's honor." As far as Santiago Macías was concerned, "there was a willingness to eliminate the words, lines, phrases or contexts which the plaintiff's believed alluded to them." On their part, the plaintiffs decided to proceed with another appeal. And this decision was in spite of the fact that, among other things, and as the accused had taken upon themselves to remind the court, the book did not include personal details nor did it mention the locale, and that the statements in the book were not libelous or offensive and were justified in the book's context. It was not, therefore, about the private lives of the plaintiffs, especially since two of them had published *Nieve roja (Red Snow)*, a historical book about the search for an uncle who disappeared in Russia (Madrid: Oberon, 2002), and also headed a national organization called Desaparecidos en Rusia (The Missing in Russia), created in the 1990s. The Court of Appeals found that the verdict of the Provincial Court was not in line with the doctrines of the High Court. The crux of the problem was not having considered the tape-recording as evidence.

A report from the public prosecutor on January 8, 2009 gave the impression that the end of the affair would perhaps be quite different. What the report said was that the key to the matter continued to be Rosa Muñoz Garrido's recorded testimony, since, according to the Constitutional Tribunal,

the Constitution's stand on the fundamental right to freely communicate veracious information in any type of media, consists of providing information regarding facts that are claimed to be true, by which it is to be recognized that this constitutional protection extends only to veracious information and not to information about facts that are not veracious, which means, in effect, that information supported according to the accepted practices of informative professionalism is included under this protection, whereas fabrications, rumors and outright deceit are excluded, but erroneous information is also included under this protection, which is to say, information regarding facts that are incorrect if the author fulfilled his or her special obligation to check the veracity of the facts he or she expounds employing the due diligence required of a professional [. . .].

In other words, inexactitudes and errors were admissible as long as they did not affect the essence of the information. The public prosecutor's report also referred to the theory of journalistic neutrality utilized by the defendants and which the ruling by the Court of Appeals considered to have been "taken from American jurisprudence," a theory which holds that the author of an article or book fulfills his or her obligation for veracity by indicating that what appears in his or her writing is really what someone else said and by identifying the provenance. And the report concludes by stating: "For all of which reasons and applying the theory of journalistic neutrality the appeal for annulment should be granted."

The Civil Branch of the High Court published its ruling on December 14, 2009. The spokesperson was Xavier O'Callaghan Muñoz, whom we have already seen performing the same function in the case of Dolors Genovés. Once again the High Court overturned the ruling of the Provincial Court, in this case the Toledo Provincial Court. There were two motives for the annulment: in the first place, the Provincial Court had made an erroneous interpretation of article 18.1 of the Constitution (the right to honor), since the object of the lawsuit was "an activity of a public nature within the context of a matter that is of public interest;" and, in the second place, by allowing the right to honor to prevail, there was a violation of fundamental rights such as the freedoms of expression and information.

The plaintiffs considered there to have been an infringement on their honor on four counts: the assertion that Miguel Garrido had an equestrian photograph of Franco in his house; the imputation of an attitude of indifference on the part of Miguel Garrido and his two sons toward, respectively, their father and grandfather; the suggestions that the two sons' trips to Russia had been financed by the government; and, finally, that the transfer of cadavers from Russia to Spain had been carried out with ostentation and pomp. In response to these complaints, the spokesperson proposed starting from various premises:

a) the doctrine of journalistic neutrality, of American origin and already in use by the European Court of Human Rights since 1986, to which we have alluded before and which in this case required the identification of the person who had made the statements and in the "appearance of sufficient verisimilitude" of the information;

b) the context, since, given what is being narrated, the ideas can be the object of all types of debate, but cannot be considered an offense, so it is the researchers and writers who should deal with the matter, not the judges. In other words: "the criteria for historical interpellation cannot be put on trial, since they form part of the ample field granted scientific historical evolution and the free expression of thought"; and

c) none of the four counts set forth by the plaintiffs can be considered infringements on their right to honor.

Consequently, the High Court accepted the arguments of the appeal for annulment of the ruling handed down by the Toledo Provincial Court in May 2006, which was annulled and, in so doing, the prior ruling by the Toledo 2nd Court of First Instance, which dismissed the Garrido Polonio family's lawsuit, was upheld. Furthermore, the plaintiffs were then sentenced to pay all court costs. Besides the spokesperson O'Callaghan Muñoz, the ruling was signed by Antonio Xiol Rius, Jesús Corbal Fernández, José Ramón Ferrándiz Gabriel and Antonio Salas Carceller.

Notes

1   Gloria Olmedo Sánchez-Cabezudo was born in 1921. While her lawsuit was making its way through the legal system she published a book entitled *Julio de 1936. Lo que yo viví (July 1936. What I Lived Through),* (Madrid: Nuevos Escritores, 2006). It tells what happened to her family and places her father's assassination against the backdrop of the atmosphere created from the microphones of Radio Madrid. Gloria Olmedo attributes the following tirade to the Communist leader and passionate orator Dolores Ibárruri *La Pasionaria (The Passion Flower)*: "Kill them! Grab your sickles and your shotguns and kill them! Now they are paying for their crimes!" (p. 33). The author explains what happened to her father by referring to the "hatred built up over the years that now, with nothing to hold it back, was unleashed on those who represented Christian values or who demonstrated their adherence to the forces that opposed Spain's disintegration" (p. 47). And she laments the state of the country since the transition to democracy: "Again there are two Spains, may the Virgin protect us" (p. 50). She concludes: "We have learned to remember without rancor and I would even dare to say that we have forgotten our grievances" (p. 73), at which point she says that this acceptance may have been influenced by the fact that her brother Miguel was in the process of being beat-

ified as a "Martyr to his Faith" (according to what she says he died shouting "Long live Christ the King!"). And she closes her book as follows: "I have related all of this because lately, when we are determined to put all this barbarity behind us, those who have clamored for a clean slate seem to take pleasure in stirring up the old hatreds, airing in public the memory of grandparents and ancestors who were victims of a civil war and, as such, of evident injustices, as if it were a badge of honor; as if being the descendant of those who fell victim to that terrible chaos were a new kind of nobility [. . .] 'Historical memory' belongs to both sides; let it not be appropriated by one side alone (the losing side which is now the winning side). My loved ones did not die in order to be ridiculed and scorned. They were assassinated without a trial. Let us leave everyone at peace in their graves" (p. 74). It is significant that she never mentions the court-martial that judged the events surrounding her father's assassination nor her mother's intervention in that court-martial.

2 Emilio Silva and Santiago Macías, *Las fosas de Franco* (Madrid: Temas de hoy, 2003), 212–13.

Dionisio Pereira and the Orally Transmitted Memory of Cerdedo

Dionisio Pereira González's research on the repression in Cerdedo, a locale near Pontevedra, was published in 2003 and 2006. I am referring to his article "Os mortos esquecidos: radiografía da represión franquista nun pequeño concello rural. O caso de Cerdedo" (The Forgotten Dead: An Exploration of the Francoist Repression in a Small Rural Municipality. The Case of Cerdedo) and his book *A II República e a represión en Cerdedo (The Second Republic and the Repression in Cerdedo).*[1] The article was a synthesis of local data: political forces, victims of the repression and the war, people humiliated in various ways, fugitives, exiles, etc. In Cerdedo there were eighteen persons, mostly socialists and anarchists, who were assassinated by the fascists. Among the forces that participated in the repression, Pereira named the Falange, the Civic Guard and the Civil Guard.[TN1] Pereira also dedicated a section to the "persons who stood out for their participation in the assassinations and abuses or as instigators of the same," in which there appeared the names and nicknames of twenty-four persons, including a civil guard, two priests, a leader of the Feminine Section,[TN2] a schoolteacher and members of other professions. The first name to appear was "Manuel Gutiérrez Torres (head of the Falange, pharmaceutical inspector and apothecary from Soutelo de Fontes; mayor of Cerdedo in the 1940s and 50s)," and the second name to appear was "Francisco Nieto (haulage contractor; Falangist)."

Pereira's book, a history of Cerdedo in the twentieth century, was an expanded version of the article. Manuel Gutiérrez Torres's name appears on two occasions: in a section entitled "1936: That Hellish Year . . ." and in the appendix with data regarding the repression, in which details are given about – notice the addition of the word "alleged" in the heading – the "persons who stood out for their alleged participation in various manifestations of the repression." There were other differences. In the first place, the list included more people. Besides Manuel Gutiérrez, for example, his brothers Ángel and Luis also appear. The Falangist Francisco Nieto appears again, but now accompanied by his brother Eligio, also a Falangist. And an important change is that the people interviewed are listed by their initials, whereas in the article their full names were given. However, it is easy to identify the majority of them by comparing both lists.

According to the Galician press (Óscar Iglesias, *El País*, June 7, 2007) the plaintiffs, represented by the lawyer Santiago Taibo, decided to sue "because Pereira refused to make a retraction," and "it was a question of safeguarding the honor of their ancestors." They also disputed the historian's claim that Gutiérrez Torres was a member of the Falange from 1936 until 1940 because, according to them, he was studying pharmacy during those years. As if one could not be a pharmacy student and a member of the Falange at the same time. "What kind of historical rigor is that?" the plaintiffs asked. Their lawyer, Taibo, even asked Pereira at the trial if he had conducted psychological examinations of his sources prior to the interviews to find out if they were in their right minds. For her part, Pereira's lawyer, Jacoba Millán, reminded the court that there was sufficient evidence, including Gutiérrez's membership card, to prove his militancy in the Falange without having to rely on the witnesses who had collaborated with the historian. The plaintiffs, who originally asked for a retraction of the two texts and indemnification, eventually limited themselves to the retraction because they did not want to appear to be motivated by "economic considerations." Furthermore, they were aware that the word "alleged" had been added to the appendix implicating Manuel Gutiérrez and Francisco Nieto in the repression.

Dionisio Pereira had provided the missing element in the history of the repression in Cerdedo. When Pereira published his research, historians had been going public for many years with the names of the victims of the repression and the circumstances of their disappearance. The innovation in Pereira's work is that he named the assassins and the persons who gave the assassins their orders.

According to the plaintiffs – Ramona, Manuel, Elisardo and María del Carmen Gutiérrez Nieto, María Emilia Gutiérrez Mosquera and Enrique Gutiérrez Gil – the right to honor was violated by the words, already cited, in the article from 2003. They therefore demanded a public retraction by the author as well as "payment of court costs for having acted in bad faith." In his defense, Dionisio Pereira maintained that the proceedings of the conference in Narón "had a very limited dissemination because they were from a Historical Congress and their only repercussion was in academic circles." He also said that in the book published in 2006 the word "alleged" had been added and that "its dissemination did not extend beyond historical circles either." Furthermore, he affirmed that his research had been carried out with rigor, employing scientific historical methodology, and that his intention was not to impugn anyone's honor but simply to conduct a historical study of the repression and, especially, of the repression's victims. This affirmation was corroborated by the historians Andrés Domínguez Almansa, José Antonio Meigueiro Rey and Lourenzo Fernández Prieto.

The ruling, dictated by Judge María Pedreira García, accepted the existent contradiction between the right to rectification and the right to freedom of information, and more so in this case in which the information came from a Historical Congress and not from the mass media. The ruling then discussed the abundant precedents regarding conflicts between the right to freedom of expression and the rights to honor, privacy and protection of one's image. There was special emphasis placed on the Dolors Genovés case. The conclusion was clear: it is not the mission of the courts to pass judgment on historical truths, nor on those instances in which "a relevant cultural, scientific or historical interest predominates," for which reason the lawsuit should be dismissed. Furthermore, the content was neither of a defamatory nature nor did it represent for the plaintiffs "a rejection or prejudice toward their persons on the part of the residents of Cerdedo." But, as expected, the ruling was appealed.

In a statement to the press, Dionisio Pereira's lawyer said, "We are satisfied with the ruling because it is fair." The following is a summary by Óscar Iglesias in the Galician edition of *El País* (December 14, 2007):

> During ten months of judicial proceedings, Dionisio Pereira's case has served to focus the debate in Galicia over the use of oral sources on the part of researchers. Last February Pereira was asking himself, "How does one document extralegal assassinations without recourse to oral sources?" Along the way, the historian and economist from A Coruña, renowned expert on anarchism and a point of reference for the study of the repression in Galicia, received the support of his professional peers, from Ángel Viñas to Paul Preston, and from every strata of Galician society. The ruling [. . .] legitimizes the historian's methodology.

Shortly thereafter the association Verbo Xido published a communiqué entitled "Conducting Research in the Name of Freedom" which ended as follows:

The association expresses its agreement with the ruling and with the principles upon which it is founded because we believe it will serve to facilitate
the work of those who, like Dionisio Pereira, only seek the truth. We
believe it is the minimum tribute that is owed to those who blazed a trail
to the future with their example, working in a field which, despite the
more than three decades that have elapsed since Franco's death, continues
to be openly hostile territory. What happened during the Civil War and
the Franco dictatorship will cease to be an open wound and will be transformed into a lesson from history when the government fulfills its
responsibilities and historians are able to follow their research wherever it
leads them.

The case of Cerdedo's mayor also had an interesting consequence. In solidarity with Dionisio Pereira, the archeologist and member of Verbo Xido,
Alfredo González Ruibal, who was then at Stanford University on a research
grant, decided to post an article in English on his university webpage.
Under the title "The Killers," it alluded to Pereira's research on Cerdedo
and spoke of the victims and the assassins, without using the word
"alleged," and included a photograph of Manuel Gutiérrez Torres at a
wedding where he was the godfather. The report was on the website from
October 2006 until June 2007. The family sued him, demanding a retraction and one hundred thousand euros in compensation, conditions he
refused to meet. The lawyer Jacoba Millán clarified that her client had
included the photograph with the intention of showing that "the repressors
also have their genial side." She also said that on the webpage the mayor's
photograph was not presented as related to the victims: "The assassinations
were not attributed to him."

   In July 2008, Judge Enriqueta Sanmartín Carbón, recognizing the right
to freedom of expression and the absence of intent to slander, dismissed the
lawsuit brought by Gutiérrez Torres's family against González Ruibal.[2]

The lawsuit against Dionisio Pereira was finally resolved on March 26, 2009
when the Third Section of the Pontevedra Provincial Court, composed of
Antonio Juan Gutiérrez R. Moldes, president, Javier Esain Manresa and
Francisco Javier Romero Costas, presented its ruling. In the part dedicated
to juridical principles, after emphasizing the prevalence of the freedoms of
expression and scientific creation over the right to honor, it was pointed out
that:

   a review of the publication written by the defendant reveals that, as a
   whole, it is a historical study of a very specific time and place, presenting

a very ample collection of data about many persons, among whom the relatives of the actors play a minimal role. This data is offered with apparent objectivity, with no personal or subjective value judgments and with a few small conclusions that in no way affect the actors. The historical character of the work is complemented by bibliographical references and references to the persons who were interviewed, as the primary source of the majority of the data that was described [. . .].

The paragraph indicated in the lawsuit does not justify civil protection of the right to honor because there is no evidence in the text of any type of offensive aim or intention toward the actors or toward the family members who brought the lawsuit, who have no relevance in the work as a whole. The actors are identified by their name and personal information which according to the rest of the evidence corresponds to reality but which, by this point in time, does not represent harm to their dignity. The object of the study is not the specific actions of the persons, or of a particular person, but rather of a collection of events which, given the time that has elapsed, now have a historical value and public relevance, for which reason the historical interest predominates, making article 8.I.L.O. I/1982 applicable, because the scientific freedom of the historian deserves legal protection.

The ruling dismissed the appeal and held the plaintiffs responsible for court costs.

Notes

1 The first was published as part of the Actas do Congreso da Memoria (Proceedings of the Congress on Memory), Narón (Pontevedra), 2003; and the second was published by the association "Verbo Xido" – Xunta de Galicia in 2006.

2 Articles by Rocío García in *La Voz de Galicia* from May 16, 2008 to July 2, 2008.

Alfredo Grimaldo and the Honor of the Rosón Family

La sombra de Franco en la Transición (Franco's Shadow over the Transition), by Alfredo Grimaldos Feito, was published in 2004 (Madrid: Oberon [Grupo Anaya]). According to Francisco Javier Rosón Pérez and Julio, María Mercedes and Javier Eduardo Rosón Boix, the book cast doubt on the honor of Antonio and Juan José Rosón Pérez. After a long preamble on the right to honor, the ruling stated that in a case of conflict between the right to honor and the right to freedom of expression or freedom of information, the following criteria should be borne in mind: the conflicts must be dealt with on a case by case basis; the deliberation must be carried out bearing in mind that the prevalence of the right to freedom of information over the so-called rights of personality is neither hierarchical nor absolute; the public interest of the information must be apparent, since only communal relevance can justify the requirement that the consequences of the information's dissemination be accepted; "freedom of expression cannot justify the attribution to a person, identified by name and surnames, or in any manner that their identity is beyond doubt, of deeds that are reprehensible from any perspective regardless of the social customs of that time, and which would cause that person to be unworthy of public esteem and respect"; and, finally, "veracious information should mean information that is corroborated according to journalistic professionalism." Furthermore, the lawsuit recalled once again that, according to the Constitutional Tribunal, the obligatory veracity does not require that the facts and opinions utilized in the reporting be rigorously true but only that they be worthy of protection. Rumors, lies and insinuations obviously do not qualify.

The problem, although there may have been other issues as well, was Chapter 9, entitled "From Assassinations at Dawn to the Restoration of the Monarchy: José María de Areilza and Antonio Rosón." The subheading of the chapter's first section is "The Rosón Family, Scourge of Galicia." It traces the history of the Rosón clan, from the city of Lugo, and, in so doing, illustrates the continuity of Francoism after the dictator's death. According to contemporary accounts in the press (Grimaldos mentions *El Progreso de*

Lugo), Antonio, the oldest member of the clan, had been active during the repression in hunting down fugitives – "causing authentic panic among them" – conducting house to house searches and looting. And then, in 1978, he became the first president of the Xunta de Galicia and later president of the Galician Parliament. After being an ardent Francoist he joined the UCD (Union of the Democratic Center) and from there he became a member of the conservative AP (Popular Alliance). Juan José, twenty-one years younger than his brother Antonio, was a close associate of Rodolfo Martín Villa.[TN1] Juan José was the Civil Governor of the province of Madrid from 1976 until 1980, and Minister of the Interior from 1980 until 1982. He too joined the UCD after having been a Francoist. Both brothers died in 1986.

The lawsuit claimed that the author's source was an article written by José Luis Morales entitled "Matanzas en Galicia. La saga de los Rosón" (Massacres in Galicia. The Saga of the Rosón Family) published in the magazine *Interviú* in 1978 and in which the subheading "The Rosón Family, Scourge of Galicia" also appears. This is the text from Alfredo Grimaldos's book that affected the honor of the Rosón family:

[. . .] before the edition [this refers to *Interviú*] even went to the printer, Juan José Rosón and his cohorts already knew the contents of the article. He and his brothers Antonio and Luis began pressuring Antonio Asensio, president of the Sociedad Editorial Zeta, S.A., which publishes *Interviú*, to prevent José Luis Morales's article from getting to the newsstands. The three brothers tried everything: alternately playing good cop and bad cop, threatening lawsuits and promising to buy advertising space. But Asensio did not back down. Then the members of the Rosón family decided to pull out all the stops. Accompanied by a notary, they began visiting all the Lugo residents who had made declarations to Morales. Some of them retracted their statements out of fear. Others stood their ground. At the same time, the Rosón brothers got a magistrate in Lugo and another in Madrid to order the confiscation of the edition. The judge in Madrid was not chosen by chance. He was the ultra right-wing Rafael Gómez Chaparro, head of the 14th Court. Since prior censorship did not exist, they decided to confiscate a publication whose contents they could not even know officially. A strange juridical principle. Meanwhile,

TRANSLATOR'S NOTE 1. Rodolfo Martín Villa, born in 1934, held many high posts during the Franco dictatorship. He was the Minister of Public Order (1976–1979) during the first phase of the transition to democracy. The harshness with which he put down student and worker demonstrations earned him the title "the truncheon of the Transition."

policemen working under orders from Juan José Rosón surrounded the Hauser and Menet print shop and seized two copies of edition number 101 of the magazine. Furthermore, the distributors were warned of the serious consequences for them if the edition got into the hands of the public, and the supervisors of post offices were urged be on the alert for attempts to mail the publication. The Rosón family had employed coercion to prevent their past from being known. Their bullying cost the publisher twelve million pesetas . . . Subsequently, a supplement was printed with the number 101 bis . . . It too was confiscated.

According to the plaintiffs, Grimaldos was accusing the Rosón brothers of "bullying" in every sense of the word. The ruling handed down on March 14, 2008 by Judge María de la Consolación González Sánchez, agreed with the plaintiffs that the words and expressions utilized "are essentially offensive and deliberately tarnish the memory of Antonio and Juan José Rosón Pérez, as well as their professional prestige, which inevitably and directly affects their entire family, including their heirs." Regarding the right to freedom of information, the ruling admitted the public relevance of the information, "given the status of the persons implicated," but denied its veracity, since "the work's author has not demonstrated that he carried out a reasonable verification of the information transmitted and has not demonstrated that the information was based on real events." The ruling also denied the validity of the declarations by the witnesses who testified at the trial, "given that they did not shed sufficient light on the question of the certainty of the events that are narrated." The ruling even describes part of the work as a "mere transcription of what had previously been published at the time in the magazine *Interviú.*"

The ruling then pointed out something that Grimaldos's book never mentioned. There had been two prior resolutions of this matter: in 1981 the Barcelona Provincial Court agreed with Luis Rosón Pérez and handed down a guilty verdict against the director of the publishing group Anaya for the crime of disobedience; and in 1983 the High Court also ruled in favor of Luis Rosón Pérez and found Antonio Álvarez Méndez (better known as Antonio Álvarez Solís), director of the magazine, and José Luis Morales Suárez, author of the article, guilty of contempt, severe slander and severe disobedience. The ruling in the lawsuit against Alfredo Grimaldos recalled that the lawsuit against Antonio Álvarez and José Luis Morales had received much coverage in the most important news media on June 28, 1978 when it was filed. Therefore, Alfredo Grimaldos was considered to have withheld information by omitting a relevant fact, for which reason "the requirement of veracity for the information had been violated."

The ruling also denied that the book was protected by the aforementioned theory of "journalistic neutrality," since, according to this theory, the text should be limited to merely transmitting the declarations and information provided by oral sources with no alteration, "so if the information is reworked, there is no journalistic neutrality" and the same is true if "a specific version of events is assumed based on a specific oral source." In other words, if there is the slightest manipulation – "the artful insertion into the heart of a declaration of greater extension, interrupting its flow with the author's own assertions" – it ceases to be journalistically neutral. Grimaldos was accused, then, of adopting a specific version "within a topic of such general sensitivity as the Civil War and Transition" and of not having employed the level of diligence required for investigative reporting or historical reporting.

According to the ruling and in keeping with what has been said, the information lacked the necessary veracity, was simple rumor or invention and fell short not only of absolute truth, but of the truth that can be achieved with the necessary diligence. What had been written was an attack on the honor of the Rosón family and the plaintiffs. Thus, Chapter 9 constituted "an infringement on the right to honor of the plaintiffs, since in the deliberation of the rights in question (freedom of information and the right to honor) the right to honor of the actors must prevail since the information contained in the book under consideration cannot be considered journalistically neutral nor does it meet the requirement of veracity." And here the ruling brought forth a curious fact. The work that had been the basis for Chapter 9 of Grimaldos's book was, as we have seen, an article by José Luis Morales for *Interviú* entitled "Los Rosón, Scourge of Galicia,"[1] which, according to the ruling of the High Court in 1983, had itself reproduced in its entirety an anonymous and clandestine text from 1977 entitled "Biography of a Knave."[2]

For all of which reasons Alfredo Grimaldos and Grupo Anaya were sentenced to publicize the ruling in *La Voz de Galicia*, *El Progreso de Lugo*, *El País*, *El Mundo* and *La Vanguardia* within ten days and to pay the plaintiffs a symbolic euro, "as compensation for the damages caused." Finally the ruling insisted that only the sentence would be made public, not "the entirety of the considerations contained in the ruling, given their eminently juridical content." Naturally, the defendants filed an appeal, which was rejected by the Provincial Court. The next step would be an appeal for annulment to the High Court.

A Step Backwards: The Prevalence of the Right to Honor over Freedom of Information

The appeal filed by Alfredo Grimaldos Feito and the Anaya group against the ruling of the Madrid Provincial Court in October 2009, which had found in favor of Francisco Javier Rosón Pérez and María Julia, María Mercedes and Javier Rosón Boix, family members and descendants of the Rosón brothers, was finally resolved in May 2012. The ruling's spokesperson was the president of the First Civil Chamber of the High Court Juan Antonio Xiol Ríos, who was accompanied on the tribunal by Francisco María Castán, José Antonio Seijas Quintana, Francisco Javier Arroyo Fiestas and Xavier O'Callaghan Muñoz.

First to speak out against the appeal for annulment was the Attorney General's Office, which requested that the appeal be rejected. The appeal was based on a point already discussed on various occasions in this book: Grimaldos's lawyer recalled that the function of the chamber was not to judge history and in support of his argument he alluded to the abundant jurisprudence which already existed concerning this question, especially recalling the ruling in May 2009 with regard to Santiago Macías's book *Franco's Mass Graves*, already mentioned, which resolved the case on the basis of the doctrine of neutral reporting and the illegitimacy of historical analysis in a court of law. The High Court accepted the appeal and recalled that, when fundamental rights were at stake, as in the Macías case, the proceedings should not be based on previous rulings but should instead evaluate the concrete evidence.

According to the spokesperson in the Grimaldos case, Juan Antonio Xiol Ríos, every historiographical construction is marked by a special nature because it is not a question of simply narrating some events but rather of presenting a historiographical evaluation of those events, for which reason the freedoms of scientific production and creation must be borne in mind. The right to honor, although limited by the freedoms of expression and information, is related to the dignity of the person and includes professional prestige. For the spokesperson the conflicts between some rights and other rights should be resolved "by employing techniques for constitutional deliberation" or, what amounts to the same thing, by evaluating the respective fundamental rights.

He went on to say that the said deliberation should respect the prevalence of the alluded freedoms over the right to honor "as a guarantee for the formation of a free public opinion, indispensable to the political pluralism that democracy demands," but that the deliberation also demands an evaluation of the relative weight of the respective rights in collision; in other words, if the historiographical construction has interest and relevance and if it is veracious. According to Xiol Ríos, information is veracious when there is due diligence in checking the information according to professional guidelines. That would be the case for neutral reporting, but not for a historical construction that goes beyond an informative end and is slanderous or denigrating.

And here the spokesperson, following the norms outlined from the Court by Judge María de la Consolación González Sánchez, takes a great leap; in this case the right to honor should prevail over the freedoms of expression and information. He claims that the pertinent chapter from Grimaldos's book tries to reconstruct events that occurred in Galicia "after the outbreak of the civil war," relevant events of public interest. But for Xiol Ríos what was at stake "is not the consideration of historical personages pertaining to another era, but rather the personal and professional dignity of the Rosón brothers," now deceased and who remain in the memory of their family members and close friends.

So the object of the controversy is relevant and of public interest, dealing, furthermore, with very well-known personages, for which reason the freedoms prevail over honor, but the Chamber represented by Xiol Ríos does not believe it to be neutral reporting as far as veracity is concerned. The information has not been "checked in a diligent manner," for which reason the chapter dealing with the Rosón family "does not pass the jurisprudentially established test of veracity," because the information, as the Chamber has shown, came from an article in *Interviú* and, in turn, this article came from an anonymous text, "Biography of a Knave," both of which were criminally condemned by the justice system in the early 1980s.

For the spokesperson the requirement of veracity "rises to a high degree of relevance for the deliberation that should be applied in the case under examination," for which reason we must agree with the ruling being appealed in that, "given the gravity of the accusations being made, due diligence was not carried out," because of the omission of any reference to the verdicts in the 1980s, which demonstrate that the sources of information were not reliable. The author did not check or verify the information "with the due diligence appropriate for a good professional." For Xiol Ríos "veracious communication" means "information that can be verified according to the norms of professionalism for social media of communication." For all of which, he concludes, in this case "the right to honor should prevail over the freedom of expression and information."

Furthermore, Xiol Ríos points out that what was written by Alfredo Grimaldos goes beyond the right to criticize and "constitutes an illegitimate interference with the Rosón's honor, and with their personal and professional prestige, which are susceptible to being considered an aspect or manifestation of the constitutionally protected right to honor." So the First Chamber considers that the Provincial Court did not commit any infraction and reaffirms that the chapter under discussion does not rise to the level of neutral reporting nor has it fulfilled the requirement for veracity, for which reason freedom of information should not prevail because it had not been exercised in a legitimate fashion, since the "degree to which it has been affected is weak and the degree to which the right to honor has been affected is of great intensity." As a result the appeal for annulment was rejected and court costs were to be paid by the appellant.

Of course it is extraordinarily striking that in the case of Santiago Macías and his book *Franco's Mass Graves* the doctrine of neutral reporting was eventually applied and that in this case the application of the said doctrine was not possible. It is equally striking that in the Macías case Xiol Ríos appeared as a member of the court and that the spokesman was none other than Xavier O'Callaghan Muñoz, whom we saw serving the same function in the groundbreaking case of Dolors Genovés. The work carried out by Santiago Macías, based on the testimony of Rosa Muñoz Garrido, fell under the category of neutral reporting. Nevertheless, Alfredo Grimaldos's work, which included information gathered from the press and from oral testimonies as well as the information that José Luis Morales had already published in *Interviú*, could not have recourse to the same category.

Is it possible that having appeared in *Interviú* invalidated its interest? It is well known that the articles dedicated to the Francoist repression that were published by the magazine included a little bit of everything, from sensationalist texts devoid of any interest whatsoever to works that, at a crucial time, had preserved important stories that would otherwise have disappeared into the most absolute oblivion. What I mean by this is that having appeared in *Interviú* does not a priori constitute evidence either for or against Grimaldos's work. In the same way, nothing is proved by pointing out the events that were known because of the anonymous pamphlet "Biography of a Knave," which circulated from reader to reader back in the days when no one dared speak of the repression or name the assassins.

On the other hand, as usually happens in such cases, the spokesperson's lack of understanding of the civil war is revealed unintentionally when he refers to "the events that occurred in Galicia following the outbreak of the civil war." Juan Antonio Xiol Ríos has no desire to know that there was no "outbreak" but rather a savage military coup that triumphed in more than half the country and failed in the rest, setting the stage for the civil war that would follow; nor does he need to know that in Galicia, as in the better part of the country, there was never a civil war of any kind, but rather a terrible process of a repressive nature that put an end to the lives of several thousand persons and which lasted for decades. It is even possible that he does not know that the said repression was directed from start to finish by the insurgent military leaders and that the Falange was the paramilitary group most involved in the massacre.

The idea that "the civil war broke out" on July 18, 1936 dates back many years and has been discarded by serious historians. And while it is clear that the spokesperson has no reason to take up these matters that are outside his area of expertise, it is incomprehensible that he would take up the question of whether Alfredo Grimaldos's writings affected the honor and the personal and professional prestige of the Rosón family. Xiol Ríos believes that the writer lacks a basis to say what he says about the Rosóns. It is possible that if a man so intimately involved with the Rosón brothers as Rodolfo Martín Villa[TN2] had not decided, when he was Minister of the Interior, to destroy the archives of the so-called Movement,[TN3] we would now be able to access the curricula vitae of the Rosón brothers from the moment they joined the military coup. Naturally it was illegal to destroy those documents, but people like Martín Villa, who knew exactly what those documents contained, decided that nobody but themselves should see them. Nonetheless, a few things have survived that destruction.

Although we are dealing with a publicly known event, the justice system has yet to take action against the person who ordered that historicide. On the other hand, the justice system does indeed take action, and has been doing so since the Transition, against researchers who dare to speak out about the repression and name those responsible, without having been able to rely on that documentation or with the documentation related to the repression that the army, the Civil Guard and the police still have in their possession. Such researchers risk being hauled into court, as has happened

---

TN 2. See translator's note 1, p. 117.

TRANSLATOR'S NOTE 3. During the Republic the Falange united with several right-wing groups to form FE de las JONS (Falange Española de las Juntas de Ofensiva Nacional Sindicalista). During the civil war Franco forcibly united this organization with the Carlist or Traditionalist party to form FET y de las JONS (Falange Española Tradicionalista y de las Juntas de Ofensiva Nacional Sindicalista). This agglomeration came to be called "the National Movement," especially toward the end of World War II when the Spanish government sought to distinguish itself from the other forms of European fascism. Eventually the word "Movement" came to refer to everything related to the military coup of July 18, 1936.

time and again. The lesson is clear; the justice system tends to protect the word of the victors in the civil war, whose position has been consolidated with the amnesty of October 1977 and with the pact of silence, a veritable pact of amnesia. The most that has been achieved with this democracy is that after passing through a judicial Calvary, which is always full of hardships and vicissitudes, the High Court or the Constitutional Tribunal may decide that the defendant has not committed any crime for bringing to the light of day certain matters and the case is closed, although we can see that, at least here in Spain, the widespread idea that a prior ruling creates jurisprudence belongs more to the field of fiction than to reality. Evidence of this is precisely the case of Alfredo Grimaldos Feito, who is still mired in a morass of rulings and appeals in 2012 because of a chapter in a book he published in 2004 with the unintentionally significant title *Franco's Shadow over the Transition*. And all to defend the honor and dignity of the Rosón family.

Who were the Rosóns?

It is well known that the three older brothers – Luis, Antonio and Pascual Rosón Pérez – belonged to the Falange, in other words, to the fascist party. Luis, for example, lawyer and later a military man, was one of the Falange leaders in Becerreá. It is also well known, from a statement by another brother, Javier, to the magazine *Blanco y Negro* (May 3, 1978), that Antonio was a lawyer who, starting in October 1936, collaborated in the military/judicial farce put in place by the insurgent generals. Javier Rosón stated in *Blanco y Negro* that his brother Antonio was "the defense attorney at the courts-martial of 400 persons that took place in Lugo during three months in 1936." Antonio Rosón himself boasted of having defended republicans, communists, Galician nationalists and socialists.

What Javier and Antonio Rosón did not say is that those courts-martial had no connection whatsoever to the legal world as we know it, but rather to that world in which terror had replaced the rule of law, and that there was no merit at all in acting as a "defense attorney" at those "trials," since the roles of defense attorney and prosecutor were assigned at random and formed part of a theatrical performance that lacked any juridical value whatsoever. In fact, starting in November 1936 a decree established that the role of defense attorney would always be assigned to a military man. To say that Antonio Rosón had acted as a defense attorney in those courts-martial – in fact, as far as we know, he acted as secretary and court-appointed defense council – as if it were something meritorious is something the Rosón Pérez brothers could get away with in 1978 when we had not seen nor could we have access to the transcript of a single courts-martial; today they could no longer get away with it. They were playing with the general ignorance caused specifically by those who, knowing the contents of those documents and who could be affected by their being made public, were either destroying or hiding them.

They also did not say that it was the newspaper *El Progreso* that, in 1936, published information on the stellar role played by Antonio Rosón Pérez during the first moments of the military coup. This information was later gathered in the historian María Jesús Souto's book on the Francoist repression in the province of Lugo. Antonio Rosón had earned his law degree a short while before the coup and had completed his military service with the rank of second lieutenant,[TN4] which was sufficient, along with his being a Falangist, for him to be assigned the task of "liberating" Becerreá and the surrounding area, where he served as the commanding officer. According to María Jesús Souto, "As a Falangist and commanding officer of the area he was charged with organizing the Falangist forces which apparently sowed terror (verified by documents in Cervantes [a town in the area]) among all those who had sympathized with the F.P. [the Popular Front]."[3] Do the judges who sentenced Alfredo Grimaldos know the functions carried out by a commanding officer after the 1936 military coup? I will put it succinctly. He was the maximum authority in the area and the one who decided where each person should go, whether back out on the street, to prison or to the firing squad. The only authorities above him would be the highest echelons of those involved in the coup, who no doubt knew and appreciated him since they assigned him to that post.

Well then, this same Antonio Rosón Pérez was the one who during the Transition, when already ensconced in the UCD (Union of the Democratic Center), presented himself as a Galician nationalist and a lifelong democrat and got to be president of the Xunta de Galicia.[4] He denied his Falangist past by stating that if he was in the Falange it was because of his military status; and he explained away his involvement in the courts-martial by presenting himself as the defense attorney for Republican prisoners. In the ruling against Grimaldos the spokesperson Xiol Ríos states, "The appellant insists that Antonio Rosón Pérez was a Falangist in 1936, when in fact he did not join the Falange until 1942 according to the record." Something does not add up here. Not only because María Jesús Souto mentions his membership in the Falange from the moment he joined the coup but rather because, even if that were not so, he would have been a Falangist starting

TRANSLATOR'S NOTE 4. Alférez de complemento.

in August 1937 when Franco issued a decree imposing automatic membership in the Falange on all military men.

Let us take a look at what Antonio Rosón told the magazine *Cambio 16*
on May 7, 1978:

> On July 18th I was in my home town and I remember that on the morning
> of the 19th – it was a Sunday – I went to mass with my father. That after-
> noon they burned the church and put up some barricades in the town. In
> spite of all this, I did not make a move from my house. It is true that we
> listened to the radio because those were tense moments in Madrid and else-
> where. On July 21 they called me to the Military Command in Lugo, where
> my records were on file. They knew that I had been a second lieutenant
> and they were calling everybody in. They selected me out of everyone
> because I had done my military service as a second lieutenant. When I
> arrived in Lugo they commissioned me so I could go to my home town
> with the Civil Guard and with other groups of armed men who had been
> in the San Fernando barracks, with the objective of putting an end to the
> barricades and the house-to-house searches. When we arrived we made a
> bit of noise so the people would flee. You understand?[5]

On September 19, 1936 the newspaper *El Progreso de Lugo* again highlights
Rosón's activity:

> Due to the military activity of the commanding officer of this town, the
> second lieutenant Don Antonio Rosón, many firearms have been collected
> in this judicial district. The long firearms that have been gathered are
> calculated to number more than one hundred and there are approximately
> fifty small firearms, many of them so old that not even their brand names
> are familiar.

A short while later, starting in October 1936, the newspaper regularly
published the names of those who, accused of different degrees of the crime
of rebellion, appeared before emergency summary courts-martial and were
then shot. Antonio Rosón was incorporated into the repressive
judicial/military machinery in early October and on October 7 *El Progreso*
bade him farewell with a recital of his accomplishments as the commanding
officer between July and September, in other words, during the harshest
stage of the fascist repression. What was an insurgent military man, a rebel
and an outlaw like Rosón doing "defending" from his own crime of rebellion innocent persons when the only thing they had done was to remain
loyal to the legally constituted government? The alleged "defense" these

delinquents, now armed with judicial authority, put into practice is now well known to us through the transcripts of these courts-martial, which were nothing more than a mockery of justice from beginning to end. Each person acted out their role the best they could, even though the results were always foreseeable: death or thirty years imprisonment for the most prominent Republicans, for political leaders and for union leaders; twenty years imprisonment for less prominent leaders; and twelve years imprisonment for those who had stood out in any way, etc. In order to pull off this farce the rebel general's faction had to invent some category of crime that would justify these sentences and that was the role that, in a display of limitless cynicism, was played by the "crime of military rebellion."

Here is what *El Progreso* said about Antonio Rosón, his brother Luis and other family members on August 23, 1936:

> . . the highly patriotic labors carried out by Messrs. Antonio Rosón, Commanding Officer of this town, Don Fermín Pérez Rosón, doctor and head of Falange in Nogales, Don Luis Rosón and Don Manuel Pérez Rosón, local heads of Falange in Becerreá and Cervantes respectively are worth pointing out. With their enormous souls they are performing a magnificent task in defense of the Fatherland.
>
> We would be remiss if we failed to mention the brave Falangist Manuel Díaz Vilela who, with the keen sense of smell of a detective, goes directly to the lairs where the fugitives hide, causing them genuine terror.[6]

It seems to me that the declarations by Rosón himself, no matter how much he has been able to soften or distort the facts, as well as the news items in *El Progreso*, make it clear what kind of a personage we are dealing with. He himself tells us whom he was serving, the rebel generals, and what tasks he carried out, namely the occupation of the towns that remained faithful to the constitutional legality of the Republic. He even describes how they accomplished the occupations by making "a bit of noise," a phrase that needs little explanation. Anyone interested can consult the vast bibliography on the subject – Galicia is one of the regions most thoroughly investigated – if they wish to find out what these groups armed by the rebels would do when they occupied a town: indiscriminate gunfire, assaults on houses, arrests, searches, vandalism, looting, plundering, murder, etc. That was what he called making "a bit of noise."

And finally, there is Pascual Rosón Pérez. In 1936 he was named by his own father to the post of secretary of the municipal government of Cervantes, a town near Becerreá and under its jurisdiction. And that is what caused problems for him. The Cedrón family, who wanted complete control of the town, took actions to remove him from the post he had taken up. To that end the Cedróns followed two procedures: they reminded the authorities that during the Republic Pascual Rosón had been the secretary of the Galician Regionalist Party (local bosses like the Rosóns were accustomed to adapting themselves to whatever the circumstances required) and they brought to the light of day the outrages he committed from his post as secretary following the military coup. María Jesús Souto's book acquaints us with a dossier from 1937 in the Lugo Provincial Historical Archive that describes some of Pascual Rosón's activities during the final months of 1936 according to declarations of the town's residents themselves.

The portrait that emerges is that of a fascist and extortionist who robs at will, is extremely violent and aggressive, and who allows and even encourages his subordinates to abuse female detainees, takes part in beatings and persecutions, and who, as lord and master of the townsfolk's lives and property, is fond of issuing death threats to those residents he dislikes.[7] The military men and the Civil Guard, aware of Pascual Rosón's excesses, tried to rein him in, not because they considered his behavior criminal but because it encroached on their monopoly of violence. However, they did nothing serious to stop him. In fact, if his excesses were brought into the light of day in 1937 it was for no other reason than that it was in the interest of the Cedrón family. On the other hand, nothing serious could have resulted from the inquiry since, during the years of the Transition, we find Pascual Rosón Pérez holding the post of secretary general of the Pontevedra Provincial Government.

Given what we now know, it would seem that the article by José Luis Morales in 1978 and the section on the Rosón family in the book by Alfredo Grimaldos were persecuted by the justice system not because they did not reflect a well-known reality, later investigated by the historian María Jesús Souto in 1998, but simply because that part of the past of such distinguished people should not be brought into the light of day. That was why the 1977 Amnesty Law was passed, to erase that past. Another doubt arises. One wonders how the lawsuit against Grimaldos would have turned out if there had not been prior successful lawsuits, in 1981 and 1983, for the article about the Rosón family that appeared in the magazine *Interviú* in 1978. The Rosón family wielded far greater power in the late 70s and early 80s. One family member was a general; another was a second lieutenant and president of the Xunta de Galicia; another was the secretary of a Provincial Government; and another, much younger, was a military lawyer and, among many other things, Minister of the Interior. In 2004, things were different. It is possible that without their successful lawsuits from more than twenty years before, and with María Jesús Souto's book in circulation for the past six years, the Justice System might have decided that there were insufficient grounds for the lawsuit against Grimaldos. On the other hand, it would be best to treat those prior rulings with the utmost caution and not let them serve as precedents for today's decisions. After all, they were handed down during those peculiar early years of the Transition when openly Francoist judges could still do whatever they pleased.

In this sense, Alfredo Grimaldos could be called a belated victim of the Transition. He has become the last one to pay for what was said about the Rosón family in those years. The ruling against him is the most recent, but it is the one that brings us closest to the case of Fernando Ruiz Vergara and represents a closing of the circle. In the lawsuit against Fernando Ruiz for his film *Rocío*, although he had no documentation to prove it, everyone knew who José María Reales was and what he represented; but the justice system protected him, convicted the man who fingered him and silenced those who came forth to tell who he was and what he had done. The Grimaldos case is much more serious since there are documents that demonstrate who the Rosóns were and what they did following the military coup on July 18, 1936. We are clearly in the presence of a family that belonged to the network of Galician bosses – two of them who were simultaneously lawyers and military men – who joined the fascist military coup, in which they had leadership roles and who prospered throughout the dictatorship and during the Transition.[8] And whoever does not believe it should inform themselves about what happened in Galicia following the coup. They should read any one of those farces called courts-martial in which Antonio Rosón played the role of "defense attorney," they should request a copy of the 1937 dossier of the investigation of Pascual Rosón or they should read María Jesús Souto's book.

Notes

1 In the ruling, it is stated that it had not been possible to identify the author of a subheading or lead sentence in the *Interviú* article – it was not Morales – which stated: "The Rosón family is Galicia's plague, now ensconced in such privileged posts as the Civil Governorship of Madrid or the Presidency of the Xunta de Galicia. There they are, hiding their dirty laundry. And what dirty laundry it is!"

2 The text of "Biografía de un Truhán," with the proper names either incomplete or reduced to initials, can be read in E. Bacigalupo et al., *Casos prácticos de la jurisprudencia penal*, 2ª ed. (Madrid: Ceura, 1986), 220–225.

3 M. J. Souto, *La represión franquista en la provincia de Lugo* (A Coruña: Ediciós do Castro, 1998), 157.

4 See Antonio Rosón's statements during a press conference in *El País* on May

7, 1978. Rosón allowed himself the luxury of having the correspondent from *Interviú*, José Luis Morales, expelled from the press conference.

5 A. Grimaldos, *La sombra del franquismo . . .*, 178–9.

6 M. J. Souto, *La represión franquista en la provincia de Lugo* (A Coruña: Ediciós do Castro, 1998), 157–8.

7 María Jesús Souto tells me that the reference for the document where all this is related is Archivo Histórico Provincial de Lugo, Sección Guerra Civil, Corporaciones, Legajo (File) 12700, "Copia certificada del expediente instruido contra el secretario de este Ayuntamiento Pascual Rosón Pérez." (Certified copy of the dossier of the investigation of the secretary of this Municipal Government Pascual Rosón Pérez.)

8 In the article "Antonio Rosón: el caciquismo como fondo" (Antonio Rosón: With Bossism as a Backdrop) (*Cuadernos para el diálogo*, April 29, 1978) we can read that Antonio Rosón, in his role as "vinculeiro" (the Galician equivalent of the Catalonian "hereu") [both words mean "heir" or "firstborn son"], was the head of a clan converted into members of the "power élite with representatives in the Administration, the Army, the legal profession, banking, the Church . . ." And it added, "He assumes the presidency of the Xunta of Galicia as a result of something that seems a normal consequence of all his prior life: the exercise of absolute authority. In addition to the presidency of the Provincial Government, he has occupied the presidencies of the Cámaras Oficial y Sindical Agraria (local Francoist organs in charge of controlling peasant activities), of the Unión Territorial de Cooperativas del Campo – UTECO – (Territorial Union of Rural Cooperatives), of the Caja Rural Provincial de Lugo (Rural Savings Bank of the Province of Lugo) and has also been an attorney for the Francoist Parliament . . ."

The Spanish Justice System, Baltasar Garzón and the Crimes of Francoism

When working on a case, it is so easy to say: there is no technical basis for this little article that says who knows what. You write forty-seven pages citing articles and snippets from the internet. You take rulings from the Constitutional Tribunal and you cut and paste them and so on, and in no time at all, in one afternoon, you have freed yourself from a mess that would have given you nothing but headaches and no personal satisfaction, and they pay you the same. They pay you the same! What do I care? One afternoon cutting and pasting and I put together a writ saying that there is no basis here for a ruling. Let someone else deal with it. It is a temptation.

> José María Mena, ex Public Prosecutor of the Catalonian Superior Court on the television program *Salvados* ("The Saved") during an episode entitled "¿La justicia es igual para todos?" ("Is Justice the Same for Everyone?") (February 27, 2012)

The members of the High Court who sentenced Judge Baltasar Garzón to an eleven-year disbarment because of the Gürtel case – a trial against a corruption ring with links to the conservative PP (Popular Party) during which, given the seriousness of the events and the role played by the lawyers, Judge Garzón as well as others (the judge and magistrate of the Civil and Penal Chamber of the Superior Court of Madrid, the two anti-corruption prosecutors assigned to the case, the Judicial Police and the Police Chief in charge of the prison) felt it was justified to authorize wiretapping the conversations between the defendants and their attorneys – decided to publish their ruling on February 23, 2012. It is evident that none of the members of the High Court were ignorant of the symbolism of the date, since no one who lived through the events of February 23, 1981 could forget the attempted *coup d'état* involving several military units commanded by Lieutenant Colonel Antonio Tejero of the Civil Guard and General Milans del Bosch. The fact that Baltasar Garzón, the judge who tried to put the crimes of Francoism on trial, was expelled from the judiciary on the thirty-first anniversary of that neo-Francoist coup attempt could not have been gratuitous or coincidental.

There are several points in common between the case of Baltasar Garzón and the first case that was related in this book, that of Fernando Ruiz Vergara and his documentary *Rocío*. For example, when Judge Garzón was put on trial for the Gürtel case, his defense attorney was Francisco Baena Bocanegra, the same lawyer who defended Ruiz Vergara in 1981. Furthermore, the lawsuit against Ruiz Vergara for *Rocío* was filed on the morning of February 23, 1981, a few hours before Lieutenant Colonel Tejero's civil guards occupied the Spanish Parliament. The *Rocío* case involved the silencing of a man who had pointed out the party responsible for the repression in a town in southern Spain and the Garzón case involved the silencing of a judge who would have placed that repression in its juridical context. These are coincidences of course, but they provide a sense of beginning and ending to this story that covers thirty years and they provide a sense of continuity to a justice system that, thirty-six years after Franco's death, continues covering up the crimes of fascism and protecting the perpetrators.

Before taking up the story of Judge Garzón's trial, we should examine how we got here.

Background

The Failure of the Law of Historical Memory

It was in December 2006 that several associations of the family members of Francoism's victims in different parts of the country filed a series of accusations with the National Tribunal[TN1] concerning cases of forced disappearances. The PSOE (Socialist Party) had come to power in March 2004 promising a Law of Historical Memory which would be drawn up by an inter-ministerial commission headed by the vice-president of the government, María Teresa Fernández de la Vega. Nevertheless, attempts to reach a political agreement on the said law proved complicated. Between the

TRANSLATOR'S NOTE 1. National Tribunal (Audiencia Nacional) is the third highest court in Spain. Above it is the High Court (Tribunal Supremo) and above that is the Constitutional Tribunal (Tribunal Constitucional). There are no exact equivalents in the either the British or American systems. My translations of their names are somewhat arbitrary. However, I believe the functions of the Tribunal Supremo are closest to those of the British High Court and the functions of the Tribunal Consitucional are closest to those of the American Supreme Court.

outright rejection on the part of the Right (Popular Party) and the dubious and extraordinarily moderate attitude of the PSOE, a party that tends to vacillate according to circumstances between the Center-Left and the Center-Right, it became impossible to make any progress. The Right's argument was always the same: the said law was a violation of the 1977 Law of Amnesty and a departure from "the spirit of the Transition."[1] This perspective was also supported by some intellectuals belonging to the PSOE sphere. On the other hand, left-wing parties such as Izquierda Unida (United Left) or Ezquerra Republicana de Cataluña (Catalonian Republican Left) as well as eminent independent figures sympathetic to the plaintiffs' demands – José Antonio Martín Pallín, member of the International Commission of Jurists and president of the APDHE (Spanish Association for Human Rights), comes to mind – or organizations like Amnesty International or Human Rights Watch supported making the law as strong as possible.

Under these circumstances, time passed and the year 2007 arrived without a Law of Historical Memory and with events that did not augur well for a successful outcome. In April 2007, for example, it was announced, in the midst of the most absolute confusion possible, that, thanks to an agreement between PSOE and IU (United Left), the Francoist courts-martial would be declared illegitimate. What the associations had asked for in their lawsuits was a review and annulment of the Francoist courts-martial. What was now being offered to them was a document declaring those courts-martial, not illegal, but merely illegitimate, a status which lacked any juridical value. The document, which the Ministry of Justice began sending to the few family members who requested one, was claimed to be "moral reparation" to the victims of Francoism, but it lacked any juridical value and did not include any type of economic compensation. The timeframe covered by the economic compensation that was later approved for persons who died defending democracy (135,000 euros) was from January 1, 1968 until October 6, 1977. No one explained why persons who died prior to that were not covered.

Even worse, an article from the draft of the law was leaked to the press stating that the bureaucrats in charge of the archives would be given the responsibility of hiding the names of the repressors (members of the military/judicial apparatus, witnesses, etc.), whose identity should not be divulged in any way in the documentation provided to the victims' descendants. Naturally, before it was removed from the law, this absurdity only served to further discourage the already disheartened associations that had expected the Law of Historical Memory to be useful in some way. Finally, in November, when the deadline was approaching, the PSOE reached a broad agreement with left-wing and nationalist parties which allowed the law to go forward. It was published on December 26, 2007 in the *Boletín Oficial del Estado* (*BOE*, Official Bulletin of the State). Behind this agreement there was a significant distribution of public monies – several tens of millions of euros – which would, once again, compensate the said parties for old Francoist confiscations. The strange part about this distribution was that, unlike prior indemnifications, the parties were not required to demonstrate ownership of the property that was supposedly confiscated.[2]

Before going on, it is worth clarifying what was expected of the Law of Historical Memory and what the said law finally turned out to be. The principal demands of the social movement for historical memory were the annulment of the sentences handed down by the Francoist courts-martial, the assumption by the government of all responsibility for the exhumation of mass graves, the creation of a large central archive of documents related to the Francoist repression and that the Valley of the Fallen, the Pharaonical monument built by political prisoners, which contains the remains of the dictator Franco, the founder of the Falange José Antonio Primo de Rivera and thousands of combatants, be converted into a center dedicated to the memory of slave labor. None of these demands were attended to because they collided with different interests and perceptions of the problem. What the law did accomplish, besides the aforementioned document with a "declaration of moral reparation" and limited economic compensations, was the concession of Spanish nationality to members of the International Brigades and to descendants of exiles, the return of private documents from the Salamanca Civil War Archive and, the farthest reaching measure, the removal of Francoist vestiges from public spaces, which turned out to be extremely difficult to enforce. Furthermore, the government baptized the law with a strange name: *"LAW 52/2007, December 26, by which rights are recognized and expanded and measures are established in favor of those who suffered persecution or violence during the civil war and dictatorship,"* which never succeeded in supplanting the idea of a "law of historical memory" as it was originally proposed and was popularly known. It turned out that the concept of historical memory did not please some of the sectors who participated in the law's elaboration.

Garzón Initiates Judicial Proceedings against the Crimes of the Dictatorship

Meanwhile, the lawsuits were going forward. In July 2008, for example, three more lawsuits for crimes against humanity were filed with the National Tribunal and added to the prior cases. Finally, on September 1, it was publicly announced that Judge Garzón had decided to open an investigation into the crimes of Francoism. Given the fiasco of the Law of Historical Memory, the news was well received by the associations for historical memory. The Right reacted harshly and resorted to the usual argument that "the wounds of the past must not be reopened." From the beginning doubts were put forward concerning the legal viability of the proceedings Garzón was claiming to initiate. The challenge was to demonstrate that before the Nuremburg trials some type of legislation existed that would allow what had happened in Spain to be examined as a crime against humanity. Those who were critical of the judge's initiative argued that, according to Spanish legislation, these cases should be derived from the territorial courts where the crimes had taken place or from the High Court with the idea that a special judge should be designated. Very soon jurists realized that the proceedings initiated by Judge Garzón would not last long. Above all, there was a clear awareness that Garzón's proceedings went well beyond what was contemplated by the Law of Historical Memory.

On October 17, 2008, Judge Garzón published a writ attributing an extermination plan to Franco and other fascist military men. The writ requested confirmation of the demise of military and civil personnel who had held high posts and it ordered the exhumation of nineteen mass graves in different provinces. The document, which recalled that "until the present date impunity has been the rule regarding events that could be classified judicially as crimes against humanity," has historical value in and of itself. The writ also ordered the establishment of three groups: one would be in charge of the digitalization of the various documents that had been gathered, another would consist of experts who could evaluate the information the Court had received, and a third would consist of judicial police at the service of the second group. These groups were established during the following weeks.

In the following days, insults and affronts of every kind rained without respite upon the judge. The right-wing press, in the majority in Spain, was enormously perturbed at the time, which should not surprise us if we consider the concepts being applied to what many still considered the "glorious uprising of July 18": military coup, crimes against humanity, annihilation, extermination, forced disappearances . . . But the attacks did not come only from the Right but also from old communists, socialists and ex-socialists, intellectuals who were close to the PSOE and even the president of the government himself, Rodríguez Zapatero, who simply declared that Franco had already been judged by history.

For his part the Public Prosecutor for the High Court, Javier Zaragoza, insisted that, since the 1932 Penal Code did not cover the said crimes and that in any event those crimes were erased by the 1977 amnesty, they should be treated as common crimes that remained outside the jurisdiction of the National Tribunal. It was useless to recall that at Nuremberg the crimes being judged had also occurred before the creation of concepts such as genocide and that laws of amnesty are not applicable to crimes against humanity. In the end the Public Prosecutor Zaragoza thought that the affair put forth by Judge Garzón did not belong to the judiciary but to the government. In other words, it was a matter of executive rather than judicial power.

The brief period of time during which Judge Garzón's initiative lasted allowed for only one meeting, on November 4, 2008, of the groups created by his writ. The group of experts consisted of the jurists Carlos Jiménez Villarejo and Antonio Doñate, the forensic scientist Francisco Etxeberria, the historians Julián Casanova, Queralt Solé and me, and also a representative from the associations for historical memory, Manuel Escarda. The first two were designated by the judge and the other five were named by the associations for historical memory. At the time, the map of mass graves that had been opened was already significant. The number of bodies recovered was calculated to be 4054.

The Judicial System Shuts Down Garzón's Initiative

Suddenly, on November 18, Judge Garzón decided to recuse himself in favor of the seventy-two courts in whose jurisdictions there were mass graves. Apparently he saw what was coming and attempted to keep the case alive by sending it down to the territorial courts before his own colleagues on the National Tribunal could declare the task he had initiated to be outside his jurisdiction. The maneuver accomplished nothing since, as could have been foreseen, the territorial courts did nothing with the case either (only one, in Benavente, carried out the procedure of ordering a common grave in Santa Marta de Tera to be opened in the presence of a forensic specialist, members of the Civil Guard and the family members of those who had been assassinated). In any event, just in case some judge felt tempted to bring any of these lawsuits forward, the High Court did not specify whose obligation it was to carry out the investigations and, in March 2010, decided that no action could be taken until the case opened against Judge Garzón had been resolved.

Toward the end of November 2008 several manifestos were published in support of the judge and of the right of the Spanish courts to judge the crimes of Francoism. Then, once again, a declaration by the government's president Rodríguez Zapatero demonstrated the government's limitations: "Everything that happens so that this may pass into oblivion, into the most profound oblivion for the collective memory of Spanish society, will be good news." On December 4, 2008, the National Tribunal closed forever the lawsuits against the 1936 military coup and the dictatorship, and remitted the affair to the Law of Historical Memory (only three of the seventeen magistrates dissented and supported Garzón's right to bring the suit forward and his justification for his initiative).

For its part the Socialist government totally abandoned the idea of taking responsibility for the exhumations, as the associations had requested, and transferred that responsibility to the governments of the autonomic regions. A short while later, in February 2009, it would be the PSOE itself that appeared before the United Nations Human Rights Committee, which the previous October had requested the repeal of the 1977 Law of Amnesty and the granting of a free hand for the investigation of the crimes of Francoism, to defend tooth and nail the model of the transition and the aforementioned Law of Amnesty. Furthermore, in June, the PSOE and the PP reached an agreement to limit universal jurisdiction: the National Tribunal would only have jurisdiction in cases involving Spaniards.

As far as the Law of Historical Memory is concerned, reality demonstrated that even the application of the measures regarding the removal of Francoist vestiges from public spaces was not going to be easy. The Right, ever more emboldened, demonstrated a complete rejection of the said removals and what began as criticisms ended in a refusal to comply with the law. In the same fashion the autonomic regions governed by the PP refused to draw up the map of common graves that the Law of Historical Memory had proposed.

In May 2009, at the height of the Gürtel case, a lawsuit was brought by the ultra right-winger Miguel Bernard, member of the fascist group Fuerza Nueva (New Force), of which he became secretary, and his pseudo union "Manos Limpias" (Clean Hands), and the equally ultra right-wing association "Libertad e Identidad" (Liberty and Identity), against Judge Garzón for prevarication. The lawsuit was accepted by the High Court, with the support of the president of the Penal Chamber and a number of magistrates, some of whom were openly associated with the extreme Right, for example Adolfo Prego de Oliver Tolivar, head of the Foundation for the Defense of the Spanish Nation and an active militant against the movement for historical memory. Miguel Bernard, a bureaucrat and lawyer, achieved his objective after sixteen lawsuits, one for each year that he ran his illusory union "Manos Limpias." They had all been rejected until Judge Garzón's enemies saw the way clear to putting an end to him. Then they took on the suit of this lawyer whose specialty was filing lawsuits (for example against the manufacturer of Viagra and against the television series "Los Lunnis" for an episode defending gay parenthood). In December 2011, during an act commemorating the hundred and ninth anniversary of the dictator's birth, Franco's daughter named Miguel Bernard "Knight of Honor" for his "services in defense of the ideals of the Movement." During the ceremony some three hundred Francoists celebrated the expulsion of Judge Garzón from the National Tribunal and the imminent opening of the trial against him.

In the High Court as well as in the National Tribunal there were judges with ties to the PSOE, but it seems clear that not even these judges showed their support for Judge Garzón. In fact it was the aforementioned magistrate Martín Pallín who told the story of how the vice president of the government, María Teresa Fernández de la Vega, irritated by the proceedings Garzón had initiated, said to people of her circle: "Enough of Garzón's stunts! If he thought he was going to bring down the Law of Historical Memory, he has another think coming." From this moment on, and with the approval of the government, Garzón was fair game. Neither the PP nor the PSOE would lift a finger to avoid the hounding and toppling of the judge. But it was precisely in this context that forty-six groups associated with historical memory declared that the Law of Historical Memory constituted a national disgrace. A subsequent petition in July 2009 demanded the application of the European Convention on Human Rights and a series of changes in the Law.

On September 9, 2009 Garzón appeared in court as the accused before the Magistrate Luciano Varela, who was in charge of the lawsuit brought by the extreme Right. Given the turn the affair was taking, expressions of support for the judge both from within Spain and from abroad were on the rise. There was a growing sense that he was in a no man's land ever since his initiative that had dynamited the Law of Historical Memory. With the Right united against him and the government, with its habitual ambivalence, turning a blind eye, the operation against the judge was being given the green light. Proof of the profound collusion between the two main political parties was the agreement they then reached that the "war crimes" would not be the target of persecution by the Spanish justice system. In February 2010, PSOE and PP also decided together to reject the creation of a Truth Commission to examine the reality of the Francoist repression. Their rationale was that it would imply a "recognition that the transition has not ended." During this entire process there was a curious phenomenon: many of those who accepted the right of family members to provide a decent burial for the victims, a right that nobody dared deny, nevertheless opposed a rigorous and exhaustive investigation of the repressive process and its consequences.

In April 2010, the High Court decided that the judge should appear before the court and should be suspended for investigating the crimes of

Francoism. It was then that the former Anticorruption Prosecutor Carlos Jiménez Villarejo accused the High Court of carrying out a "brutal coup against democracy" and of "transforming itself into an instrument for expressing Spanish fascism." If excluded now from the National Tribunal, there was still the possibility that Judge Garzón could take on other posts outside Spain without being stripped of his functions, but neither the High Court nor the General Council of Judicial Power nor Varela, the presiding magistrate, would allow it. In the end, Garzón had to step down from the National Tribunal.

The Trial

January 24: Preliminary Matters

The chronological order of the trials was not fortuitous. The trial that raised the most expectations, the one concerning the lawsuit filed against the crimes of Francoism, was relegated to second place. First came the trial for the use of wiretaps in the Gürtel corruption case, which would be easier to control and whose sentence (eleven years disbarment which, given the judge's age, would mean definitive separation of Garzón from his judicial career) would obviate a second and far more transcendent sentence and one which would be followed closely by everyone. So with the sentence in the Gürtel case they killed two birds with one stone. It should not be forgotten that the presiding magistrate in the case concerning the crimes of Francoism, Luciano Varela, was also part of the panel of judges in the Gürtel case.

The first session of the trial concerning Judge Garzón's investigation of the crimes of Francoism, with the exposition of preliminary matters, took place on January 24. Garzón's defense attorney, Gonzalo Martínez-Fresnada, put forth several matters. The first two revolved around the nullity of the proceedings, since the presiding magistrate, Luciano Varela, was the same person who had molded the writings of the accusation, which was plagued with serious flaws, and thus avoided their being dismissed, even to the extent that the definitive text could be considered a literal copy of the writ, whose true author was Judge Varela himself. The second matter put forth by the defense questioned the legitimacy of the accusation by the ultra right-wing organizations ("Manos Limpias;" "Libertad e Identidad" and Falange, which was eventually expelled from the proceedings), since there had not been any specific accusation nor had the prosecution identified any crime. Finally, the defense contested the rejection of several of the testimonies requested, in reference to national and international jurists whose intervention would have served to put the validity of the accusation in doubt. The prosecution considered all these objections to be unfounded.

Finally, the Attorney General, Luis Navajas, agreed with the defense regarding the "unusual" decision by the presiding magistrate to accept the document of the accusation, which he described as a mere "cut and paste" of the magistrate's own writ. According to Navajas, this conduct was "radically null," contrary to juridical norms and left the accused in a state of defenselessness. He concluded by saying that these were circumstances that led the Attorney General's office to support, for the first time in history, the recusal of a Chamber of the High Court in order to avoid "the embarrassment of the European Court of Human Rights saying that our High Court had failed to observe essential procedural norms and had not acted with independence and impartiality."

Nevertheless, the Penal Chamber of the High Court, "without addressing the excesses committed that have been denounced during the hearing," rejected by four votes to three all the preliminary matters presented by the defense as well as by the Attorney General. This result was no doubt influenced by the desire not to embarrass either the presiding magistrate Varela or the court that had backed his peculiar procedures. Among the members of the Court were the president of the Penal Chamber, Luis Saavedra, who had accepted the lawsuit filed by the Falange, and the ultra right-wing magistrate on extended leave of absence, Adolfo Prego, a key element in the relentless pursuit of Judge Garzón. This Court was challenged by Garzón "for lack of objective impartiality." The Penal Chamber, presided by Carlos Granados, the last Attorney General of the State during Felipe González's time in office, also understood the legitimacy of the ultra right-wingers to bring forth their accusation (they requested a twenty-year disbarment and a fine of 21,600 euros for the crime of prevarication).

It should be borne in mind that all the members of the Court except Granados had participated in the preliminary investigation of at least one of the three lawsuits brought against Judge Garzón. Furthermore, of the fifteen magistrates in the Penal Chamber only the aforementioned Granados had not participated in the said investigations. This strange conspiracy led even a lawyer and ex-deputy of the conservative PP like Jorge Trías Sagnier, who has already appeared in this book on two occasions (see the chapters on Violeta Friedman and Dolors Genovés), to describe what was happening to Garzón as a judicial witch hunt. How was it possible that the same magistrates who had investigated the lawsuits would later become the spokesperson or members of the judicial panel trying the case? Another one of these magistrates was Miguel Colmenero Menéndez de Luarca, ex-president of the conservative Association of Attorneys General and the man responsible for the fact that Judge Varela was not recused. For his part, Luciano Varela Castro, advisor to President Felipe González's last team at the Department of Justice and Interior, where he worked with the aforementioned Vice President María Teresa Fernández de la Vega, apparently saw no contradiction between his membership in Judges for Democracy and his role in the election of the ultra right-wing Adolfo Prego to the High Court. Varela's name was already well known because he had cast the only dissenting vote in favor of the corvette captain Adolfo Scilingo[TN2], arrested on Garzón's initiative and found guilty of crimes against humanity by the High Court. Another of the magistrates in the Penal Chamber was Manuel Marchena, with close ties to Prego as well as to Jesús Cardenal, the ultra-conservative Attorney General during Aznar's term in office. Cardenal had tried by all possible means to find evidence of crimes in the financial accounts for the courses that Garzón taught in New York and had to desist, probably because of pressure from his own colleagues. There was also Francisco Monterde, of the conservative Professional Association of the Magistracy and with close ties to Opus Dei, who was indebted to the PP for his ascendancy to the General Council of Judicial Power as well as to the High Court. Finally, there were Perfecto Andrés Ibáñez and Joaquín Jímenez, president of the tribunal that judged the lawsuit against Garzón concerning the wiretaps in the Gürtel case. Both were considered progressives, a term that, in these circles, becomes as ethereal and mysterious as when it is applied to members of the Spanish Bishops' Conference.

During the exposition of preliminary matters, Garzón refused to answer the prosecutor's questions "because he was not qualified to appear in this chamber exercising the role of prosecutor." Nevertheless, the prosecutor was able to read the questions, which ranged from asking Judge Garzón if "trying the crimes of genocide committed in Spain was within the jurisdiction of the National Tribunal" to asking him if anyone had helped him in the elaboration of the historical study in the Writ, and along the way referred inevitably to his failure to include an investigation of the events in Paracuellos[TN3] (OVERLEAF) and inquired whether his intent was not to carry out another General Lawsuit.[TN4] (OVERLEAF)

TRANSLATOR'S NOTE 2. Adolfo Scilingo (b. 1947), an Argentine naval officer now serving 30 years in a Spanish prison, was convicted in 2005 of committing crimes against humanity, including having political prisoners thrown out of airplanes during Argentina's "dirty war" against leftists between 1976 and 1983.

The questions posed by the attorney for the defense allowed Judge Garzón to describe and justify the events starting when he had accepted the accusations of the associations for historical memory at the end of 2006. He explained that he had requested information about the disappeared persons from different governmental authorities and that none of them provided a satisfactory response, for which reason he had to turn to the victims' associations, which eventually enabled him to speak of 114,000 persons missing as a result of what he referred to, using inappropriate terminology, as "the national uprising," when he should have called it what it was, a military coup. Asked about the crime he was investigating, he defined it as a plan against the form of government and against the highest organs of the nation in the context of crimes against humanity. In Garzón's view, unlike that of the government or the movement for historical memory or the majority of analysts, the Law of Historical Memory was compatible with the proceeding he had initiated.

January 31 to February 7: The Witnesses for the Defense

The declarations were made on January 31 and February 2, 6 and 7, 2012. Almost all the persons who testified had a connection to the first accusation, filed at the end of 2006. In general, they limited themselves to telling the family stories that had led them to turn to the National Tribunal. On January 31, there were declarations by María Martín López (from Pedro Bernardo, Ávila, and the Association for Memory "Sierra de Gredos"), María del Pino Sosa (from Arucas, the Canary Islands) and the Galician historian Ángel Rodríguez Gallardo representing the Association for Memory of Ponteareas (Pontevedra). On February 2, it was María Antonia Oliver (Association of Mallorca) and Josefina Musulén (Association of Aragón). On the 6th, Olga Alcega Madruga (Navarra), Rafael Espino Navarro (Aguilar, Córdoba), Manuel Perona (Cataluña) and Fausto Canales (Ávila) testified. And finally, on the 7th, declarations were made by Antonio Solsona Nebot (Castellón), Emilio Silva Barrera (Priaranza del Bierzo, León) and Antonio Ontañón Toca (Association of Cantabria). For different reasons there were

TRANSLATOR'S NOTE 3 (PREVIOUS PAGE). Paracuellos del Jarama is a small town outside Madrid where between 2,000 and 4,000 right-wingers were killed in November and December 1936.

TRANSLATOR'S NOTE 4 (PREVIOUS PAGE). The General Lawsuit (Causa General) was an enormous investigation undertaken by the Franco regime of the "crimes" committed by the Spanish Republic and its supporters before and during the civil war. Wherever no real crimes were found, they were invented.

several persons who had been called by the defense who could not testify, so of the twenty witnesses initially called only twelve appeared.

According to the press, the lawyers Fernando Magán and Joan Garcés, who had filed the associations' accusations, were going to testify, but in the end, they did not. All the declarations were powerful due to the severity of the cases narrated. Some extreme right-wing commentators – the ones who considered Judge Garzón "a professional troublemaker specializing in fraud and political polarization" – maintained that there was "something obscene" in those testimonies and spoke of "paid witnesses" because of the economic support received by some associations. The lawyers for the prosecution, represented by Joaquín Ruiz de Infante Abellán who, after the first declaration by María Martín, requested of the tribunal that there by no further testimonies of this sort, limited themselves to asking the witnesses repeatedly if they had filed other accusations in the past, if there was anyone who had encouraged them to file accusations now and if they had received subsidies, an authentic obsession of "Clean Hands" and "Liberty and Identity," diametrically opposed like the rest of the Right to the moderate politics of historical memory practiced by Rodríguez Zapatero's government. Some of the accounts of the trial described the right-wing plaintiff Miguel Bernard, seated at the back of the courtroom under an enormous cross, two meters tall, squirming in his seat while the witness presented the testimonies. The webpage of "Clean Hands" would later speak of "Garzón's great circus."

Among the testimonies, perhaps the most dramatic, because of its abundant details, was that of the Galician researcher Ángel Rodríguez Gallardo. He alluded to the systematic plan to eliminate the legitimate representatives of the Republic, the persistence of unsolved crimes and the difficulties of investigating those crimes, especially in a nation that had still not opened all its archives. The prosecution, as usual, was concerned about the accusations and possible subsidies and, as proof of their conviction that it was all part of a prearranged plan, questioned the "simultaneity" of the accusations and whether the witnesses had received legal advice. Other witnesses presented their stories: Josefina Musulén spoke of the disappearance of her grandfather and her grandmother, from whom they also took their daughter who was about to give birth; María Antonia Oliver spoke of her grandfather; Fausto Canales recalled his father, killed along with nine other people in Pajares de Adaja (Ávila), whose remains were transferred to the Valley of the Fallen[TN5 (OVERLEAF)] in 1959 without his family's knowledge; Antonio Solsano spoke of his grandfather, eliminated by the Civil Guard in 1947; the terrible testimony by Olga Alcega, whose grandfather was removed from a common grave in which seventy-nine men and two women from seventeen towns in the province of Navarre had been buried; or the case of Rafael Espino, with various family members who disappeared from a town in Córdoba where fascism had eliminated one hundred and eleven people. He was the witness who, when asked by the prosecution why they had not filed an accusation before, replied: "If they did not even allow their names to be inscribed [he is referring to the Civil Death Registry], how were we going to file a lawsuit with the court?"

As brief as they were, several of the testimonies served to underline the dimensions of the Francoist repression. The members of the tribunal listened impassively to all these testimonies. Some outside observers of the proceedings must have thought that the trial, whose outcome was so uncertain, was worth the trouble, even if it was only so those testimonies could be heard in a stronghold as inaccessible as the High Court. For example, the declaration by Emilio Silva Barrera, founder and president of the Association for the Recuperation of Historical Memory, was especially relevant because, in addition to telling his grandfather's story, he mentioned the presentation to the United Nations of more than twelve thousand cases of Spaniards who had been disappeared and the presentation in Geneva of a formal complaint regarding sixty-four disappearances, which resulted in the Spanish government being urged to investigate those events. Since there was no reply whatever from the latter, the association had presented a complaint to the ombudsman. Emilio Silva added that the association had appeared as witnesses during a lawsuit against the crimes of Francoism filed in Argentina. The judge in that case, María Servini de Cubría, had requested information from the Spanish government in December 2011 and, to date, had not received any response.

The ultra right-wing press engaged in a daily campaign against the witnesses' testimonies, which disturbed them deeply. This led them to cast doubts and aspersions in their media against some of these testimonies. It happened in the case of María Martín López, the eighty-one year old woman who was the first to testify. María recalled the assassination of her mother on September 21, 1936 in Pedro Bernardo, a town in the province of Ávila, and recalled the place next to a bridge where the fascists had buried her remains, which had yet to be exhumed. The newspaper *La Gaceta*, mouth-

TRANSLATOR'S NOTE 5 (PREVIOUS PAGE). El Valle de los Caídos, the vast mausoleum and basilica carved out of solid rock in Cuelgamuros, to the northwest of Madrid, between 1940 and 1959, largely with the slave labor of Republican prisoners. Franco is buried there as well as José Antonio Primo de Rivera, founder of the Falange. There are also the remains of thousands of mostly Francoist soldiers but also an unknown number of victims of the Francoist repression whose remains were exhumed and buried there without their families' knowledge.

piece of the ultra-right group Intereconomía, responded to this declaration by recalling that in the said town two right-wing landowners had been assassinated before the town was occupied by Franco's forces. In this way they tried to eviscerate María Martín's testimony. What they did not tell us is that they had obtained the information about the assassinated right-wingers on the Internet, where it was posted on the webpage of the General Lawsuit, the mass proceedings that Francoism opened against the Republic after the war in order to justify the coup and the civil war, and which even provides the names of the persons alleged to have committed the crime along with their whereabouts.

Nevertheless, it would be useless to search for anything equivalent regarding the victims of Francoism, like María's mother, whose assassination was never investigated for the simple reason that those responsible for the crime were the same persons who were in power for decades. Naturally, *La Gaceta* also said nothing about the twenty victims of the fascist repression inscribed in San Bernardo's civil death registry nor did it provide María's affirmation during the trial that her mother was assassinated together with twenty-seven men and three women.[3] *La Gaceta*'s mission as well as that of similar right-wing organs was to undermine, day by day, anything that could cast doubt on the validity of the trial against Garzón. For example, when Caroline Edelstam, from the Swedish foundation of the same name, called the judge "a martyr, like all those who sacrifice themselves," *La Gaceta* came out with the ridiculous idea that PSOE and IU had initiated a campaign to present the judge "as a martyr confronted by the Right."

Notwithstanding, once again the principal recourse against the testimonies presented during the trial and against anything that smacked of historical memory was to bring up the assassinations in the town of Paracuellos, near Madrid, where right-wingers were massacred in November 1936 after the Republican government had fled to Valencia, Franco's columns had failed to occupy the capital and bombs pounded the city day after day. On February 2, 2012, for example, in response to the oral testimonies, *La Gaceta* dedicated its front page to the crimes in Paracuellos. And again, the Right distorted reality by concealing the fact that, unlike the events denounced by the associations for historical memory, the crimes in Paracuellos had been investigated, their victims honored and their families paid reparations, to which must be added forty decades of continuous commemoration.

And as could have been foreseen, the extreme Right represented by the prosecution managed to introduce the case of Paracuellos into the trial. Over the objection of the defense, which maintained that the crimes in

Paracuellos were not the object of this trial, and with the approval of the presiding judge, Granados, the prosecuting attorney requested and was granted permission to read into the record Garzón's ruling in 1998 rejecting the accusation filed by the Association of Families and Friends of the Victims of the Paracuellos Genocide against, among others, the former communist leader and ex-deputy to parliament Santiago Carrillo for his alleged involvement in the said crimes. Garzón's argument distinguishing the events in Paracuellos from the case brought in 2008 against the Francoist repression was of little use. In any case, Garzón thought that the Paracuellos affair fell under the jurisdiction of the court where those events occurred. The members of the association that had filed the complaint were especially upset that in 1998 Garzón had justified his refusal to investigate the events in Paracuellos with the argument that genocide was not categorized as a crime in 1936 and yet in 2008 he had decided to open an investigation of the crimes of the dictatorship.

The last declarations by the witnesses for the defense coincided with two significant events: a celebration in parliament in homage to the founder of the Popular Party and Francoist politician Manuel Fraga Iribarne, during which his party and part of the PSOE applauded while the Right-wing Catalonian Nationalists remained silent, and the Basque Nationalist Party, the United Left party and all other leftist parties were absent, since they refused to attend; and the declaration by the vice-president of the government Soraya Sáenz de Santamaría that, for the time being, there would be no changes made to the Valley of the Fallen.[TN6]

Documentary Evidence and Final Reports

Since it had not been allowed to present witnesses in the normal way, the defense decided to gather written declarations by international organizations (the United Nations, human rights organizations, the Red Cross, etc.) and statements of general jurisprudence, and requested that two documents be read into the record: a writ from the district attorney's office and the dissenting opinion of the three magistrates who had voted to support the case initiated by Garzón in December 2008. The prosecution proposed that Spanish legislation be borne in mind and not the defense's proposal, and asked that five documents be read into the record, all of them related to the judge's refusal starting in 1998 to investigate the Paracuellos massacre. The defense attorney Martínez-Fresnada responded to this request by pointing out that several of the resolutions the prosecution was requesting be read

TN 6. See translator's note 5, p. 144.

into the record were signed by a judge other than Baltasar Garzón and, furthermore, he reminded the court that the Paracuellos affair and the case brought against Santiago Carrillo had been excluded from the trial by the presiding magistrate himself, Luciano Varela. Nevertheless, Judge Granados approved the prosecution's request. The reason for the prosecution's wish that these documents be read into the record was that one of the accusations was rejected by Judge Garzón on the grounds that the crime of genocide had been created in 1944 and was not enacted into law until four years later, for which reason it was not applicable retroactively to events that had taken place previously. The prosecution also alluded to the fact that the statute of limitations expired twenty years later for everything that had occurred in 1936 and, furthermore, those responsible were the beneficiaries of pardons and amnesty granted during the transition to democracy. In its conclusions the prosecution insisted that "the presentation of the accusations was part of a coordinated effort," that the lawsuits presented in the courts had been set aside and that the proceedings opened by Judge Garzón smacked of a "general lawsuit."[TN7]

The defense did not place sufficient emphasis on the fact that the crimes of Paracuellos had already been tried and that those responsible had been condemned by the "General Lawsuit" opened during the dictatorship. Instead, the defense insisted that Judge Garzón's initiative was justified by the universality of Criminal Law and reminded the court of "the historical importance of the case," which the three dissenting magistrates stressed in their vote in favor of the investigation opened by Garzón. In response to the prosecution's argument that those responsible had already disappeared, the defense stated that such a thing was unlikely given that many of the crimes being investigated had occurred in the late 1940s and early 1950s.

The long closing speech by Ruiz de Infante Abellán, the lawyer for "Clean Hands" and "Liberty and Identity," was weak in content and monotonous to the point of stupefaction. It centered almost entirely on the formal complaint filed in 1998 against Santiago Carrillo for the events in Paracuellos and raised the following question. If Garzón had rejected the case on the basis of the expiration of the statute of limitations, the retroactive application of the law and the 1977 Law of Amnesty, why did he admit, years later, the accusations by the associations for historical memory against the crimes of those who rose up against the Republic in 1936? In Ruiz de Infante Abellán's own words, "Does Judge Garzón wish to maintain that

TN 7. See translator's note 4, p. 142.

the events in Paracuellos are not disappearances and that those of the other side are indeed disappearances? Does he want to say that those buried in one mass grave are subjected to International Law and those who are buried in another common grave are subjected to National Law?" Then the plaintiffs' lawyer added, "We make no distinction with respect to the victims." Nevertheless, in his ruling in 1998 regarding the complaint against Carrillo, Garzón never once alluded to the statute of limitations or to amnesty.

Consequently, the prosecution considered that starting at the end of 2006 with the acceptance of the accusations filed by the associations for historical memory, Garzón was guilty of the crime of continuous prevarication, the most serious type of this crime and punishable by twenty years of disbarment, since Judge Garzón had acted "for ideological motives." Ruiz, faithful to the extreme right-wing organizations he represented and in spite of saying that he respected the associations for historical memory, even cast doubt on the phrase "forced disappearance" employed by the families of the victims, since, according to what he said, they knew the date of death and the place where the remains were buried. Ruiz considered the phrase to be a cunning ploy on Garzón's part to get around problems such as the statute of limitation and the retroactive application of the laws. Ruiz even declared sarcastically that if the victims had indeed disappeared then perhaps they were still alive. He also cast doubt on the use of the concept of genocide, which did not enter Spanish legislation until the 1970s. In an attempt to ridicule the judge the prosecution said that, with the arguments set forth by Garzón, "today we could open a lawsuit against the events of May 2"[TN8] or "we could go back in time to each and every outrage that has ever occurred in Spanish history."

The arguments of the defense and of Garzón were discredited as "irrational." In Ruiz's opinion Judge Garzón "is indicting a movement, a period of time" and "is shaping the events on the basis of a bibliography that is literary" rather than scientific and that is not based on direct testimonies. The prosecution, as could have been foreseen, defended the Law of Amnesty and considered that "the victims of either side suffered an affront with the passage of the said law." Ruiz Infante even blamed Garzón for the change in the international attitude toward the Spanish Transition and toward the

TRANSLATOR'S NOTE 8. May 2, 1808, when the people of Madrid rose up against Napoleon's occupying forces. The brutal reaction of Napoleon's Mameluke troops in Madrid's central plaza (La Puerta del Sol) is depicted in Goya's famous painting *El dos de mayo de 1808 en Madrid*, also known as "La carga de los mamelucos en la Puerta del Sol."

Law of Amnesty, which had once been considered exemplary but was now regarded as a law that impeded the transition to democracy. All in all the prosecution concluded that Garzón had launched an attack "against democratic principles" when he accepted the accusations filed by the associations for historical memory.

For his part, the attorney for the defense Martínez-Fresnada summarized the proceedings and facts, sustained that the challenged arguments were "defensible and reasonable," insisted that Judge Garzón was innocent and requested that he be acquitted. Martínez-Fresnada characterized the accusations against Santiago Carrillo and against Garzón as a "counteroffensive" by the extreme-right for some cases in which the judge had intervened (Argentina and Chile) and reminded the court again that the massacre in Paracuellos, already investigated and resolved, had been introduced "through the back door" by the prosecution and had nothing to do with the case now being tried. In order to justify his allusions to the fact that the extreme-right was behind those accusations he only had to recall that two of them had been signed by Jorge Cesarsky, an Argentine right-winger tried for his involvement in a fascist murder that took place in Madrid during the Transition on the occasion of a demonstration in favor of the amnesty (the case of Arturo Ruiz),[TN9] and the Argentine military man Adolfo Scilingo,[TN10] who presented accusations against Carrillo, PSOE, PCE, etc.

The attorney for the defense stated that the prosecution had fallen into a banality when comparing Judge Garzón's initiative with the true General Lawsuit, the terrible investigation opened by Francoism against it victims. In the same way, the defense set forth the impossibility of comparing the treatment the victors gave the victims like those at Paracuellos, for whom there were investigations and reparations as well as punishment for those thought to have been involved, with the victims on the other side. He criticized the prosecution's insistence on the "coordinated action" of the associations for historical memory and drew attention to the plaintiffs' disingenuousness and their obsessive belief that Garzón had maneuvered to direct certain cases to his own courtroom. According to the defense, none of the plaintiffs, with the exception of Falange, had denied the events which were the object of the investigation opened by Garzón. What had changed was that the victims' families had decided to denounce those events before

TRANSLATOR'S NOTE 9. In 1977 Jorge Cesarsky was found guilty of the murder of Arturo Ruiz.

TN 10. See translator's note 2, p. 141.

the National Tribunal, events that were crimes of illegal detentions without knowledge of the whereabouts of the victim, equivalent to the forced disappearance of persons in the context of crimes against humanity associated with a crime against the high organisms of the state and the form of its government. The defense concluded by saying that the problem remained unresolved: "It would be sensible to think that it may be within the jurisdiction of the criminal courts and their application of internal and international norms that a judicial solution to this problem exists."

The report by the district attorney Luis Navajas was blunt. "It would be pathetic and ridiculous that while a judge in Argentina is investigating the crimes of Francoism, here we persecute the judge who brings forth the accusations filed by the families of these victims and initiates proceedings against deeds of extraordinary gravity." Navajas maintained that even if Garzón had committed "errors of approach," it would, in the final analysis, be one of many instances that do not justify a criminal proceeding for prevarication. He rejected once again the arguments of the presiding magistrate, Luciano Varela, and, after recognizing the rights of the victims on both sides, he expressed "the greatest contempt" for those on the Right who seemed to have come to the tribunal to "play the victim card." Navajas alluded to the prosecution's obsession with Paracuellos and denied its relationship to the events being judged. In order to show the differences between the repressions on both sides, the attorney general read the war decrees of two of the principle generals during the 1936 military coup (Emilio Mola and Gonzalo Queipo de Llano) which clearly demonstrated that the leaders of the coup planned to use terror from the start. According to Attorney General Navajas, Garzón should be acquitted, since a guilty verdict would have "a devastating effect," demonstrating that jurisprudence based on standard practice had yielded to a criminal legal process centered "on the name and reputation of the accused."

In his final statement Judge Garzón cited Kant, who wrote that "man's tribunal is his conscience" and declared that his was clear. He said he had initiated the proceedings in recognition of each judge's independence and capacity to interpret the Law, which constitutes the "essence of the judicial function," and he insisted that his decisions were at all times in conformity with the Law and that his objective was always to avoid "the neglect of the afflicted and the oblivion of the victims."

The multifaceted coverage of the trial during the retransmission of each session and in the daily press demonstrated, with a few exceptions, the scarce reliability with which the press informed (or misinformed) the public about the proceedings. On the other hand, the various statements by the prosecution, the defense, the attorney general and even by Judge Garzón himself provided abundant evidence, as one would expect, that their knowledge of the repressive phenomenon was superficial and riddled with vague and inappropriate concepts. This criticism could even extend to the witnesses, whose statements were tainted by Francoist propaganda when they described their families' victims as persons who were executed and not assassinated. According to Francoism, the Republicans *assassinated* and they themselves *executed*. These deficiencies, in the media, in those who took part in the trial and in witnesses who denounced events of a repressive nature, display the scarce knowledge and the lack of awareness in Spanish society regarding those events and the long road we must still travel in order to bring justice to those Spaniards who disappeared.

During the days that the trial lasted there were always people who, outside the courthouse, showed their support for the judge and their criticism of the trial. Some of them carried photographs of disappeared family members and asked for "Dignity for the Victims." They also shouted slogans such as "Disbarment for Francoist judges," "Enough impunity already," "This trial smells vile," "Truth, justice and reparations" or "Unless you agree with what they say, they'll take your freedom of speech away."

During the following days and when the sentence for the Gürtel case was made known (disbarment for eleven years), which provoked an outburst of indignation and caused Judge Garzón himself to call the sentence "predetermined," the Right continued its daily campaign through its mass media (*El Mundo*, *La Razón*, *La Gaceta*, *ABC*, *Libertad Digital*, etc.) and in its numerous Internet pages and forums. It was in this context that, on February 10, 2012, the office of the United Nations High Commissioner for Human Rights, Navi Pillay, asked Spain to repeal the 1977 Law of Amnesty because it was in violation of international norms. She also asked Spain to eliminate all obstacles to the investigation of human rights violations during the Franco dictatorship and the indictment of those responsible. These requests were supported by a report from eighteen experts of the said organization who based their findings on the International Covenant on Civil and Political Rights, ratified by Spain in 1985. And with respect to the sentence in the Gürtel Case, eighty-two organizations related to human rights from thirty countries lamented that "in a democracy like Spain the independence of the justice system could be violated by incriminating a judge" and urged that the judge's good name and status as magistrate be restored. To the same effect, on February 25 a statement was published with the signature of the Nobel Peace Prize winner

Adolfo Pérez Esquivel, Head Prosecutor on the International Criminal Court, along with two thousand other signatures "in memory of a great judge, a great person and a great companion."

Confronted by criticism coming from all sides, the judiciary took offense and went on the attack. On February 10, 2012 the spokesperson for the General Council of Judicial Power, Graciela Bravo, considered it "inadmissible" and "intolerable" that the members of the High Court were being insulted. She lamented the statements by the ex-Anticorruption Attorney Carlos Jiménez Villarejo, who characterized the members of the High Court as "a caste of bureaucrats bent on revenge." She affirmed that Garzón had had a trial "with every guarantee" and an impartial tribunal that had acted "without any type of ideology" and which had handed down a unanimous sentence. Furthermore, Graciela Bravo expressed concern "for the image of Spanish Justice that is being projected," when it is "at the forefront of Europe when it comes to justice with guarantees, whatever anyone might say." Two days later it was the president of the High Court, the ultraconservative Carlos Dívar, named for the post by President Rodríguez Zapatero, who, in the Congressional Justice Commission, answered the criticisms for the verdict against Judge Garzón. The only party that supported Dívar was the conservative Popular Party, which warned that these criticisms could be punished. Dívar also expressed concern about the commentaries made by Spaniards to the foreign media denigrating the High Court and the Spanish justice system for the trials against Judge Garzón. The bluntest of these came from Gaspar Llamazares, of the United Left party, who compared it to the Dreyfus affair and said, "I do not comply with an unjust sentence that is a barbarity and a scandal. The verdict against Garzón is an embarrassment to the citizens." The deputy from the Catalonian Republican Left party, Joan Tardá, was equally outraged. "The general perception that the citizenry has with respect to you judges, and even with respect to the Justice Administration, is that you are off the mark, way off the mark; perversely politicized; excessively inbred and corporative."

The Ruling

On February 23 the General Council of Judicial Power ratified the disbarment of Judge Garzón from the judicial profession according to the sentence handed down in the Gürtel case. The measure was adopted unanimously by the nineteen spokespersons of the Council and the president, the aforementioned Carlos Dívar (only one spokesperson was missing,

Félix Azón, who refused to attend because he did not agree with the date chosen). The spokespersons were selected by the Popular Party and the Socialist PSOE. The sentence disqualified Baltasar Garzón from serving as a judge or magistrate "with the definitive loss of his post and of the honors that go with it, as well as with his invalidation during the time of the sentence for any employment or post with jurisdictional functions or any governmental post within the Judiciary, or with jurisdictional functions outside the same." His post in the Fifth Chamber of the High Court will be opened for competition.[4]

On Monday February 27 it was made public that he had been acquitted in the trial for his investigation of Francoist crimes. For many people, this was no surprise. It was what they expected. The text of the ruling recalled that since a very early date the Prosecutorial Ministry warned Judge Garzón that, in addition to the non-retroactive nature of criminal laws and the 1977 Law of Amnesty, in accordance with the present penal code, the events under investigation could only be classified as common crimes. Nevertheless, in October 2008, Garzón claimed that opening an investigation of Francoist crimes was within his jurisdiction, but only a few days later the Prosecutorial Ministry declared Garzón's proceedings null, after which the judge withdrew from the case in favor of the territorial courts. In early December it was the Criminal Chamber of the National Tribunal itself that declared the investigation of those events to be outside the jurisdiction of Garzón's Fifth Chamber and of the National Tribunal itself.

After describing this sequence, the juridical fundamentals set forth in the ruling establish that in the Spanish court system there is no place for a mere inquiry without the goal of imposing a penalty on someone. In other words, if what the victims intend is a report similar to those of "truth commissions," the Spanish penal system has nothing to offer them since "the right to know the truth does not form part of the penal process and can only be satisfied tangentially." For the members of the High Court, the penal system "does not lend itself to the declaration of historical truth concerning such polyhedral events as the civil war and the subsequent postwar." And it adds:

> The methods of judicial investigation are not those of the historian. All things considered, if the differences between memory and history are obvious, then equally obvious are the differences between historical research and a judicial inquiry carried out with a purpose distinct from that of the historian. (. . .). The investigative methods of the judge in a court of inquiry have nothing to do with the investigative process of the historian. It is unwise to confuse historical truth with forensic truth, since historical truth

is general and subject to interpretation (. . .) and, frequently, requires a certain temporal distance in order to achieve an objective analysis.

According to the ruling, Garzón's description of events was designed to surmount the problems of retroactive application of the law, the statute of limitations and the 1977 Law of Amnesty. International Law should be incorporated into Spanish jurisprudence "in a way provided for in the Constitution and with effects provided for in the same." For the magistrates of the Second Chamber the Martens clause [TN11] "seems to be framed in very generic terms" and the Nuremburg principles were incorporated into our body of laws after the events Garzón intended to investigate occurred. Neither can one resort to the International Covenant on Civil and Political Rights, which went into effect in Spain in 1986. Furthermore, the crimes that could have been committed between 1936 and 1952 fall within the statute of limitations; and specifically, the crime of illegal detention and disappearance, of permanent character at present, was not regarded as such at that time.

And as far as the international norms that would consider amnesties like the Spanish one to be null, they are not binding for Spain. On the other hand, it is not a function of judicial power to repeal laws but of legislative power.

The ruling also contains an encomium to the Transition and to the Law of Amnesty, "very important landmarks of historical evolution," ". . . the goal was to avoid two Spains in conflict with each other" and ". . . in no way was it a law approved by the winners, those holding power, in order to cover up their own crimes," all phrases that can be read in the text. On several occasions the spokesperson, Andrés Martínez Arriete, has recourse to the report by the Interministerial Commission of 2006. He alludes to the *coup d'état*, describing it as a "military uprising" and characterizing the war as "fratricidal revenge," since "both factions committed atrocities," "authentic massacres such as, among others, the events in Granada, Belchite, Málaga, Paracuellos del Jarama, Guernica, Badajoz, (. . .), which are sources of

TRANSLATOR'S NOTE 11. The Martens Clause first appeared in the preamble to the 1899 Hague Convention and has formed a part of the laws of armed conflict ever since. The words of the Russian delegate Fyodor Fyodorovich Martens were: "Until a more complete code of the laws of war is issued, the High Contracting Parties think it right to declare that in cases not included in the Regulations adopted by them, populations and belligerents remain under the protection and empire of the principles of international law, as they result from the usages established between civilized nations, from the laws of humanity and the requirements of the public conscience."

shame for the human species." And he speaks once more of two factions, as if the legitimate government of the Second Republic, the object of a military coup and which is never mentioned, were a faction, when he says:

> It is obvious that in the territories of both factions of the civil war atrocities were carried out and that the two factions, at least their military and political leaders, did not observe the so-called rules of law.

The ruling recognizes the existence of crimes against humanity and systematic actions directed at the elimination of the political enemy, but it denies that an investigation of those events falls within the jurisdiction of Judge Garzón and the National Tribunal, although it admits that

> There still remain concrete actions to undertake with respect to the localization and recuperation of cadavers for the purpose of paying homage to the victims and procuring that genuine reconciliation which the Law of Amnesty pursued.

Nevertheless, in spite of everything, according to the High Court, Judge Garzón argued erroneously but did not prevaricate.

The dissenting vote of the magistrate José Manuel Maza Martín deserves its own separate section. According to this magistrate Garzón clearly committed a crime of prevarication with intention to deceive by taking on a case that was outside his jurisdiction, by pursuing persons who had been granted amnesty, by investigating crimes whose statute of limitations had expired, and for abuse of his judicial powers. Maza reminded the court that the National Tribunal only has jurisdiction to try crimes against humanity when they have been committed outside Spanish territory, a condition to which was later added another condition by an agreement between PSOE and PP: that there must be a connection with Spanish interests. "Trials of truth" are not recognized by Spanish legislation and, even less, by the criminal process. According to Maza, Judge Garzón was perfectly conscious that the laws could not be applied retroactively, that he could not have recourse to the crime of illegal detention with disappearance to get around the statute of limitations, that there was a Law of Amnesty and that the Fifth Chamber of the National Tribunal which he headed did not have jurisdiction in this matter, but nonetheless he went forward. He asks, sarcastically, if Garzón claims

> that some persons, victims of forced disappearance under the dictatorship,

have remained in a situation of privation of freedom, in some unknown location, during such an extended period of time that it includes the last thirty-six years, in spite of the freedoms fully recuperated in our democratic system.

Of course Maza also takes the opportunity to recall on several occasions Judge Garzón's ruling in 1998 concerning the lawsuit against Carrillo for the events in Paracuellos. After enumerating all the deeds contrary to the law committed by Judge Garzón, "an authentic sham of a criminal investigation which, in the final analysis, would have inevitably and predictably led the plaintiffs to yet another frustration in the difficult and commendable search for their loved ones in order to honor them properly," Maza affirms that the ruling should have been a guilty verdict. And he asks himself, "Perhaps from now on a Spanish judge can disobey the nation's laws, the laws dictated by our sovereign parliament, because he finds criteria and opinions that are foreign to our system of law but which coincide with his particular way of looking at things?" And he concludes, "Seldom has a clearer example of judicial prevarication been seen . . . ," showing his "deep concern for the precedent that this ruling could represent . . .". Maza Martín's dissenting opinion could hardly omit an allusion to the District Attorney Navajas, who he assumes to be satisfied with the ruling, and to Navajas's criticism of the presiding magistrate Luciano Varela. Maza was worried by these criticisms because they implied that the attack on Judge Garzón was motivated by his celebrity status.

Conclusions

From the presentation of the first lawsuits by associations for historical memory in December 2006 until Judge Baltazar Garzón's trial, more than five years transpired, which in fact can be reduced to two sequences, not counting the lawsuits themselves: the brief history of Garzón's writ opening an investigation of Francoist crimes in the autumn of 2008, which was immediately cut off by the judicial authorities themselves, and the harassment of Garzón beginning in 2010, which ended two years later with his disbarment from a judicial career because of the use of wiretaps in the Gürtel case and his acquittal for the crime of prevarication in the investigation of Francoist crimes. There was another lawsuit that had been brought against him but that case was closed because the statute of limitations had expired.

I do not know to what extent we can speak of judicial independence in a country in which the key posts on the most important tribunals are divided among the majority parties, which in turn name the persons to fill those posts. Judicial power in Spain is conservative by its very nature when not openly reactionary, which should not surprise us in a country where the military coup of July 18, 1936, the civil war and the dictatorship led to a complete purge of the judicial bureaucracy from the offices of the Justices of the Peace to the highest tribunals. It is well known that the Spanish Transition did not represent a change of any sort for these bureaucrats who one night went to bed as Francoists and the next day woke up as democrats. During the 1970s, most of those holding high posts in the judiciary had been collaborators with and servants of Francoism from its very beginning, even though their biographies conceal that fact.[5] They were all rewarded for their service. In this closed world in which high-sounding last names reveal the predominance of certain social classes there are unwritten rules that everyone has to obey.

When Judge Garzón decided to go forward with the investigation of the crimes of Francoism he was already known and admired throughout the world, especially since 1998 when he managed to have the Chilean dictator Pinochet arrested in London. From the time the lawsuits regarding forced disappearances were delivered to the National Tribunal by the associations for historical memory until Garzón decided to go forward with an investigation almost two years had gone by, during which he had plenty of time to think about the case's possibilities. From the beginning Garzón was warned even by some lawyers, jurists and groups close to the associations for historical memory that it would be impossible to initiate the investigation from the National Tribunal, which turned out to be true given how short-lived the initiative was. He was also warned that the decision to recuse himself and send the lawsuits to the territorial courts would come to naught, which also turned out to be correct. What no one could have imagined is that all this would end up costing him his career. Other judicial organisms more sensitive to the basic problem, the crimes of Francoism, would have declared the matter outside the jurisdiction of the head of the Fifth Chamber of the National Tribunal, but would have found another pathway so that the investigation initiated by Garzón could proceed. In fact the exact opposite took place. The High Court put a stop to the initiative and, while doing so, seized the opportunity to get rid of a judge whose independent behavior had left a trail strewn with enemies.

The process that leads to this ending can only be understood if we bear in mind that, given what I have explained above, the moment a holder of a high judicial post loses the political backing of one of the two largest parties, he or she is thrown to the wolves. Judge Garzón's trajectory explains perfectly well why neither the conservative PP nor the socialist PSOE tried to cover his back when it was clear that his enemies were closing in for the kill. We have already noted that the reaction of the socialist vice-president María Teresa Fernández de la Vega was crucial. She was upset to see *her* Law of Historical Memory upstaged and her critical and derogatory comments suggested that the way was open to eliminate the judge. And so the Penal Chamber of the High Court initiated the opportune motions and took up the lawsuits filed by the extreme Right, lawsuits which they had turned down numerous times before. And, finally, there were the trials. The first was for the use of wiretaps in the Gürtel corruption case, which was extremely complex legally and susceptible to antithetical interpretations. Garzón's enemies used it to solve the problem once and for all. The judge would never again serve on the bench, for having violated the rights of the defendants.

Nevertheless, the second trial was more important because of the expectations it raised both within Spain and abroad. For anyone who followed the trial, the outcome could just as easily have gone the other way. Proof of that is the dissenting vote by the magistrate Maza Martín, which was entirely in keeping with the trial's logic and clearly shows how surprised one of the members of the tribunal was by the reasons which led his colleagues to acquit the defendant. But there were three motives for the acquittal: because Judge Garzón had already been taken out of the game by the verdict in the Gürtel case, because the scandal would have been enormous if there had been a guilty verdict and because what really mattered, however much Garzón's fame may have overshadowed it somewhat, was to make clear that the Spanish justice system would never do anything about the crimes of Francoism. The ruling represents one more step backward in the defense of human rights to such an absurd extent as to admit that Spanish justice can try crimes against humanity committed abroad but its own laws prevent it from trying the same crimes committed at home. In the final analysis, lawsuits related to historical memory will not find a single channel in any judicial sphere and Universal Justice has no place in the Spanish legal system, which has armor-plated itself against these sorts of innovations. The reference points will continue to be the same as always: the Law of Amnesty, the Constitution, the Transition and the Law of Historical Memory, in other words, all the elements that make up the model for Spanish impunity.

Notes

1   During the second half of 2006 the so-called "War of the Death Notices" took place. On the occasion of the seventieth anniversary of the military coup of July 1936 and coinciding with the high point of enthusiasm for the historical memory movement, there were those who thought it an opportune time to

publish death notices in the press – primarily in *El País* – in remembrance of family members who had disappeared as a consequence of the Francoist repression. Beginning in July there was a trickle of such commemorations. The Right's response was immediate. Death notices began to appear in their newspapers (*El Mundo, ABC*, etc.) for right-wing victims. What was peculiar about the phenomenon was that the death notices for victims of fascism were being published for the first time while the others were being published for the second time and had had four decades of dictatorship to appear in the press. The phenomenon showed that the Right was not only obstinately opposed to everything related to historical memory but even denied such a fundamental act in the process of grieving as the publication of a death notice by those who had never been able to do so.

2　It should be pointed out that the economic compensations for the property of leftists plundered by those who carried out the military coup has only covered the damages caused to political parties and labor unions but has never extended to individuals who suffered the confiscations and expropriations that took place from the very beginning of the military coup.

3　On February 15, 2012, the same newspaper affirmed that María Martín had spurned the help offered her by Pedro Bernardo's right-wing mayor. The town hall also refused to remove the plaque on the church's wall commemorating the right-wing victims, promising to place another in memory of leftist victims. Between the years 2007 and 2008, the tables turned and the socialist party came to power in the town and the plaque on the church was removed in July 2008 despite the protest of the Ávila bishopric. What no one anticipated was that, under the plaque, there was an inscription with the names of the town's victims of the fascist repression.

4　The information utilized for the elaboration of this section comes from the recorded sessions of the trial itself and from articles written by the following journalists: Selina Otero (*Faro de Vigo*), Julio M. Lázaro and José Yoldi (*El País*), Alicia Moreno, Lidia Vicente and Javier Chinchón (*Rights International Spain*), G. Moreno and J. Cordero (*La Gaceta/Intereconomía*), Pere Rusiñol (*Público*), Natalia Junquera (*El País*), L. Aranzábal (*La Gaceta/Intereconomía*), María Peral (*El Mundo*), N. Villanueva (*ABC*), D. Carrasco (*La Gaceta/Intereconomía*), Unnamed authors (*La Vanguardia*), R. Coarasa and F. Velasco (*La Razón*), A. Bartolomé (*La Razón*), Laura G. Torres (RTVE.ES) and Alejandro Gutiérrez (www.proceso.com.mx).

5　One significant example would be Antonio Pedrol Rius (1910–1992), dean of the College of Lawyers in Madrid (1973), president of the General Law Council (1976), senator by royal designation in the first general sessions of Parliament under the monarchy (1977–1978). Nevertheless, his biography omits the fact that in the months following the 1936 coup he served in the insurgent generals' military/judicial machinery, specifically in the service of the Army of the South's department for military/judicial investigations.

General Reflections

When we dispense with living testimonies or historical documents
we reduce the scope of our own consciousness. In spite of this truth,
at certain times nations [...] choose to disregard certain archives
or to tolerate their being plundered or abandoned.

HERMES TOVAR PINZÓN, "Archives, corruption
and human rights: the body as testimony," 2005.

An examination of the different cases that have been described, in order to
systematize them, will reveal that, although they all deal with history, the
predominant element is *the denial of oral history*, of the personal testimony
of those who lived or knew of the events that occurred as a consequence of
the military coup. That was how it was in cases like those of Fernando Ruiz
Vergara, Isidoro Sánchez Baena, Marta Capín, Santiago Macías and Dionisio
Pereira, to which we will have to add those of José Casado Montado and
Ramón Garrido Vidal. The first group went public with the results of their
investigations while the second group consists of authors who decided to
write down their own memories. Midway between these two groups would
be the case of Dolors Genovés, which I would place beside the very best
examples of investigative reporting. Here it is not a question of oral testimony but rather of some declarations gathered from the transcript of a
court-martial and the conclusions drawn by the author. What the lawsuit
questioned was the author's work, in an attempt to censor her documentary
in which some Catalonian Francoists did not come off well. In the case of
Alfredo Grimaldos we could speak of recidivism, since the information that
led to the Rosón family's lawsuit, with rulings favorable to the family
handed down by the National Tribunal in 2009 and the High Court in
2012, was the same information that led to two other trials that ended in
rulings favorable to the Rosóns in the 1980s.

The stories of Amparo Barayón Miguel and Antonio Martínez Borrego
deserve a separate category. Even though there are differences, at their core
they are similar; two innocent persons, the first one murdered and the second one condemned to prison and forced to live under harsh conditions,
whose reputations were tarnished by serious slanders. In the first case by
putting the reason for her death in doubt with a public declaration that she

was suffering from syphilis – all to avenge the book written by her son –, and in the second case by falsely accusing him of betraying his comrades. In the case of Amparo Barayón the slanderer was a professor at the University of Castilla-La Mancha and in the case of Antonio Martínez the slanderer was a worker with a dubious past who took advantage of the fact that someone interviewed him, believed him and published his invented story.

Separate from all the cases already mentioned is that of Violeta Friedman, whose novelty is that it took place in Spain and that the justice system took the side of a Rumanian Jewess rather than the side of a Nazi who had been protected by the Franco regime. The reason for its inclusion in this book is that it allows us to reflect on what might have occurred in Spain if the honor of the victims or of the defeated in general had been taken into consideration. Even accepting the exceptionality of the Holocaust, which I do not doubt, I am one of those who believe that the Spanish insurgents of 1936 committed a crime of mass forced disappearances wherever they took control, a crime which is not protected by the statute of limitations due to the permanent nature of the crime until its resolution. In 1936 the concept of genocide had not yet been created but, even though the concept cannot be applied in the case of Spain, we are dealing with the first genocide of the cycle opened in 1936 and closed in 1945.

Furthermore, the regime not only exterminated tens of thousands of persons, they also said and wrote whatever they wished about their victims for decades during which the victims' dependents lived in total neglect and without the most fundamental rights. The first difference between what Violeta Friedman's family and friends had suffered and the Spanish experience is that to deny the Shoah constitutes a crime in much of Europe whereas to deny the Francoist extermination plan – and I do not intend to place it on the same level as the Holocaust – is permissible. Another difference between Violeta Friedman and the Spanish women who had seen family members disappear is that Ms. Friedman could rely on considerable support of all kinds during her legal confrontation with the Nazi Degrelle whereas those Spanish women have always been completely on their own.

Nor can we disregard another important element; even while recognizing the important role played by the Constitutional Tribunal, the fact is that the Spanish justice system had little at stake in Violeta Friedman's case. By this I do not mean to dismiss the work of the justice system and the important precedent that was established but rather to underscore what Violeta Friedman's lawyer, Carlos Trías Sagnier said, which is that "the stories of Spanish Republicans or Palestinians in Israel may be tragic, but they have nothing in common with the Holocaust and its survivors." In other words, that the Friedman case could not be used to put any Spanish

Degrelles in their place or to open any doors to those for whom the reality of their lives and suffering is not only denied, but is not even acknowledged. Furthermore, although a few years later this defect was corrected, the definitive text of the ruling omitted the allusion to considering it a crime "to manufacture, distribute or exhibit symbols or propaganda representing or defending events considered to be genocide." Therefore, since in Spain one ought not to speak of genocide because most of the Francoist repression occurred before 1945 – the year when Raphael Lemkin's concept of genocide was applied during the Nuremberg Trials – the ruling would have little transcendence.

There is more. Léon Degrelle's error was to deny the Holocaust and exonerate Josef Mengele. Naturally, his greatest surprise must have been that such statements could cause him problems in Spain, where a fascist regime related to Hitler's Germany, Mussolini's Italy and Salazar's Portugal came to power in 1936 and lasted until only ten years before he was sued. We should not forget that from the Court of First Inquiry where the lawsuit had been filed all the way to the High Court, the rulings all gave protection to the Belgian Nazi's freedom of expression. It is impossible to judge what the outcome would have been if the Constitutional Tribunal had consisted of different judges.

Nevertheless, and in spite of the fact that the ruling established that freedom of expression is limited by respect for honor and human dignity, and that to trivialize or justify genocide is a crime, unfortunately the ruling does not extend to those here in Spain who deny, trivialize, minimize and justify the political extermination carried out by Francoists between 1936 and 1945. Freedom of expression cannot protect professional rabble-rousers and purveyors of mere propaganda. Such people – and not historians – are the ones who should be hauled into court. I do not wish to imply in any way that only one version of history should be imposed by law, something that in any event would be impossible in a democratic society. When I say this I am referring, for example, to what France did with a secondary school teacher who, in front of his students, denied the massacre of Oradour-sur-Glane, and was temporarily suspended from his post and made to pay a fine. Unfortunately, in Spain the chaotic state of its archives and deep-rooted customs (the expurgation or destruction of "troublesome" documents or the taking home of "papers that should not be seen by others' eyes" after one's term in office) have always provided impunity for propagandists and agitators. Just one example. If the archives allowed us to truly know the consequences of the occupation of Badajoz[TN1 (OPPOSITE)] by the Africanists,[TN2 (OPPOSITE)] we would not have to put up with those who continue to deny the extraordinary horror of that event. And the worst part is that while this denial continues, Juan Yagüe's archive remains in the hands of his family, as if the papers from his years as a military bureaucrat belonged to them. Varela's archive can be consulted in Cádiz but it has been expurgated by someone chosen by Varela himself, who pointed out the documents to be removed; we know nothing of the whereabouts of the archives of Castejón, Asensio and Tella.[TN3]

Finally, the case of the attorney Jorge Trías Sagnier is unquestionably suggestive and would make a good novel. We have seen him, on the one hand, defending the honor of a Rumanian Jewess who lost her family at Auschwitz and, on the other hand, suing the journalist and historian Dolors Genovés for revealing the truth about a Francoist crime committed on the person of the moderate and respected Catalonian politician Manuel Carrasco i Formiguera, whose only "crime" was being a Republican and a Catalonian Nationalist. In the second case, it was because the honor of Trías Segnier's own family was at stake. It is incredible to discover that, in order to achieve his objective, he even conceded legal validity to Carrasco i Formiguera's court-martial and the socio-political reports contained therein.

Having placed the cases discussed in their appropriate categories, it is worth stopping to reflect on each case individually. That of Fernando Ruiz Vergara, which took place in the first half of the 1980s, exudes pure Francoism, with all the judicial authorities on the side of the Reales family and against a pair of young documentary filmmakers and an old leftist who had seen and remembered the massacre carried out by the fascists in the town of Almonte. Furthermore, the Ruiz Vergara case left us with the priceless discourse of the court's spokesperson Luis Vivas Marzal, filled with such phrases as "the impertinent and unfortunate reminder of episodes that occurred before and after July 18th" and with his affirmation that it was not

TRANSLATOR'S NOTE 1 (PREVIOUS PAGE). According to Francisco Espinosa Maestre, the number of victims massacred following the occupation of Badajoz is impossible to estimate with the available data, but from August 14, 1936 when the city was occupied until about 1943 when the killings diminished there were probably between 3,000 and 3,500 victims.

TRANSLATOR'S NOTE 2 (PREVIOUS PAGE). "Africanistas" is the term for the Spanish officers who served during the brutal Moroccan war. The generals and many of the officers who took part in the military coup of July 18, 1936 were Africanists.

TRANSLATOR'S NOTE 3. Colonel Juan Yagüe Blanco, an Africanist, commanded the column that occupied Badajoz. Major Antonio Castejón Espinosa and Lieutenant Colonels Carlos Asensio Cabanillas and Heliodoro Tella Cantos served in the column. They were all Africanists, as was General José Enrique Varela Iglesias, who later replaced Yagüe as commander of the column before the occupation of Toledo.

"wise to rekindle the embers," an image that would later be taken up by Manuel Gutiérrez Mellado,[TN4] who would pass it on to the President of the Socialist government (and labor lawyer) Felipe González to justify his firm decision to "not look back" during his fourteen years in power. There is no doubt that we are dealing with one of the harshest and saddest cases set forth in this book. That chapter should be required reading for those who are forever extolling the Transition or for those who endlessly proclaim that there is nothing left to say about the Francoist repression and that freedom of investigation has put an end to silence and amnesia.

The lawsuit against Isidoro Sánchez Baena came about in the same way as the one against Ruiz Vergara, except that it was an article rather than a documentary film, so the author was able to conceal the identity of the witness who told him who killed the watchman at an estate and, consequently, the witness did not become involved in the trial like Ruiz Vergara's witness, Gómez Clavijo, whose testimony was filmed. However, we saw how harsh the district attorney was, encouraging the plaintiffs to ask for millions of pesetas. Fortunately for the historian, the Córdoba provincial court absolved him and the High Court upheld the ruling.

José Casado Montado's "crime" was the same as Ruiz Vergara's and Sánchez Baena's. He named the assassins. This man's courageous testimony must have caused a commotion in the town of San Fernando. If he had limited himself to listing the names of those who were assassinated day after day starting in July 1936, nothing would have happened, but José Casado wanted to talk about the executioners and tell their stories, and that was the source of his problems. The children of the 1936 assassins refused to accept that their fathers were involved in the apparatus of terror, from the offices where the lists of *reds* to exterminate were drawn up, to the bullet-scarred walls where the massacres took place, not to mention the emergency summary courts-martial where so many of the victims were selected. That was the reason for the 1977 amnesty as a starting point and the so-called "spirit of the Transition" as the ideological motto for reconciliation. Where the past has been erased there are no crimes or criminals.

The story of Dolors Genovés and her documentary film *Sumaríssim 477* would not have existed without the transcript of the court-martial of

---

TRANSLATOR'S NOTE 4. General Manuel Gutiérrez Mellado was appointed Chief of Staff of the Spanish army in June 1976 and was Deputy Prime Minister of Spain (equivalent to Vice President) during Adolfo Suárez's term as President of the Government.

Manuel Carrasco i Formiguera, because then few people, except for the protagonists and witnesses, would have known that Carrasco i Formiguera's trial took place with the collaboration of important representatives of Catalonian fascism, among them the Falangist Carlos Trías Bertrán, father of the lawyer Jorge Trías Sagnier. With all the journalistic and historiographic logic in the world, Dolors Genovés decided to emphasize the testimonies of these Catalonian Falangists, thus illuminating a piece of history previously unknown. What the Trías family could not accept was that Genovés maintained that those testimonies were a decisive justification for the assassination of Carrasco i Formiguera; in other words, that the intervention of their father and others was the determining factor at the trial. The Trías children rejected the methodology and conclusions of Dolors Genovés's work, which they labeled a "deception." The Court of Preliminary Inquiry and the Barcelona Provincial Court agreed with the Trías family, but the High Court and the Constitutional Tribunal did not. The work of Xavier O'Callaghan Muñoz and María Emilia Casas Bahamonde, spokespersons respectively of the High Court and the Constitutional Tribunal, was especially important because of the stress these magistrates placed on "the scientific freedom of historians."

In its first phase, the lawsuit against Dolors Genovés and *Sumaríssim 477* was played out in extrajudicial spheres. Let us not forget that in 1995 there was an election in Catalonia, the year when Convergència i Unió (CiU), the party of the Trías family, lost its absolute majority. There were many people who, for different motives, aligned themselves with the Trías family and joined the fray. From among the historians, Josep Benet, witness for the prosecution, was the harshest, perhaps because he felt that his field of expertise had been invaded. It is also worth mentioning Joan Maria Thomas and Javier Tussel. After having supported the author and the documentary, Tussel changed his mind in September 1995 and declared that "*Sumaríssim* lacks the least bit of historical rigor." The journalist Arcadi Espada of *El País* also played an important role in attacking Genovés and her film.

TV-3 was the mouthpiece for CiU and if, on the one hand, it provided Dolors Genovés the legal consultation that was her due as a member of the television station's staff, on the other hand, the station's management even apologized to the Trías family through the then general director of Radio y Televisión, Joan Granados, a man in the sphere of Jordi Pujol (CiU), president of the Catalonian government. A letter sent to Eugenio Trías stated that the problem was due to "some journalists' obsession with taking their work to its ultimate consequences in an eagerness for professional perfection that ignores the values that public television should always bear in mind" (Ana Aguirre, *El Mundo*, April 14, 1995). TV-3's staff replied with a manifesto in defense of Dolors Genovés signed by fifty journalists. For Ana Aguirre "what the controversy demonstrates is that the wounds of the past have not yet healed."

For many people, *Sumaríssim 477* had attacked the honor of "one of our own" – since, setting aside his youthful Francoist vagaries, Trías Bertrán was above all a Catalonian and his descendants were an active part of the Catalonian intellectual élite – and it was essential to finish off the author, who was subjected to a full-scale siege which, lived day by day, became almost unbearable. According to Dolors Genovés, her case was really deliberated in the press and in Parliament. But she armor-plated herself, went on with her work and finally, after ten years, she won. It also must be said that she counted on the support of, among others, Josep María Huertas Clavería, Joan B. Culla, Baltasar Porcel, Josep Fontana, Ernest Lluch and Raimon Obiols,[TN5] and that in 1995, in the middle of the anti-*Sumaríssim 477* campaign, she received the Popular Memory Prize for her trilogy of documentaries on aspects related to the civil war (*Operació Nikolai*, *L'or de Moscou* and *Sumaríssim 477*), a prize awarded by historical foundations that are part of the socialist sphere. Furthermore, during the trial she received an unexpected testimony in her favor from the son of the doctor who attended to Manuel Carrasco i Formiguera in prison.

I do not doubt in the least that the Trías Sagnier siblings would have preferred that the transcript of Carrasco i Formiguera's court-martial had remained under lock and key. The fact that the transcript was made available to Hilari Raguer, Carrasco's biographer, and to Dolors Genovés, was most unusual at the time. Otherwise, it would not have been available for consultation until 1997, the year the military/judicial archives were opened to researchers and *Sumaríssim 477* would not have been made or would have been a very different film. And if in this case – a work based on such an irrefutable document – the author was forced to live through a ten-year Calvary, during which her professionalism was under constant attack, we can imagine what would have happened if the information regarding the involvement of Catalonian fascists in the military/judicial farce against Carrasco i Formiguera had come to her from an oral testimony. It astonishes that, in their desperation, the Trías family would actually validate the procedures of the Francoist military "justice" system. The court's

TRANSLATOR'S NOTE 5. These were all Catalonian intellectuals: Josep Maria Huertas Clavería, journalist; Joan B. Culla, historian; Baltasar Porcel, author; Josep Fontana, historian; Ernest Lluch, politician, economist and historian; and Raimon Obiols, politician.

spokesperson, María Emilia Casas Bahamonde, felt obliged to tell them that their approach was unseemly.

Going beyond the mere concepts of freedom of expression and freedom of information, the spokesperson's forthright defense of the scientific freedom of the historian regardless of his or her moral and ideological perspective, and considered by the spokesperson to be necessary for the formation of a collective historical consciousness, is a gift to posterity.

It would have been interesting to see how a lawsuit filed by Amparo Barayón's descendants would have turned out if it had gotten to the courts in 2005. Would Ana Isabel Almendral's slanderous public statement have passed the test of public interest and veracity? I have no doubt that Dr. Almendral's granddaughter would have been obliged to make a public retraction and that Amparo and her descendants would have received the justice they were due. Unfortunately, the family's situation, scattered as they were throughout the world, impeded a response that would have put the slanderer and the newspaper that published her slander in the place they deserved. As we have seen, Ramón Sender Barayón was not asking for much, but he did not even achieve that.

Ana Isabel Almendral Oppermann's spiteful comment had nothing to back it up except the impunity of the victors, the conviction that nothing would come of an attack on a woman to whom the Francoist justice system "had already given her just deserts." Once again no one, not even a woman who was an eyewitness, should make a comment about a doctor at the service of fascism. Pilar Fidalgo's testimony should disappear so that Dr. Almendral's reputation would remain untarnished. And the same fate should befall Ramón Sender Barayón's book for having reproduced Pilar's story. But since neither of these two things came to pass, Almendral's granddaughter decided that the best course would be to attack Amparo Barayón's son where it would hurt him the most; if Ramón Sender Barayón had "attacked" her grandfather's reputation, she would attack the reputation of Ramón's mother, claiming that, rather than a victim of Zamoran fascism, Amparo was suffering from a venereal disease that would have killed her in any event.

Almendral Opperman's case also poses questions concerning the role of the press. How is it possible that the journalist who interviewed her and the management of the newspaper allowed this to happen? Perhaps anything goes as long as it increases sales, even slander? *La Opinión de Zamora* demonstrated, in this case, the profoundly reactionary spirit of the old provincial press that Spain inherited from the dictatorship. Especially since the journalist as well as the newspaper must have been aware that the attack on Amparo Barayón overshadowed the true motive for the interview. Later, when Amparo's family members complained to the newspaper, the editors also showed their true colors by giving absolute preference to the ridiculous musings of Zamora's local chronicler and relegating everyone else to the back pages. The result – with the exception of Almendral, the local chronicler and *La Opinión de Zamora*, which probably saw a rise in its readership for a while – was the bitterness of impotence for all concerned: for Amparo's children in the United States, for her niece in Málaga, for her great-niece in England and for those of us who intervened in defense of the memory and honor of Amparo Barayón Miguel.

In the story of Antonio Martínez Borrego, Juan Gila Boza and the journalist Mercedes de Pablos, just as in that of Dolors Genovés, the transcript of a court-martial is central, except that in this case the journalist originally thought that the transcript no longer existed and then, when she was encouraged to consult it, she refused to do so in order to avoid confronting the problems it would have caused for her book. If she had consulted the transcript of the court-martial she would have realized that Gila Boza had deceived her and she could have made the appropriate revisions to her book but, instead, she preferred not to admit her mistake. I am convinced that a person who is lying would find it difficult to deceive a historian with expertise in a given area, since the historian has so much information that, in a very short time, alarm bells would go off. That is what happened to the historians Benito Bermejo and Sandra Checa in the case of the false deportees Enric Marco and Antonio Pastor.[TN6] But this was not the case for Mercedes de Pablos, who never knew that Gila Boza was deceiving her for the simple reason that she was not an expert on the subject. She displayed an obvious lack of professionalism in the preparation of the book and, subsequently, a complete lack of ethics when she was advised of the serious wrong she had committed with Antonio Martínez Borrego, whose reputation was tarnished by Juan Gila Boza and by the author, who was supposedly in favor of the recuperation of historical memory.

Just as in the case of Amparo Barayón, here too it is necessary to examine the role played by the press, specifically the Andalusian edition of *El País*. In the long-established and purest tradition of old-fashioned journalism, the "independent morning daily" behaved from the start in a partisan fashion, favoring "a colleague" regardless of whether she was right or wrong. The newspaper prevented information from getting to the reader, did not

TRANSLATOR'S NOTE 6. The story of the historians Benito Bermejo and Sandra Checa and the impostors Enric Marco and Antonio Pastor is detailed on pp. 70–71.

worry about whether the transcript of the court-martial really required a complete revision of the book, never weighed the author's declarations against the opinions of those of us who had pointed out the problem and, throughout the entire controversy committed itself to avoiding negative fallout and to conduct that does not conform to journalistic ethics, but does indeed conform to their habitual style. To top it all, and as the final act of this chain of nonsense, the ruling on the lawsuit filed by Antonio Martínez Borrego's children favored Mercedes de Pablos and the impostor Juan Gila Boza.

The story of Fabien Garrido's webpage containing the memoir by his father, Ramón Garrido Vidal, is actually the story of a rather peculiar judge, Juan Carlos Carballal Paradela, whose court was in the town of Cambados. The family of the ex mayor of O Grove did not like what was said about him in Ramón Garrido's memoir and turned to the justice system where, by chance, they found a judge who saw no problem whatsoever in handing down a ruling that ordered the disappearance of that memoir from the Internet. We are talking about an autobiographical text by a person already deceased who wrote of events he had lived through and knew about. But the Cambados judge decided to do away with that testimony because, according to him, it did not fulfill the requirements for protection by the freedoms of expression and information. Carballal knew that Ramón Garrido was not a historian and that his testimony was of value to history because it was the first-person account of a protagonist. But the judge came to the conclusion that Garrido Vidal had no right to say what he had said about the Francoist mayor, even if it was a personal testimony. Consequently, the judge condemned him to silence.

It may be sufficient to read the judge's allusion to "the recollection so many decades later of what is now called 'historical memory' in a malicious, uncontrolled and vengeful fashion or without true and serious facts [. . .]," in order to know what sort of man he is. But one really ought to have heard the judge from Cambados publicly expound his opinions – his participation in the conference on historical memory in O Grove was not anticipated; he seems to have invited himself – in order to know why he ruled against Fabien Garrido's webpage. In the appendix to the chapter on Ramón Garrido I have transcribed some of what he said at that conference, but something essential is lacking – his tone of voice and the style of his presentation. His sense of absolute superiority over the audience and his total disdain for dialogue were palpable. Fabien Garrido was not even advised that a judicial proceeding was going to take place; and the ruling arrived later, addressed to Fabien's deceased father. This, along with family problems and the distance involved – he was living in France – prevented Fabien from appealing the ruling handed down by the judge, who boasted in September 2007 during his presentation at the conference that no one as yet had ever suggested that the ruling was mistaken. In the words of Fabien, ". . . until I received the ruling, an announcement of the hearing which would decide to do away with my webpage was never sent either to my address or to my father's address."[1]

I harbor no doubt whatsoever about how any of the cases dealt with in this book would have ended if they had all been heard by the judge from Cambados. It is a question of logic. If Judge Carballal ruled in favor of the family members of the Francoist mayor of O Grove, why would he not rule in favor of the plaintiff from Luque, the plaintiff from San Fernando, the children of Doctor Quirós, the plaintiffs from the town of Domingo Pérez in the province of Toledo, the children of the mayor of Cerdedo or the Rosón family. Carballal's ruling was based on the denial *per se* of oral testimony. This means that for Judge Carballal to believe in testimonies about the repression, he needs either eyewitnesses or documents, even though he knows perfectly well that for those events there are neither the former nor the latter. People who think that way do not take into account that we live in a country in which, if you want to know what happened to a right-wing victim, all you need to do is go to the National Historical Archive, ask to see the Causa General (General Lawsuit) and there you will find the most complete information possible for each case, which normally includes even the names of those responsible and their whereabouts. Nevertheless, if you want to know what happened to a leftist victim, it is often the case that you will not even find their name in the Civil Death Registry, because he or she was never inscribed. That is why it is necessary –nay essential –to resort to oral sources. And it will always be so as long as the Army, the Civil Guard and the Police maintain the archives of the repression without possibility of access.

All of this was brought up at the conference in O Grove – that, given the lack of available documentation, research on the Francoist repression required reliance on the testimonies of persons who lived through or knew of what happened. But the judge from Cambados would have none of it. He demanded proof that the Francoist mayor took part in the elaboration of lists of persons to be assassinated. He maintained that if what Ramón Garrido said had appeared in a work of historical research with appropriate methodology there would have been no problem, but that the way Ramón Garrido had related it in his memoir constituted an insult to the honor of Joaquín Álvarez Lores. Unfortunately, Judge Carballal did not properly appreciate the consequences of the fact that, between the honor of a witness who had suffered repression and exile and had seen friends and family members disappear, and the honor of the fascist mayor of O Grove, he had opted for the latter. Inversely, the judges we have discussed, from Córdoba, Cádiz, Oviedo and A Estrada, would have ruled in favor of Ramón Garrido's testimony and the webpage created by his son would still be available today. The fact is, as we all know, the justice you receive depends on which judge you get.

The story of Marta Capín is, once again, that of a family aggrieved by the harm caused to their father's honor. He was a doctor who, according to various testimonies, was involved in the killing of the personnel of the sanatorium at a hospital in Valdediós. The story caused an especially strong public reaction because the majority of the victims were women. There was also a boy. What the passage of time and the lack of any investigation had turned into a legend, the exhumation and subsequent investigation revealed to be a carefully planned massacre. The Oviedo judge, following the criteria established by the Constitutional Tribunal, recognized the investigative work carried out by the author and exonerated her, a ruling that remains important since the evidence that implicated Dr. Quirós in the elaboration of the list of persons assassinated in Valdediós depended on the words of a witness who is still alive and was twelve years old at the time of the massacre (his mother, who also saw the list, was advised to return home by a soldier who was a relative of hers and who was standing guard at the door of the sanatorium). It is likely that if the case had been tried by Judge Carballal, Marta Capín's fate would have led her to "end up in jail" for having cast doubts on Dr. Quirós's honor without providing evidence (since for this judge, oral testimonies do not count). Marta Capín's case was still unresolved when the conference in O Grove took place. Judge Carballal sat at the same table as Capín during lunch at the conference and told her that she would "end up in jail."[TN7]

Santiago Macías and Emilio Silva were tried for including Rosa Muñoz Garrido's testimony in their book. She told them about the results of the inquiries she had made as she followed the trail of clues that led to information about an uncle of hers and two other residents of the town called Domingo Pérez. In this case a court-martial also plays a part. It is what allowed Rosa Muñoz to discover what happened to these men from their arrest in 1937 until their deaths in 1938. As a non-specialist in the area,

TRANSLATOR'S NOTE 7. Marta Capín's description of her conversation with Judge Carballal is on p. 99.

her testimony contains certain contradictions, but this was not the problem. What Rosa Muñoz Garrido says is simply that the three men were sentenced to death, without evidence, for the murder of a landowner in 1936; that the transcript of the court-martial itself proves that other men were responsible for the crime and that the landowner's wife and other right-wing residents of the town took advantage of the murder to denounce whomever they pleased, among them Rosa's uncle and the other two victims.

The magistrate who tried the case agreed that doubts had been cast on the validity of the Francoist military/judicial system and that the three men were innocent, but she found it unnecessary to have referred to two persons, the landowner Besa Olmedo and his wife, as responsible for their deaths, since the former had been murdered shortly after the military coup of July 18, 1936 and the latter because, according to Rosa Muñoz, it was other persons who had denounced her uncle and his companions. From this perspective, Muñoz's affirmation that "what triggered those three men's story involved a fourth person: Besa Olmedo, one of the largest landowners in the area" was unfortunate, since what was indeed the origin of those three men's story was the repression unleashed as a consequence of the landowner's murder. Neither does the reference to his wife, Adriana Sánchez Cabezudo, seem entirely appropriate since, regardless of how many dozens of innocent persons she may have denounced, it seems that the said three men were implicated by others. Personally, I believe that if the information provided by the transcript of the court-martial had been more clearly presented and the text in question had been more carefully written, this case would not have come to trial.

As always, it was oral testimonies that led the family of the Francoist mayor of Cerdedo to sue the Galician historian Dionisio Pereira, who continually refused to reveal his sources while steadfastly defending the methodology he had employed. We have already mentioned how, in an attempt to invalidate oral sources, the lawyer for Gutiérrez Torres's family even asked Pereira if the persons who gave their testimonies had been previously subjected to psychological tests. It is questions such as this that demonstrate in a vivid fashion the absurdity of forcing history to pass through the justice system.[2]

Pereira himself altered the direction the case was taking. In order to avoid greater problems, and having heard that the ex-mayor's family was "lawyering up," he decided to introduce nuances that toned down the initial text while he was preparing the expanded version. Consequently the lawsuit was only against the text that had been published in the proceedings of the Congress on Memory in 2003. As in the next case we will deal with, Dionisio Pereira received the support of, among others, several Galician historians who testified at the trial. One of them, Lourenzo Fernández Prieto, professor of Contemporary History at the University of Santiago, recalls the prosecutor's ignorance and aggressiveness, and his obsession to prove that Pereira was not an authentic researcher but rather a non-specialist making undocumented accusations. His attitude was so extreme that even the judge had to request that he be more prudent. All of this in a courtroom whose wall was decorated with a Francoist escutcheon.

Finally, the story of Alfredo Grimaldos and the Rosón family takes us back to the Transition. There is no doubt that this present-day case has a great deal in common with the lawsuits filed by the Rosón family in the 1980s. In fact, the basis for the information that motivated both lawsuits is the same: a mysterious anonymous work entitled "Biography of a Knave," source for the articles published by José Luis Morales in *Interviú* in 1978 and also for the section of Grimaldos's book which is the object of the recent legal action. And the title of Morales's articles and of that section of Grimaldos's book is the same: "The Rosón Family, Scourge of Galicia." The peculiarities of the case prevent us from delving more deeply into what makes this case exceptional, since it does not seem possible for the time being to grasp all the connections that exist among the different texts and their possible authors. Indeed, Grimaldos does not even allude in his book to the earlier lawsuits. Of course the ruling did not accept the character of "neutral reporting" in his work. Nonetheless, the worst part is that the ruling censures the author for having taken on "a topic of such general sensitivity as the Civil War and Transition."

This is precisely what could not be forgiven in Grimaldos's work. He had revealed the dark underside of the Transition and the dominant role played during that period by persons who had been openly involved in the military coup in July 1936 and in the fascist repression that followed. These lines of continuity are demonstrated by the Spanish judicial apparatus which decided against Grimaldos even though other recent ruling on very similar cases had protected the authors' freedoms of expression and information. The judge's problem was that to have found Grimaldos innocent would have been recognition that the rulings on the lawsuits filed by the Rosón family against José Luis Morales during the Transition were unjust. Once again, doubt was cast on the sources used by José Luis Morales or Alfredo Grimaldos when attempting to bring to the light of day a story for which there could be no other sources but oral testimonies. The historian Mirta Núñez Díaz-Balart, who testified in support of Grimaldos, recalled the aggressiveness of the Rosóns' lawyer and wondered if lawyers like him, or other lawyers mentioned in this book, model their behavior in court on the lawyers in the dozens of trials seen in movies, excluding of course Atticus Finch, the unforgettable character created by Harper Lee in her novel *To Kill a Mockingbird* and interpreted by Gregory Peck in the film of the same name directed by Robert Mulligan. The ruling handed down in May 2012 in the Grimaldos case put things in their place once and for all: the honor and dignity of the Rosóns, dyed-in-the-wool Francoists and fat cats during the Transition, should be protected at all cost.

For the present English edition, I have added a thirteenth case, the one against Judge Baltasar Garzón Real. When the Spanish edition was published in 2009 the judge had already seen how the investigation he had initiated against the crimes of Francoism from the Fifth Chamber of the National Tribunal had been aborted shortly after it had begun. At the time, the eventual outcome of the case against Garzón would have been unimaginable. Now, as I write this, and with the perspective that all the cases in this book have provided, I can say with certainty that from the judges who condemned Fernando Ruiz Vergara in the 1980s to those who, on February 23, 2012, expelled from the legal profession a judge who tried to bring a little justice to the victims of Francoism and closed the door on the accusations presented by associations and family members, there is a line of continuity which characterizes the quintessence of the permanent Right — in other words, the same right-wing that prepared the transition from dictatorship to democracy with the aid of those sectors, from a range of ideologies, who joined forces with the Right to accept the obliteration of the past and to accept the Transition as the only reference point.

Notes

1 E-mail, February 9, 2009.
2 Part of the trial can be seen at http://www.youtube.com/ watch?v=ETIGkxKZ74k.

Conclusions

History is objective but not impartial.

JOSEP FONTANA

It would be interesting to carry out a study of comparative law to find out how different European nations handle conflicts between the freedoms of expression and information and the right to honor, especially in countries with a complicated past, such as those in which the fascist experience left a profound mark or even in France with its collaborationist Vichy regime. What differentiates Spain from all those countries is that the persons who overthrew the democratic Republic in 1936 remained in power until the dictator's death in 1975, and that it was sectors of the Francoist élite who controlled the political transition. In the final analysis, and even though the purge of those responsible in Germany and Italy seldom went beyond the higher echelons, Nazis and fascists lost the war and adapted themselves to the new times by taking advantage of the numerous opportunities to remain in the centers of power. But they were conscious of having lost. Fascism had been violently defeated. The Nazi leadership either committed suicide or were condemned at the Nuremberg trial. The image of Mussolini's cadaver hanging upside down in a Milan plaza must have terrified more than a few Francoists in Spain, the only fascist island left after the Second World War. Everywhere else fascism was regarded with suspicion and during the following decades each country, to the extent permitted by their possibilities and according to the tangle of complicities involved, developed legislation that addressed the past.

Here in Spain, the story was different. Two years after Franco's death and one year before the approval of the Constitution, an amnesty was declared that wiped the past clean with the stroke of a pen. But even though the pardoning of Basque terrorists was part of the equation, what really disappeared as if by magic was the fascist past, the only past that no one knew quite what to do with after four decades of dictatorship. The decision to declare this amnesty was presented as the product of a national reconciliation and, with time, came to be regarded as one of the more precious achievements of the so-called "spirit of the Transition." The type of transition that evolved between 1973 and 1978 had positive aspects for all the forces that participated in the process and benefitted to a greater or lesser extent, but Spain's democratic memory was ignored as was the fact that in more than half the country there was no "civil war" at all, but simply a military coup and a plan for extermination. And that in the rest of the country there was a failed military coup, civil war and the great military/judicial purge of the postwar.

In other words, the transition ignored the previous democratic experience destroyed by fascism, a fact which those who agreed to cast aside the past gave another interpretation. According to them, they did what they did precisely because they had learned the lesson of 1936. And what was the lesson of 1936? Something that had caught on in the greater part of Spanish society by the end of the long dictatorship as a result of forty years of propaganda: the Second Republic, which had aroused so many hopes, was a failure that had led the country into disaster. One more ingredient was added to this and that ingredient was fear. The populace had to avoid provoking the beast because it was still strong and could cause great damage. Thus, what came out of that critical historical moment was the result of decades of one-sided propaganda and accumulated fear. In addition, it was necessary to find a way out of that dead-end street at all costs.

The political parties began to accommodate themselves to the possibilities in play but not a single party ever contemplated the possibility of vindicating Spain's democratic past, a decision the parties would justify by saying that, above all, it was necessary to look to the future. Only in this way can we explain why the parties, whether of the right or of the left, accepted without batting an eyelid that no party could run in the first elections with the word *república* or any of its derivations in its name. In this way the country killed off from the very start the possibility that Parliament would have any political party with ties to the rich tradition of Spanish republicanism.

All things considered, what the "lesson of 1936" meant to the new political parties was the assumption that the Republic had been mistaken and had gone too far on several fronts, which led to a tragic outcome, and therefore one had to be cautious and practical so as not to upset the Francoist powers still in control of the polity and judiciary. Once the members of the democratic opposition began to share some of the power and form part of the system, they moved even further from what should have been an obligatory commemoration of the Republic. Logically, and in accord with the motif that runs through the judicial cases related in this book, nothing was done with regard to the victims of the Francoist repression except for a 1978 Law of War Pensions that provided a miserable stipend for victims' dependents if they could prove the disappearance of their loved ones. And in 1997, when people in many parts of Spain decided on their own to commemorate their loved ones and even give them a decent burial, the government as well as the political élites turned a blind eye to these initiatives; indeed, many politicians did whatever they could to put a stop to them, convinced as they were that these initiatives were as inopportune as they were unseemly. "After all," these politicians were probably thinking, "everyone must be aware that Spain has gotten over 'the Civil War' by official decree." Those were years when to speak of *all that* was impertinent. *All that* simply did not exist.

Behind this ongoing denial of the past are hidden various keys to understanding what has been described in this book. It is the way the transition transpired, *artificially* closing down the past, that abandoned and left defenseless all those who would approach that past in order to uncover and transmit what had happened. The transition armor-plated Spanish fascism's right to honor and left its memory intact while, at the same time, it forgot the right to honor and the right to memory of the victims of the military coup and the terror that devastated the country until the end of guerilla resistance in the 1950s. We have already seen throughout these pages that the honor of the vanquished does not count. The vast majority of Francoist courts-martial represented a frontal attack on the right to honor of those who were obliged to appear before them; yet it has never occurred to any judge or judicial authority to request their annulment en masse. Furthermore, the justice system has even denied individual requests for review and annulment, arguing that democratic rights and values cannot examine further back than 1978. Nevertheless, with those same rights and values we can indeed haul into court and condemn someone who has purportedly tarnished the honor of persons involved in events that occurred in 1936. Evidently, a justice system that behaves in this fashion leans to the right or, at least, that is its proclivity.

At the same time, and as evidence of what we have been saying, it was Rodolfo Martín Villa, Falangist and Minister of the Interior in 1977, who ordered the destruction of the Movement's archives.[TN1] These would not be the only collections of documents to disappear, but their loss is irreparable. And such losses occurred because of the total lack of legal protection for similar documentation at the time – and even today if we consider the military/judicial collections – since there would not be a Law of Documental Patrimony until 1985. That law included provisions for the creation of a Law of Archives, which Spanish researchers are still waiting for, which means, among other things, that we can only inquire about the

TN 1. See translator's note 3, p. 123.

location of documents that were generated by the State Administration starting in 1985.

And so . . . amnesia and silence, destruction and neglect of documentation. This is what the transition did with the recent past. It is very likely that if it had not been for the destruction of the personal dossiers of those who gave life to the Movement, some of the lawsuits we have described in this book would have been rejected in short order. It would have been enough to turn to the personal dossiers and corroborate the curricula vitae of some of the protagonists in order to place their lawsuits in the appropriate context. And not because the dossiers contain detailed accounts of the crimes in which they participated – that would be unthinkable – but rather because the dossiers would provide the chronological and biographical particulars and the degree of complicity in "the grand task" carried out by members of the Movement. In reports and documents about members of the Falange, repressive activities are concealed behind set phrases such as "participated in tasks of cleansing" or "obeyed punctually all he was ordered to do," especially if those phrases refer to events during the period immediately following the military coup. It would be interesting to be able to see the dossiers of the Rosón brothers, those of the Catalonians who testified in Burgos at the court-martial of Manuel Carrasco i Formiguera, those of the various Francoist mayors we have mentioned, those of "Sergeant Venom's" gang members from Zamora, or those of the Reales family in Almonte. But it will be impossible unless for some reason, as in the case of Juan Gila Boza, something turns up in the transcript of a court-martial.

It is sufficient to read the Constitution to know that the solution to the problem we are describing cannot lie with the justice system: article 18 guarantees the right to honor and to one's own image and article 20 recognizes the right to the freedom of expression and of information. It cannot fall to judges to decide whether a historical work has been executed well or not, or if the work's interpretation of events is the correct one; or if the methodology employed is the appropriate one or if, on the other hand, there is a better methodology. Above all because judges are not qualified to do so, nor is it their responsibility. Only the historian, the researcher or the documentarian knows how to evaluate the worthiness and reliability of a witness. And only they are fully conscious of the road they have travelled in order to arrive at a series of conclusions, glimpses of which road appear in the notes, the bibliography and the sources, etc. And specifically with respect to the repression, we who have studied it know that those who joined the coup voluntarily or by force, whether sooner or later, became involved in different aspects of the repressive task: drawing up the lists, making the arrests, establishing files on the prisoners, locking them up, interrogating and torturing them, transporting them in trucks, assassinating them, digging the common graves, filling those graves with the dead, sprinkling the dead with quicklime, waiting for the next group to arrive, closing the grave, cleaning up the blood there where it remained . . . and then starting all over again. And these labors, which in Spain lasted for years, required the cooperation of many people at all levels. A democratic judge should at least be aware that if all this never fell into the hands of the justice system it is because of the long duration of the dictatorship and the nature of the transition.

It is possible that at the beginning of the Transition – I am thinking of the era of the UCD (Unión del Centro Democrático) – judges were delighted to take on the task of protecting the glorious past (for instance Judge Luis Vivas Marzal and his phrase "the impertinent and unfortunate reminder of episodes" from the past), and it is even possible that there are judges today – some cases have been seen in these pages – who believe that that past should still be protected from the menace of historical memory, but it is incomprehensible that at this late date such an attitude exists in a normalized democratic society. Although I hasten to add that, without a doubt, once the period from 1976 to 1981 was superseded, it has been the lack of action on the part of politicians that handed the problem over to the justice system. But the rulings in the trials of Judge Baltazar Garzón erase all doubt. The justice system will in no way allow the legacy of Francoism to be dismantled or questioned.

And if politicians had fulfilled their obligation to protect the collections of documentation when there was still time and to make it available to the public, the situation would be very different. And if, years ago, there had been a moderately coherent national policy regarding archives and those archives had been provided with adequately trained personnel, the means to understanding the past would have existed and the possibility of reconciling our differences would have been greater. And if the collections of documentation still preserved by the Army, the Civil Guard and the Police – or should still be preserved by those institutions if they have not already been destroyed by the said institutions – had been taken over a long time ago by the National Archive and by qualified personnel from the Corps of Certified Archivists, the truth would be more accessible. And if the various democratic parties and governments had clarified, at some point, their condemnation of the military coup and dictatorship, and their assumption of the democratic values represented by the Second Republic – and not as a merely formal declaration forced by circumstances as in November 2002[TN2 (OVERLEAF)] – the memory of those events from the past would be perceived differently by all Spaniards. Let us not forget that the feeble policy of historical memory adopted by Spain would not have come about without the social pressure that began to exert itself toward the end of the 1990s. If it had been up to the different governments and political parties, Spain would still be just like it was during the Transition.

From this perspective, the examples of the journalists, documentary filmmakers, researchers and historians whom we have seen pass through the pages of this book are the product of the way the transition was imposed and the policies of amnesia applied in Spain from the Transition to the present. Does it make any sense that in the midst of a timid attempt to establish a policy with respect to historical memory there are still trials being held for attacks against the right to honor (half the cases dealt with here are from after 2005)? Should we tolerate a judge who prohibits access to a person's memories because someone has approached him and said, "Hey, look at what they are saying about my grandfather . . .," when it turns out that the grandfather was the first fascist mayor of O Grove thanks to a savage military coup? Must we really respect the honor of persons who, regardless of the consequences, joined, or even participated in the preparations for, an armed conspiracy against a democratic regime and found themselves involved, one way or another, in the repressive process? It is striking that the distinguished judge from the town of Cambados mentioned as a justificatory argument for prohibiting testimonies like those of Ramón Garrido that "[. . .] it is a serious concern that the descendants of one side or the other find themselves having coffee together in the same café." Nevertheless, Judge Carballal seems not to remember the four decades during which the family members of persons who were assassinated by the fascists in O Grove and throughout Spain had to live day after day not just with people who say, "Your father is an assassin," but with the assassins themselves.

It is appropriate to recall that if the war had ended with a Republican victory all the fascists, whether military men or civilians, would have been treated as what they were, i.e. delinquents, many of whom would have ended up in jail. They could boast of having the laws on their side during

TRANSLATOR'S NOTE 2 (PREVIOUS PAGE). In the summer of 2002, *El País* published a long and profusely illustrated article about the exhumation of a mass grave in Priaranza del Bierzo (León), putting a spotlight on the Movement for the Recuperation of Historical Memory. Not wanting to appear completely out of touch with this social movement, various politicians prepared a condemnation of Francoism which was passed on November 20, the anniversary of the dictator's death. Presented as a great achievement, it was mere window-dressing that did not commit the government to anything.

the dictatorship, but a democracy cannot tolerate that that farce be perpetuated. It is no longer a question, as some sarcastically say, of undoing the results of the military coup, the Civil War, and the dictatorship, but simply, from the perspective of the times in which we are living, of putting each person in the place where they belong and that they deserve.

It is significant that out of all the cases described in this book, of those accused of being involved in the repression only Luis and Antonio Rosón were military men. And I say this because when the Archives of the Territorial Military Tribunals were opened to researchers we learned that, although the executioners were Falangists, requetés,[TN3] civil guards or soldiers, the repression was always organized under military control, either by the delegations of Public Order or by the military commander of each locale, where the "local bigwigs" drew up the lists of persons whom others should arrest and kill. Most people were only aware of the final phase of the process and knew absolutely nothing about how the name of a family member got to be on the list. Naturally it is easier to name those you could see than to name those who stayed in the shadows or were just passing through like the post commanders.

The protagonists of this book can never be compensated for the years of worry and heartache they were forced to endure. Let us not forget that the justice system works slowly and its road, full of appeals and counterappeals, is long and narrow. And if that is not enough, the outcome is unforeseeable; the justice system eventually agreed with Violeta Friedman, Isidoro Sánchez, José Casado, Dolors Genovés, Marta Capín, Santiago Macías, Emilio Silva and Dionisio Pereira but not with Fernando Ruiz Vergara, Fabien and Ramón Garrido, Alfredo Grimaldos and Baltasar Garzón.[1] None of them deserved what they had to go through for performing an act of courage and personal commitment that would deserve to be rewarded with approval in a democratic society. They had forgotten Judge Vivas Marzal's demands for "[. . .] rigorously historical narratives, impartial and not for consumption by the 'common folk.'" Here we find the source of part of the problem. Histories of the repression are written precisely for the "common folk." It is striking that of the eleven lawsuits dealt with in this book — setting aside the cases of Violeta Friedman, Amparo Barayón and Baltasar Garzón[TN4] — the majority occurred in Andalucía (4) and Galicia (3), two of the zones where the fascist repression was most severe and which have been

TN 3. See translator's note 2, p. 10.

TRANSLATOR'S NOTE 4. These cases are not included because in the case of Amparo Barayón there was no lawsuit and in the cases of Violeta Friedman and Baltasar Garzón the lawsuits were not against historians or documentary filmmakers.

most thoroughly investigated. Furthermore, it is significant that most of the lawsuits took place in territories where the coup triumphed and the fascist repression began immediately.

How can we measure the personal damage suffered by those who have spent years subjected to the enormous pressure of the law for having made this or that assertion, who have seen their work and professionalism questioned, and who have been subjected to aggressive and relentless questioning merely for having passed along what others have told them? There is no way to measure the harm. Nothing and no one could compensate them for what they have been through. The only thing that can be done is to prevent it from happening to others, something we can attempt to do in three ways: by admitting the reality of what happened in 1936 with all its consequences, by repealing the Law of Amnesty passed in November of 1977,[2] and by guaranteeing the freedoms of investigation, expression and information. I conclude with these words from Judge María Emilia Casas Bahamonde:

> The possibility for our contemporaries to form their own world view based on the evaluation of others' experiences depends on the existence of a historical science freely and methodologically founded. Without a dialogue with the value judgments of others – with those of the historian, which is what concerns us here – we would be unable to form our own value judgments. Neither would there be space – which can only be attained through freedom – for the formation of a collective historical consciousness.

APPENDIX

CONCLUSIONS FROM THE CONFERENCE "THE REPRESSION IN GALICIA: FREEDOM OF INFORMATION AND THE RIGHT TO ENGAGE IN RESEARCH" (O GROVE, SEPTEMBER 19–22, 2007)

1. The events that are uncovered by means of the scientific methodology of History cannot be put on trial by Courts of Law, which should also protect the historian/scientist's rights to freedom of expression and freedom of scientific creation and to opinions or subjective criticisms regarding those events, their causes and their consequences.

2. We propose that the principles described in the Report by Diane Orentlichar as an amplification of "the collective principles updated for the protection and promotion of human rights through the

struggle against impunity" by the United Nations Human Rights Commission during its 61st session be incorporated into all administrative and legislative actions.

3. Manifest institutional support for the movement for the recuperation of historical memory is a necessity.

4. We propose that for the historians and associations that work for the recuperation of the memory of the events that occurred between 1936 and 1978 the following specific rights be legislatively recognized:

- Unrestricted access to all archives.
- Access to all places of interest for the research.
- To produce and obtain pertinent evidence for the reconstruction of the Memory and honor of the victims.
- Immediate judicial protection whenever any type of evidence that can be of value for the reconstruction of memory related to that historical period is in danger.
- Economic help from the State for all activities directed at proving events or actions relative to the said period and from which violations of human rights were derived.
- A guarantee, depending upon the procedure that is established, of the power to preserve the anonymity of the sources that provide, or may provide, data according to the criteria protected by historical science.

5. Finally, we consider it basic to establish meeting places and networks for unity for historians, researchers, collectives for the recuperation of memory and propagators of information about the Francoist repression, with the goal of cooperating more intensely and maintaining complete solidarity in the face of judicial harassment of our colleagues.

Notes

1 It is interesting to observe how a similar phenomenon occurs with regard to the exhumation of mass graves. There are judges who agree to proceed with the requests filed by family members for the localization of their loved ones, requiring the State to cover all expenses, and others who refuse to take action. Among the former we find María del Carmen Santos González, the first judge to agree to proceed with such a request and who took charge of the opening of a mass grave in Piedrafita de Babia (León); Rosa María Serreta, who took charge of the mass grave discovered in Gordaliza del Pino (León); Jesús Marina, who proceeded with the identification of the remains found in the mass grave in

Otero de los Herreros (Segovia); and Julio Álvarez Merino, chief judge in Talavera de la Reina (Toledo), under whose supervision the mass grave in Pepino was opened. Among the judges who refused to accept the requests to open mass graves we find Olga Ruiz, in Viguera (La Rioja); Macarena del Rosal, in Santaella (Córdoba); and two more cases in Asturias, Mónica Casado Gobernado and Beatriz Serrano Díez. This information is from Ana María Pascual, "Los otros 'Garzones' de la Memoria Histórica" ("The other 'Judge Garzones' of Historical Memory"), in *Interviú*, October 6, 2008.

2   The fact that José Luis Rodríguez Zapatero's Socialist government, in spite of claims to the contrary, remained insensitive to these requests to repeal the Law of Amnesty could be seen in a news item that appeared about the time the Spanish edition of this book was coming to completion. It was entitled "Confronted by the United Nations, the Government Defends the Transition and the 1977 Amnesty" (M. Sáiz-Pardo, Colpisa, Madrid, February 3, 2009). This was the government's answer to a recommendation from the United Nations in October 2008 that the Law of Amnesty be repealed "so the courts could pursue, without legal impediment, the crimes of Francoism" and "because that law is in conflict with the international precept that 'statutes of limitation do not apply to crimes against humanity'" (report approved at the 94th meeting of the committee that watches over the enforcement of the International Covenant on Civil and Political Rights, which supported the Law of Historical Memory and the investigation initiated by Judge Baltasar Garzón). According to the news item, "The Executive, with an unusual bluntness for a diplomatic communiqué, replied to the United Nations' recommendation saying that it 'laments' that the Committee has involved itself in an affair of which it has 'no knowledge' and reminds the Committee that the Law of Amnesty, which will not be repealed, was a pillar of the Transition." Furthermore, the communiqué accuses the Committee of "ignorance of the origin and social significance of the Law of Amnesty." And it concluded, "The Spanish State would like to emphasize that the Committee is disqualifying a decision backed by all of Spanish society and that contributed to the transition to democracy," and it also recalled that "the said law was requested by the entire democratic opposition" and "was one of the first laws passed consensually by the same body that passed the 1978 Constitution." "Further," it added, "not only Spanish society but also world public opinion, is aware of and has always supported the process of transition in Spain, a process that was made possible, in part, thanks to the said law."

When the conservative Popular Party came to power in 2011, the government did nothing but intensify these tendencies to see everything through the prism of the Transition. And it ended the Law of Historical Memory with the stroke of a pen. All that remained of the law was a budget for exhumations and it is anybody's guess as to how that budget will be administered. It only exists because, from the sectors of the socialist PSOE opposed to the historical memory movement to the most reactionary members of the Right, after more than a decade of struggle, it has finally been accepted that the victims of the repression cannot remain in the mass graves where their assassins buried them. Nevertheless, the steps that would really be necessary to confront the problem have not been taken, starting with mapping the mass graves, an initiative that was rejected at the time by all the autonomous communities governed by the Popular Party. The reality is simply that the Spanish Right sees no reason to break with Francoism or admit to its criminality, which explains the Right's rejection of the social movement for historical memory that began in the late 1990s and its continued adherence to the justificatory versions of the military coup and the dictatorship.

About the Author

Francisco Espinosa Maestre (Villafranca de los Barros, Badajoz, 1954), historian with a Doctorate in History, was the scientific coordinator of the website todoslosnombre.org (all the names), which attempts to put names to all the victims of the Francoist dictatorship, and the author of *Informe sobre la represión franquista* (*Report on the Francoist Repression*), which was part of the investigation of the crimes of Francoism initiated by Judge Baltasar Garzón. He was also a member of the judge's advisory commission during the investigation.

Among his numerous books it is worth mentioning *Guerra y represión en el Sur de España* (*War and Repression in Southern Spain*), 2012, *La primavera del Frente Popular. Los campesinos de Badajoz y el origen de la guerra civil (marzo-julio de 1936)* (*The Spring of the Popular Front. The Peasants of Badajoz and the Origin of the Civil War (March-July 1936)*), 2007, *Contra el olvido. Historia y memoria de la guerra civil* (*Against Amnesia. History and Memory of the Civil War*), 2006, *La columna de la muerte. El avance del ejército franquista de Sevilla a Badajoz* (*The Death Column. The Advance of the Francoist Army from Seville to Badajoz*), 2003, *La justicia de Queipo* (*[General] Queipo [de Llano]'s Justice*), 2000, and *La guerra civil en Huelva* (*The Civil War in Huelva*), 1996. In 2010 he coordinated the writing and publication of *Violencia roja y azul. España, 1936–1950* (*Red and Blue Violence. Spain, 1936–1950*).

About the Translator

Richard Barker (New York, 1945), Professor Emeritus of Spanish at the University of Wisconsin–Stevens Point, was sidetracked from the field of literary criticism, traditional for his profession, following a conversation in 1986 with an older man in his wife's home town. During the following twenty years he did research in many archives and recorded interviews with scores of the town's residents who had lived through the Spanish Republic, the Civil War and the Franco dictatorship. His research was first published in Spain as *El largo trauma de un pueblo andaluz: República, represión, guerra, posguerra* (Castilleja del Campo, Sevilla: Ayuntamiento, 2007) and subsequently in Great Britain as *Skeletons in the Closet, Skeletons in the Ground: Repression, Victimization and Humiliation in a Small Andalusian Town: The Human Consequences of the Spanish Civil War* (Brighton, Portland, Toronto: Sussex Academic Press, 2012). He has also published *Fugitive from Spanish Fascism: A Memoir by Miguel Domínguez Soler* (Stevens Point, WI: Cornerstone Press, 2009), a translation.